SECRET GARDENS

HUMPHREY CARPENTER

SECRET GARDENS

*A Study of the Golden Age
of Children's Literature*

faber and faber

This edition first published in 2009
by Faber and Faber Ltd
Bloomsbury House, 74–77 Great Russell Street, London WC1B 3DA

Printed by CPI Antony Rowe, Eastbourne

A CIP record for this book is available from the British Library

ISBN 978–0–571–24914–5

CONTENTS

ILLUSTRATIONS

PREFACE

About twenty years ago, when I was an undergraduate, it occurred to me that the great English children's writers from Lewis Carroll to A. A. Milne formed some sort of identifiable literary movement, like (say) Bloomsbury or the Georgians or the Romantics. And the vague ambition began to gather in my mind of one day writing a book about them. It was to be concerned largely with their personal psychology, which I could perceive to be in many ways very odd. Literary criticism was not to play much part in it. I wrote a couple of papers, one on Carroll and the other on J. M. Barrie, and put these and a few other fragments into a big ring-binder optimistically labelled 'Children's Writers'. And that was that, though occasionally I would come across a book – for example, Peter Green's life of Kenneth Grahame – which stirred the ambition again.

Many years later I found myself co-editing *The Oxford Companion to Children's Literature*. I thought that this would get the original project out of my system, but it didn't. I became more certain than ever that the work of the great children's writers between about 1860 and 1930 formed some sort of discernible pattern of ideas and themes. But the entries for them in the *Oxford Companion* could scarcely do more than hint at a web of connections, influences, and common purposes. Of course, studying them in detail showed up the differences as much as the similarities. And I had begun to realise that the important thing they had in common, whatever it might be, was not simply warped private lives. Certainly most of them were in some respect psychological curiosities, people whose personal difficulties in the real world had driven them inwards and helped to develop the childlike side of their imagination. But I didn't now feel that this was what I was chiefly looking for.

With the end of work on the *Oxford Companion* in sight, I began to contemplate writing something about these authors, in depth; and almost at the same moment came a suggestion from a publisher friend that I might 'do a study of the great children's writers from the time of *Alice* to *Winnie-the-Pooh*'. So I set out on my quest, feeling at times that I was adding yet one more to the already appalling number of books about children's books, yet all along wondering why nobody had ever tried to explain why so many children's classics, and classics of a particular kind, should have appeared in England in the space of about sixty years. What was it that possessed the late Victorians and the Edwardians to create a whole new genre of fiction?

The book changed beyond recognition as I wrote it. I suppose my original notion had still been to concentrate on the biographies of the writers I was dealing with; but again and again the links between these authors proved to be not in their lives, but on the deeper levels of the books themselves. I examined the books as closely as I could, in the hope of coming to understand what Carroll, Milne, and the others were really trying to say, and to perceive why so many authors in this period of English history had chosen the children's novel as their vehicle for the portrayal of society, and for the expression of their personal dreams.

The book claims to be 'a study of the Golden Age of children's literature', but it is selective, dealing only with those authors whose work seems to me to require, and deserve, investigation of this kind. Many who wrote for children during this period, and were deservedly popular, have been omitted or treated skimpily, because their work scarcely touches on the themes that preoccupied their more puzzling contemporaries; Robert Louis Stevenson and Rudyard Kipling are the most obvious examples among British writers, and Mark Twain among American. Indeed I have said very little about American writing at all, selecting only Louisa Alcott for enquiry, because I believe *Little Women* to be largely a misunderstood book, and also because her choice of subject matter – a realistic novel about family life – throws into relief the British writers with their preference for fantasy. And it must be said that the wave of great books for children between the 1860s and the 1930s, though it certainly swept over the United States and gathered authors from that country into it, was all along predominantly British in character.

I had originally intended to call this book simply *The Golden Age of Children's Literature*. The expression 'Golden Age' is often applied to the period of English children's books from Carroll to Milne,[1] and it is appropriate in more ways than one. Quite apart from the sheer quality of the books, one observes that many of them seem to be set in a distant era when things were better than they are now. And childhood itself seemed a Golden Age to many of these writers, as they set out to recapture its sensations; Kenneth Grahame even called his first book about childhood *The Golden Age*. In the end, however, I relegated this label to my subtitle, hoping that the main title I had chosen would convey the more subtle nature of the theme of so many children's writings: Arcadia, the Enchanted Place, the Never Never Land, the Secret Garden.

*

I would like to express my gratitude to Gillian Avery, who read the first draft of the book, and made many helpful comments; to Colin Matthew, for steering me towards some background reading on the social history of the period; to Julia Briggs, for looking through what I had written about E. Nesbit; to Susan Hamilton, for inadvertently helping me to find the final title for the book; and to my wife and co-editor of *The Oxford Companion to Children's Literature*, Mari Prichard, for constant advice and support. Rona Treglown very kindly read the revised text and saved me from a wide variety of lapses and errors.

Secret Gardens

PROLOGUE
The Road to Arcadia

All children's books are about ideals. Adult fiction sets out to portray and explain the world as it really is; books for children present it as it should be. Child readers come to them hoping for a certain amount of instruction, but chiefly for stories in which the petty restrictions of ordinary life are removed: they want to encounter people who can fly, geese that lay golden eggs, frogs that turn into princes, spaceships piloted by children, anything which measures up to their ideals of adventure and imagination. Adults, on the other hand, are more likely to want to feed the children a set of moral examples. By all means let them have their fun, but the opportunity of providing models of ideal behaviour is not to be wasted.

These days we are accustomed to children's books which fulfil both needs at once. For more than a century it has been possible to pick up stories which both satisfy the child's desire for excitement and contain some moral truth or lesson. In fact, we would think fairly poorly of a modern children's novel which did not satisfy both criteria. Occasionally one appears: Roald Dahl's *Charlie and the Choco-late Factory* (1964) has been loved by children and hated by adults because it is full of fun and virtually amoral. And during the fashion in the 1970s for 'problem fiction' about the disabled and the socially deprived, it was possible to discover new books for children that were as joyless and heavily didactic as the Victorian evangelical novel at its worst. But these are exceptions. Far more typical of modern children's authors are, say, Alan Garner and Philippa Pearce, to name two of the very best; their books are on the primary level full of excitement, but have a carefully conceived moral structure beneath the surface. Garner's *The Owl Service* (1967) and Pearce's *Tom's Midnight Garden* (1958), in which both writers are working at full pitch, have narratives which deal largely in magical events: figures on china plates coming alive (the Garner story) and a child time-travelling each night into the Victorian age (Pearce's book). But Garner is using a myth-come-alive plot as a way of examining relationships between modern adolescents, and Pearce is allowing her hero to learn about the necessity of growing up.

Nowadays we take this dual purpose for granted, but it was not always so. Until the middle of the nineteenth century there was plenty of material for the sheer entertainment of children, and plenty that gave them moral instruction, but the two scarcely ever met between one set of covers. 'Instruction' predominated over 'Amusement', to use the terminology favoured by the first English booksellers for children, who began business in the mid-eighteenth century. The greater number of children's books published in England between the 1740s and the 1820s were sternly moral, using simple stories to convey whatever ethical message was then in fashion, whether it be that hard work always leads to improvement in one's financial and social position (a moral much favoured from the 1750s to the 1780s), or that idle and thoughtless children would soon die an unpleasant death and then suffer everlasting torment in Hell (a message that became fashionable with the rise of the evangelical movement, early in the nineteenth century).[2] As to entertainment, that was left chiefly in the hands of the pedlars of the popular literature known as chapbooks, which played much the same part in society as lowbrow television drama does now. For a few pence children could buy the thrilling adventures of Jack the Giant Killer, or Fortunatus who could travel round the world in a few seconds with his Wishing Cap, or Guy of Warwick who slew such splendid monsters as the fearsome Dun Cow, not to mention Robin Hood, whose interminable exploits were usually narrated in doggerel. The young themselves loved such stuff; Boswell, Wordsworth and Lamb were among those who looked back at it nostalgically when they were grown men, and regretted the moralists' attempts to suppress it.

Those attempts were never really successful, and the chapbook tales kept pouring from the presses until well into the nineteenth century, to be succeeded in due course by the Penny Dreadfuls, yarns of hardened criminals and highwaymen, which again were lapped up by children. The moralists were, of course, playing Mrs Grundy, and their objections to the cheap popular literature as entertainment for children seem largely ridiculous to us now. But it was not entirely a case of blinkered prudery. There was a sense among the more intelligent moralists – such as Maria Edgeworth and Anna Laetitia Barbauld, to name two who stood out from the crowd at the beginning of the nineteenth century – that an opportunity was being wasted. Surely it must be possible to write entertainingly for children and convey a moral at the same time?

Miss Edgeworth and Mrs Barbauld, and one or two others, tried their best; but the results were very limp – handfuls of little stories about ordinary children discovering the nature of the world around them by careful observation and reflection. There was no vital spark in what Charles Lamb disparagingly called 'Mrs Barbauld's stuff'. Ironically it was the evangelical movement, growing daily in numbers and fervour at the beginning of the nineteenth century, which turned out stories that, despite their triply underlined morals, had real

excitement in them. Take Mrs Mary Martha Sherwood's
hellfire tract *The Fairchild Family* (1818): this, the best known of
evangelical tales for children, is peppered with gruesome but all
readable descriptions of rotting corpses, shown to his children by Mr
Fairchild so as to demonstrate the transience of the earthly body. It may
be deplorable, but it is far more exciting than the predictable stories by
Maria Edgeworth about the daily doings of little Harry and little Lucy.

There were a few sensible books which managed to combine
excitement with some sort of moral message. *Aesop's Fables* was one
such, and *Robinson Crusoe* and *Gulliver's Travels* (suitably abridged)
reigned almost unchallenged in their popularity with children simply
because they held both tale and message in balance. And of all things
one of the most genuinely enjoyable writers for children had emerged
from the ranks of the seventeenth-century Puritans, a group that in its
time had been especially fervent in denouncing imaginative literature
for children. John Bunyan, in writing *The Pilgrim's Progress*, produced
a book which, though it was not meant primarily for child readers,
continued to attract them for more than two centuries after its first
appearance in 1678.

And there were fairy tales, at first just the native English ones (not
very many in number or particularly distinctive in character), but from
the early eighteenth century imports from France as well (all the
Perrault tales), and the *Arabian Nights*, and then (a century later) the
discoveries of the brothers Grimm. By the time the Grimms' work
began to reach England in 1823, the old opposition of the moralists to
fairy stories had begun to fade away. But a little earlier they had
opposed them as vociferously as they had opposed the chapbooks. Mrs
Sarah Trimmer, self-appointed censor and reviewer of English children's books at the very beginning of the nineteenth century, would
have liked to see every single fairy story taken out of nurseries and
burnt. 'The terrific image,' she told readers of her *Guardian of
Education*, when reviewing a new printing of *Cinderella*, 'which tales
of this nature present to the imagination, usually make deep impressions, and injure the tender minds of children, by exciting unreasonable
and groundless fears. Neither do the generality of tales of this kind
supply any moral instruction level to the infantine capacity.'

This was not complete nonsense. No child is likely to be very
frightened by *Cinderella*, but it is difficult to say what sort of notions
about the world she or he might carry away from it. Fairy stories are
only vaguely moral, usually in a haphazard way. What does *Cinderella*
have to teach? It is not a rags-to-riches story, because Cinderella is just
as nobly born as her step-sisters. One might assume that its message is
that virtue will out, and true worth of character will be discovered;
certainly many fairy stories are about things being perceived in their
proper shape (the frog is really a prince). Yet Cinderella gets to the ball

er virtues but because she has a fairy godmother.
himself, who was responsible for the form in which
nown, seems to have had no clear idea what message
He added two rhymed *moralités* to his original French
first states that the quality which won the prince's hand
as 'Charm', and the second that you will never get
anywhere   ut a fairy godmother. The cynicism behind these
'morals' is far from inappropriate to the story. The main emotion that
Cinderella is likely to summon up is delight at the downfall of the Ugly
Sisters; many fairy stories, as the American critic Jack Zipes has pointed
out, have a considerable 'subversive' element in them.

Fairy tales in fact occupy a moral no-man's-land. Does Red Riding
Hood really deserve to be eaten up by the wolf? In a sense, yes; she has
been absurdly careless. But understandably children find her punishment too extreme, so a happy ending is usually added. Do the ogre's
daughters in *Hop o' my Thumb* really deserve to have their throats slit
while they are sleeping, through a trick played by the hero? They have
done him no harm. As a reflection of the real state of the world, such
stories are uncannily accurate. Reward and punishment, happy endings
and disasters fall on people with just that degree of unpredictability and
unfairness. The modern psychologist Bruno Bettelheim has indeed
argued that the fairy tale contributes subtly to the emotional health of
children by helping them to adjust to the external world. But as a
vehicle for organised moral instruction the fairy story leaves a lot to be
desired. One's success or failure in life seems to depend much more on
whether one is a third son, or has happened to meet a mysterious old
man coming through the wood, or has found a firebird's feather, than
on any innate qualities of character, or even on making the right moral
or emotional choices. The Grimms themselves seem to have been aware
of this. According to a recent examination of their work by an
American scholar, John M. Ellis,[3] they reorganised much of their
original folk material so as to reduce the ethical irrationality of the tales,
and to present their readers with something approaching an ordered
moral universe. Hans Christian Andersen, of course, writing original
fairy stones rather than retelling or adapting traditional ones, was free
to do this from the start, and his tales always have a clear moral
structure. Unfortunately the emotion which ruled most strongly in
Andersen's mind seems to have been self-pity, and the feeling that his
true worth had never been appreciated, so that his stories, while
incomparably crafted, have a maudlin self-regarding streak that limits
their moral applicability. They began to be read in England in the mid-
1840s; it is interesting that they inspired few English imitations.
Andersen's particular form of introspection does not seem to have
struck a chord in the British literary imagination.

*

Round about 1810, it seemed as if something out of the ordinary was happening in English writing for children. The moralists were still firmly in command of much of the market, but the bolder London juvenile booksellers (John Harris most notable among them) were starting to produce jolly little hand-coloured books which were intended simply to amuse young readers, and did not draw only on the old chapbook stories or the traditional fairy tales. They were mostly in doggerel verse, chiefly imitations of a rambling poem about Old Mother Hubbard and her dog that Harris had published in 1805, or of an equally vacuous verse-tale called *The Butterfly's Ball* which he put into print two years later. For a time it seemed as if facetious rhymes about Old Dame Trot and her Comical Cats, or Dame Wiggins of Lee and her Seven Wonderful Cats, or Dame Deborah Dent and her Donkeys, or 'The Peacock "At Home"' and 'The Lion's Masquerade' would edge the moral tale right out of the nursery. Harvey Darton, the outstanding historian of English children's literature,[4] has called this period 'the dawn of levity'. But the gaiety of Regency life faded, and with the 1830s and the advent of the Reform Bill all this jocose stuff for children vanished too. Its place was taken by whole bundles of dreary books of facts, published under such titles as *Pinnock's Catechisms* and Mrs Marcet's *Conversations*, in which young people were catechised (and thereby instructed) in every subject from the Kings and Queens of England to Vegetable Physiology. Dickens eventually satirised this fashion for fact-cramming in *Hard Times* (1854); a decade earlier, at the height of the fashion, the *Quarterly Review* for June 1844, discussing recent children's books, observed that 'the one broad and general impression left with us is that of the excessive ardour for *teaching*'. And it hinted that a renaissance in children's books was overdue: 'We should be happy if . . . we could assist in raising the standard of the *art* itself . . . What indeed can be a closer test of natural ability and acquired skill than that species of composition which, above all others, demands clearness of head and soundness of heart, the closest study of nature, and the most complete command over your materials?'

The writer of this piece clearly set the value of good children's books very high; he or she was perhaps the first person to regard juvenile literature unequivocally as an art form. But it would be some years before the hopes expressed in this article were answered. The next voices to be heard were the strident, familiar tones of the evangelicals, returning to the field this time not with such straightforward hellfire tracts as *The Fairchild Family*, but with rather a different genre of children's fiction.

The social unrest of the 1840s, and the growing awareness of the terrible plight of Britain's urban poor, publicised by Dickens and later by Mayhew, led to the devising of a new form of evangelical fiction. It was up to date in that it dealt with slum life, and heart-wringing in that its heroes were wide-eyed raggedly clothed children. On the other hand, it preached not the relief of social misery through practical, earthly reforms (improvement in working and living conditions, higher wages), but taught that the poor should tolerate their lot in this world in the secure knowledge that there were better things to come hereafter. 'We shall all be well-off in the "better land",' says a character in a typical evangelical novel of this sort.[5] The riches of faith were the only kind of affluence authors of such books were prepared to allow the poor. One of the pioneers of this type of fiction, the Revd Leigh Richmond, addressed his Sunday School readers on this subject: 'My *poor* reader, the Dairyman's Daughter was a *poor* girl, and the child of a *poor* man. Herein thou resemblest her; but dost thou resemble her, as she resembled Christ? Art thou made *rich* by faith?'[6] It was no doubt comforting to a middle-class affluent readership still haunted by the spectre of the French Revolution, and suffering deep anxieties at the sight of Chartism, to be told that the poor did not need better housing, food, and clothes so much as they needed the word of God.[7]

Nevertheless, the evangelical message was not to all tastes, and many parents must have wished that the less extreme factions in the Church of England could produce a literature with equal popular appeal but a different spiritual doctrine. By the late 1850s something of the sort was indeed happening. Charlotte M. Yonge, encouraged by her neighbour and friend John Keble and spurred on by the success of her novel *The Heir of Redclyffe*, had started to turn out tales about high-spirited daughters of the gentry who were attracted by the Oxford Movement and spent their spare energies collecting money to build new churches in poor districts. A little lower down the doctrinal barometer, Thomas Hughes, disciple of F. D. Maurice and a leading figure in the Christian Socialist movement, produced a tract which preached spiritual moderation combined with a large degree of physical aggression – the fists, he suggested, could be used when necessary in the service of God and right-mindedness. The tract, published in 1857, was called *Tom Brown's Schooldays*.

It was from the point on the spiritual map occupied by Hughes, rather than by Charlotte Yonge, that the new movement in children's literature was to begin. The Christian Socialists, whose doctrinal liberalism was combined with some rather vague attempts at social reform, played no small part in the creation of more than one of the outstanding children's books that were about to appear. But they alone were not responsible for what was to happen. A change was now taking place in the attitude of adults to children, a change closely bound up with the Romantic movement.

*

When Wordsworth published his 'Ode: Intimations of Immortality' in 1807 he was issuing a call to revolution against the view of childhood which had persisted throughout the eighteenth century, a view which had dominated both education and the writing of children's books. To the typical writer of the Enlightenment, a child was simply a miniature adult, a chrysalis from which a fully rational and moral being would duly emerge, providing parents and educators did their job properly. There was no question of children having an independent imaginative life of any importance, or of their being able to perceive anything that was invisible to adults. The only necessity was for instruction to be poured into their ears, and the only argument was about what sort of instruction it should be.

The mainstream of English child-rearing in the eighteenth century worked along lines laid down by Locke, practised moderation in all things, and gave children virtually nothing to stimulate their imaginations. Had not Locke inveighed against such 'perfectly useless trumpery' as fairy stories? *Aesop* and *Reynard the Fox* were the only imaginative works he thought fit for the nursery. Then there was the Rousseau school of child nurture, which had pockets of following in England in the late eighteenth century. Rousseau's *Émile* was to have the noble savage in him cultivated more subtly than by Locke's methods. Yet Rousseau had just as narrow a view as Locke of what children should be allowed to read. According to Émile, just about the only tolerable book was *Robinson Crusoe*. And alongside the Locke and Rousseau factions was a third group of educationalists, typified by Mrs Sarah Trimmer – the indomitable lady who delivered the tirade against *Cinderella*. Severe piety was their characteristic; they were concerned that children should be taught the true principles of religion, and they deplored both Locke's emphasis on the child's unaided use of his reason and Rousseau's concept of the noble (and potentially God-less) savage. Yet they too agreed with Locke and Rousseau about not giving children reading matter that would merely excite the imagination.

The Romantics' view of childhood turned this upside down. In England the first stirrings of change came in 1789 with Blake's *Songs of Innocence*. Though they were in no way polemic, and made no statement about the nature of the child's imagination, the *Songs* were nevertheless an ardent affirmation that children have access to a kind of visionary simplicity that is denied to adults. Blake's introductory poem describes his 'happy songs' as those which 'Every child may joy to hear'. Adults, it is implied, will not have the same instinctive understanding of their visions. Nine years later came *Lyrical Ballads*, to which Wordsworth contributed several poems describing the child's view of the world. One of them, 'Anecdote for Fathers', celebrates a child's simple directness of thought, and concludes:

Oh dearest, dearest boy! my heart
For better lore would seldom yearn,
Could I but teach the hundredth part
Of what from thee I learn.

One imagines that Locke, if not Rousseau, might have scratched his head and wondered precisely what it was that Wordsworth claimed to be learning from the child. But such poems in *Lyrical Ballads* contained only a hint, the first approaches to a thesis. That thesis was worked out more fully in Wordsworth's 'Intimations of Immortality from Recollections of Early Childhood', to give the poem its full title:

There was a time when meadow, grove, and stream,
The earth, and every common sight,
    To me did seem
    Apparelled in celestial light,
The glory and the freshness of a dream.
It is not now as it hath been of yore; –
    Turn wheresoe'er I may,
        By night or day,
The things which I have seen I now can see no more.

    Not in entire forgetfulness,
    And not in utter nakedness,
But trailing clouds of glory do we come
    From God, who is our home:
Heaven lies about us in our infancy!
Shades of the prison-house begin to close
    Upon the growing Boy . . .

The notion that children are in a higher state of spiritual perception than adults, because of their nearness to their birth and so to a pre-existence in Heaven, was not a new one in English poetry. The metaphysical poet Henry Vaughan expressed it in much the same terms in the mid-seventeenth century in 'The Retreate', which looks back nostalgically to 'those early dayes! when I / Shin'd in my Angell-infancy', and speaks of early childhood as a time when God's face was still visible; growing up, says Vaughan, consists of putting on a 'fleshly dress' over this angel-innocence. The poem concludes:

O how I long to travell back
And tread again that ancient track!

Vaughan's contemporary Thomas Traherne shared this view; in 'The Approach' he writes of the child's nearness to God:

He in our childhood with us walks,
And with our thoughts mysteriously he talks . . .
O Lord, I wonder at thy love
Why did my infancy so early move . . .

And he speaks of childhood itself as being 'My tutor, teacher, guide'.

In all these poems there is surely a hint of Eden. Certainly it is not a far step from the Genesis story to the notion that, to children, the earth appears as beautiful and numinous as it did to Adam and Eve. Growing up becomes synonymous with the loss of Paradise. Does this perhaps have a little to do with the Victorian and Edwardian children's writers' fondness for the symbol of a garden or Enchanted Place, in which all shall be well once more?

Wordsworth's Ode was perhaps not as directly influential on attitudes to children as the writings of Locke and Rousseau had been in their time. But by the mid-nineteenth century there had been a discernible alteration. The old view of the child as miniature adult, as moral chrysalis, had largely receded. On a purely practical level there were suggestions that children might simply be allowed to be themselves. *Holiday House* (1839), a novel for children by a Scottish writer named Catherine Sinclair, has some claim to attention as the first work of fiction in which children's propensity towards naughtiness is actually enjoyed by the author, even praised. The book describes the pranks of young Laura and Harry Graham, left in the charge of a rod-of-iron housekeeper called Mrs Crabtree, and a jolly, tolerant uncle. At every turn of the story Mrs Crabtree is mocked for her severity, and the uncle delights in the children's high spirits, even when they nearly burn the house down. (Harry is given a shilling for helping to put out the fire which he himself started.) *Holiday House* was too revolutionary to inspire imitations – its own author was sufficiently unsure about it to write some rather lugubrious closing chapters in which a dying brother exhorts Harry and Laura to reform themselves – but it is an indication of the reaction that was going on against the old view of childhood. It proved popular enough to be reprinted several times, and C. L. Dodgson ('Lewis Carroll') gave a copy to Alice Liddell and her sisters at Christmas 1861, a few months before he told them the story of *Alice's Adventures*.

Around the middle of the nineteenth century the change of attitude towards children became visible in adult novels. *Jane Eyre* and *Wuthering Heights*, both published in 1847, accept that children have a clear, even heightened, vision of the world. The child Jane's imprisonment in Lowood School is narrated exactly as she herself sees it, and Emily Brontë's melodrama is largely an instance of childhood passions being carried forward into adult life. Something of the same understanding of childhood may be found in George Eliot's *The Mill on the*

Floss (1860) and *Silas Marner* (1861), and, more than any other novelist
of this period, Dickens fully perceived the value of the child's-eye-
view. One notes how the Oliver Twist type of hero was also taken up
and used for their own purposes by many evangelical writers in
England and America, so that by the 1860s and 1870s the market was
being flooded by novels in which orphan waifs were leading their elders
spiritually by the hand and inculcating in them a true love of God.
Gillian Avery writes of such books:

> Children are not only shown as better than their parents, but are
> frequently the instruments of their parents' salvation. It is not,
> however, Blake's Innocent Child that we are shown. The tract book
> writers gave us a child who although appearing sinless to our eyes,
> knew he was sinful but was conscious that he had turned to Christ
> and Christ had saved him, and now urgently wished to pass on the
> message.[8]

Wordsworth's child, trailing clouds of glory, had been put to a use that
Wordsworth himself certainly did not have in mind.

By the second half of the nineteenth century, then, the child had
become an important figure in the English literary imagination. The
detritus of the moralists had not been entirely cleared away: alongside
Holiday House on the bookshelves of Alice Liddell and her sisters, in
the deanery of Christ Church, Oxford, seems to have stood a recent
reprint of Isaac Watts's *Divine Songs*, first published in 1715 and still
going strong in the 1860s. These little verses, with their pious
injunctions ('Satan finds some mischief still / For idle hands to do'),
were to be parodied wickedly in *Alice's Adventures in Wonderland* – a
sure indication that they were still being read in nurseries. Copies of the
old moral tales were still lying around too, and, despite the fact that
fairy stories were no longer dismissed as useless trash, there was little
imaginative fiction for children appearing from the presses. The typical
mid-Victorian nursery would have its Grimm and Andersen alongside
its Perrault, and a book of nursery rhymes too (these had been collected
by scholars since the late eighteenth century), but as late as 1860 there
was scarcely anything in the way of full-length imaginative children's
novels. Ruskin and Thackeray had attempted to provide something to
fill this gap, but Ruskin's *The King of the Golden River* (1851) was
really only a Grimm-type story on a larger scale, with the moral all too
clearly pointed, while Thackeray's *The Rose and the Ring* (1855),
though witty and deservedly popular, scarcely extended the bounds of
imaginative writing for children, being a comic squib chiefly intended
as a parody of the then fashionable style of London pantomime.

A few other British writers had produced a little of what might be
called 'fantasy'. A Staffordshire clergyman named F. E. Paget, calling

himself 'William Churne', wrote *The Hope of the Katzekopfs* (1844), which is strictly speaking the first original full-length English fantasy for children; but with its mixture of unimaginative fairy-tale narrative and heavy moralising it soon passed into oblivion. One or two other writers, such as the humorists Mark Lemon and Tom Hood, turned out original fairy tales, but nothing made a deep impression. Typical of the time was the *Home Treasury* series of traditional fairy stories, issued (under the pseudonym 'Felix Summerly') by Sir Henry Cole, mid-Victorian public servant and a founding father of the Great Exhibition, the Albert Hall, and the South Kensington Museum. Cole engaged 'eminent modern artists' to illustrate his *Little Red Riding-Hood, Jack and the Beanstalk*, and the rest; but the results, published during the 1840s, were heavyweight and reminiscent of a Royal Academy exhibition rather than exciting.

In fact, though in many respects the soil had been ready as early as 1830 for the development of imaginative writing for children, nothing could really happen in Britain during the first half of the nineteenth century. It was not enough for writers in general to perceive the qualities of a child's mind and imagination: before anything of value for children could come out of this, individual authors would have to feel themselves driven away from an adult audience towards a child readership. That apparently could not really happen before the 1860s, because up to then the adult world seems to have been (despite its political and social troubles) too hopeful, too inviting, for men and women of literary genius to reject it and seek a private, childlike voice for themselves. The Great Exhibition of 1851 was a celebration of Britain's position as a leader of industrial society, a leadership established painfully but in the end peacefully, for by 1851 even the working-class ferment visible during the previous decade in the Chartist marches, the Peterloo massacre, and the Bristol riots, had died down. Britain was indeed almost the only nation in Europe to have escaped the 1848 revolutions, and an enormous growth in the national economy was under way by the time of the Great Exhibition. The middle-class Englishman of 1851, like his counterpart a century later, had never had it so good.

Yet in the middle of this complacency a lone voice was beginning to mutter, chiefly into the ears of children. Its message was that the public world was vindictive and intolerant, and that the man of vision, the true artist, must alienate himself from society and pursue a private dream. Edward Lear's *Book of Nonsense*, a collection of limericks, first appeared pseudonymously in 1846, five years before the Great Exhibition, and slowly established itself as the common property of English nurseries. The dedication of the 1861 reprint, to the great-grandchildren, grand-nephews, and grand-nieces of the thirteenth Earl of Derby, for whose parents 'the greater part of . . . this book of drawings and verses . . . were originally made and composed', might suggest that Lear had a comfortable niche in society. But by 1861 Lear had long ago abandoned his job as resident water-colourist to the Earl, and had exiled himself to the Mediterranean, where he scraped a living as an itinerant 'dirty landscape painter' – words which a passing English traveller once used of him. He was homosexual, depressive, and suffered from epileptic fits. Not surprisingly he felt himself to be an outcast. He lived his Mediterranean life largely in a state of deep unhappiness, but usually became cheerful when chance threw him into the company of children, whom he could reduce to helpless laughter with his comic drawings, funny alphabets, and rhymes. His alienation from society is the real subject of his *Book of Nonsense*, with its catalogue of eccentric individuals, many of whom suffer the contempt, hostility, and often violent reactions of the public world – which is always labelled as 'They':

> There was an Old Person of Buda,
> Whose conduct grew ruder and ruder;
>   Till at last, with a hammer,
>   They silenced his clamour,
> By smashing that Person of Buda.

After the *Book of Nonsense* was published, Lear was able to turn his mind to more positive things, and his later verses for children consist largely of explorations of the possibilities of Escape:

> They went to sea in a Sieve, they did,
>   In a Sieve they went to sea:
> In spite of all their friends could say,
> On a winter's morn, on a stormy day,
>   In a Sieve they went to sea!

The purpose of such strange journeys is stated bluntly enough. As the Duck observes to the Kangaroo,

> 'My life is a bore in this nasty pond,
> And I long to go out in the world beyond!'

The Nutcracker remarks much the same thing to the Sugar-Tongs: '"Don't you wish we were able / Along the blue hills and green meadows to ride? / Must we drag on this stupid existence for ever?"' And Lear's strange travellers, despite their often perilous means of journeying, usually get to their destinations. The Jumblies cross the Western Sea in their leaky craft and come to an earthly paradise where 'they bought an Owl, and a useful Cart, / And a pound of Rice, and a Cranberry Tart.' The Yonghy-Bonghy-Bò is borne away from a broken love affair on the back of a turtle, who carries him 'Towards the sunset isles of Boshen', and even the Pobble Who Has No Toes lands up in comfort at his Aunt Jobiska's Park, while of course the Owl and the Pussycat come to the Land where the Bong-Tree grows. In these and other rhymes, published from the 1870s to the 1890s, Lear is stating a theme that becomes central to the great children's writers: the search for a mysterious, elusive Good Place.

Such a place had in a sense been the goal of the religious writers for children from John Bunyan to Mrs Sherwood. But Lear rejected their view of the universe. He could not accept any form of hellfire teaching. The notion that, as he put it, 'the Almighty damns the greater part of His creatures' seemed ridiculous to him. He described himself as one of those 'who believe that God the Creator is greater than a Book, and that millions unborn are to look up to higher thoughts than those stereotyped by ancient legends, gross ignorance, and hideous bigotry'.

These sentiments are extraordinarily close to those expressed in 1939 by A. A. Milne. In his autobiography, *It's Too Late Now*, Milne condemned organised religion for its narrowness of view, and pleaded for the recognition of 'God' as something far huger and more mysterious than the deity of Christian doctrine. A thread of connection runs here between Lear and Milne; for, almost without exception, the authors of the outstanding English children's books that appeared between 1860 and 1930 rejected, or had doubts about, conventional religious teaching. The doubts, as we shall see, are less visible in the writers who operated earlier in this period. Charles Kingsley, Lewis Carroll, and George MacDonald were all three clergymen, and their religious uncertainties can only be detected beneath the surface of their writings for children, though they were a very strong motive behind them. The group of writers who followed later – Kenneth Grahame, Beatrix Potter, J. M. Barrie, and A. A. Milne – were more conscious of their rejection of conventional Christianity. Their search for an Arcadia, a Good Place, a Secret Garden, was to a very large extent an attempt to find something to replace it.[9]

*

By the time that Edward Lear published his *Nonsense Songs* (1871), the book which contained 'The Owl and the Pussy-Cat', his urge to comment sardonically on the public world was beginning to be shared by writers of a very different kind. The mid-Victorian belief in progress, which had steered Britain to her recent economic successes and had motivated the Great Exhibition, was starting to be shaken. The realisation had dawned that the apparent triumphs of the Industrial Revolution had produced widespread misery for the working classes. First Dickens in fiction, then Henry Mayhew in his documentary survey of London poverty (concluded in 1862), revealed this truth. Many writers tried to find some solution to the dilemma. Among them were Ruskin, whose *Fors Clavigera* (1871–84) inveighed against working-class poverty (and incidentally attacked complacent Sunday School teachers for showering the children of the poor with useless little moral tracts), and Charles Kingsley, who before turning to a child readership with *The Water-Babies* wrote adult novels about the insanitary lives of the poor. The Pre-Raphaelites, and William Morris in particular, started to preach that the route back to a healthy society lay through a flight from industrialisation, a return to medievalism, and the revival of the old methods of craft. Morris's ideals led him to write *The Earthly Paradise* (1868–70), a narrative poem which describes the search for a land 'across the western sea where none grow old'. George Borrow went searching for earthly paradises on the real map, escaping from industrial England to Europe and the East; in such books as *Lavengro* (1851) he created his own literature of Escape, which was to influence Kenneth Grahame. And in 1871, the year of 'The Owl and the Pussycat', Matthew Arnold, whose voice was among the loudest being lifted against industrial society, had this to say in *Friendship's Garland* on the subject of urban life:

> Your middle-class man thinks it the highest pitch of development and civilisation when his letters are carried twelve times a day from Camberwell to Islington, and if railway-trains run to and fro between them every quarter of an hour. He thinks it is nothing that the trains only carry him from an illiberal, dismal life at Islington to an illiberal, dismal life at Camberwell; and the letters only tell him that such is the life there.

This growing vein of scepticism about the quality of contemporary life was accompanied, during the final quarter of the nineteenth century, by a certain faltering in Britain's fortunes in the public world. The prosperity of the 1850s and 1860s gave way to a period of economic uncertainty and even depression. François Bédarida, in his *Social History of England, 1851–1975* (1979), observes that during this period the economic health of Britain 'was not so radiant as it had been in the past', and describes a crisis of confidence which 'shattered all the old certainties', so that 'pessimism and anxiety became the rule'. For contemporary confirmation of this, one need turn no further than to the private journal of Beatrix Potter, compiled in code during the 1880s and 1890s. Potter draws a picture of the English middle class (to which her family belonged) deeply worried by workers' protest marches, by explosions set off by Irish Home Rulers, and by the supposedly incompetent and wrong-headed Prime Ministerial behaviour of Gladstone. 'I am terribly afraid of the future,' Beatrix Potter wrote in 1885. No wonder that she turned away, in her Journal, from the contemplation of public affairs to a meditation about her own happiness in early childhood, and eventually began to create a series of books set in a world which, though far from safe and untroubled, was not touched on by politics or other overtly adult concerns.

This widespread uncertainty, from the 1870s onwards, came despite the great expansion of the British Empire, just then taking place. The imperial spirit (certainly to be found alongside the pessimism) did not go unnoticed by writers for children, but the books it inspired were ephemeral. During the 1880s such writers as G. A. Henty turned out sheaves of stories about brave British lads abroad; but this optimistic school of fiction was to produce no classic, no narrative of more than trivial interest. Probably the nearest that one can find to an 'Empire' classic for children is Kipling's *Stalky and Co* (1899), an apparently amoral book which is in fact subtly organised to demonstrate that boyish anti-authoritarian pranks at school are a good training for manly service in the cause of one's nation. In the final chapter Stalky is seen putting into good effect as an officer on the North-West Frontier the lessons in cunning he learnt from his pranks at the College, with Beetle and M'Turk. But almost no other children's book of note reflected the imperial spirit, while Kipling's own children's writings spread into an area not far from that occupied by Kenneth Grahame and A. A. Milne; their stories have certain affinities with his *Jungle Books* (1894 and 1895) and his *Just So Stories* (1902). Moreover, *Kim* (1901), Kipling's brilliant study of a white child adrift in the Indian underworld, has something of the Arcadian yearnings of the great introspective children's authors, with its account of the old lama's search for a sacred River, an Enchanted Place where he can find peace.

Kipling was almost the only writer who straddled the two streams of children's literature, which divided in about 1860 and never really came together again until the 1950s. On the one hand was the breezy, optimistic adventure story, set firmly in the real world (though greatly exaggerating certain characteristics of that world). Stories of school life, pioneered by Thomas Hughes and then mass produced by hack writers from the 1880s, belonged in this category, as did the girls 'stories by L. T. Meade, Angela Brazil, and other popular novelists of the same sort.' Realistic' fiction of this kind attracted few writers of any quality – besides Kipling, Robert Louis Stevenson was almost the only outstanding author to involve himself with it, in *Treasure Island* (1883) and *Kidnapped* (1886) – and it was not, of course, 'realistic' in any deep sense. Except in the hands of a Kipling or a Stevenson it dealt in stereotyped characters and ideas and presented a thoroughly rose-coloured view of the world. Its ideals were a *reductio ad absurdum* for children of the notion of 'chivalry' which dominated Victorian society and was derived from a spurious Arthurian-style medievalism.[10] The ethic of this strand of children's fiction – a belief in heroism for its own sake, a condemnation of the coward or 'muff', and a conviction that the English were the best race in the world – may have contributed to the causes of the First World War.

The other strand of writing for children, the one with which this present book is chiefly concerned, was introspective, and is generally described as 'fantasy' in that its stories, more often than not, involve some impossible thing, such as talking animals or toys, or inexplicable or magical events.[11] To this strand belong most of the great names of the late Victorian and Edwardian nursery: Kingsley, Carroll, MacDonald, Grahame, Potter, Nesbit, Barrie, with Milne as a latecomer. While it was not overtly 'realistic' and purported to have nothing to say about the 'real' world, in this fantastic strain of writing may be found some profound observations about human character and contemporary society, and (strikingly often) about religion. It dealt largely with utopias, and posited the existence of Arcadian societies remote from the nature and concerns of the everyday world; yet in doing this it was commenting, often satirically and critically, on real life.

It is notable that this fantasy writing took root most quickly and deeply in England. Other European countries produced only a tiny handful of memorable children's fantasies before 1914: Carlo Collodi's chaotic but charming *Pinocchio* (1883) and *The Wonderful Adventures of Nils* (1906–7) by the Swedish writer Selma Lagerlöf are really the only examples of note. America was almost equally unproductive before 1900, and most fantasies that did appear there were imitative of British writers. Only with *The Wonderful Wizard of Oz*, published in the first year of the new century, did the United States produce a fantasy which, like its great British counterparts, examined society critically in fairy story terms. Baum's was an isolated voice (and a rather shaky one: he wrote sloppily and scarcely bothered to work out the implications of his subversive tale); no one managed to equal his achievement for more than half a century after the first appearance in print of Dorothy, the Tin Man, the Scarecrow, and the Cowardly Lion. America was still possessed with the kind of optimism that had infected British society around the time of the Great Exhibition; and optimistic societies do not, apparently, produce great fantasies. It was to take the Vietnam War and the general loss of national confidence during that period before fantasy could flower in America to the extent that it had in England. J. R. R. Tolkien produced the seeds: his English-made *The Lord of the Rings* (1954–5), with its lyrically melancholic portrait of a society in decline and threatened with total destruction, became the subject of a 'campus cult' just after the assassination of John F. Kennedy, and during the time when the international arms race was building up. The eventual consequence of this was the creation of a whole breed of native American fantasy novels, some of them of high quality.[12]

*

All books, of course, require readers, and the upsurge of introspective, non-realistic writing for children in Britain during the late nineteenth century suggests that a new audience had arisen. The general market for children's books had been active for a century before this; the business of being a 'juvenile bookseller' really became economically viable in the 1740s, concurrent with the rise of a middle class sufficiently leisured to undertake the 'instruction and amusement' of its children's minds, and sufficiently affluent to pay for the books that this required. The audience for the books of Lewis Carroll and his successors, more than a century later, was in a sense unchanged: almost entirely middle class and affluent. Comfortably off parents bought *Alice and The Water-Babies* for their children, while the children of the poorer classes had to make do with the pious trash that the Sunday Schools handed out as 'reward books'. But there was a certain difference between the middle-class child readership of the mid-eighteenth century and that which greeted the works of Carroll and Kingsley in the 1860s.

During the second half of the nineteenth century small families were coming into fashion among the middle classes in England, America, and Western Europe. Until the middle of the century it was perfectly acceptable socially, indeed almost the norm, to produce large families. One only has to look at the authors themselves to see this. Edward Lear, born in 1812, was the youngest of twenty children. Charles Kingsley (born in 1819) and George MacDonald (1824) were each one of six; C. L. Dodgson ('Lewis Carroll'), born in 1832, was one of eleven. Then around the 1850s the birth rate fell, at times steeply. Rosalind Mitchison writes, in *British Population Changes since 1880* (1977):

> The birth rate in Britain began to decline in the last quarter of the nineteenth century. The decline was not uniform: it was faster in times of economic recession and slower in booms, but on the whole it became progressively steeper until [it] reached a low point in 1933 . . . This decline in fertility has its parallels in other European countries and in other developed parts of the world. Most such countries maintained a high birth rate until the 1870s, then experienced a fall, and the fall continued until the 1930s.

The reasons for the decline have never been entirely explained. Mitchison observes that 'similar changes took place in countries at very different stages of their economic development', and it appears that factors other than the purely economic were in operation. The middle classes, themselves still a comparatively new element in society, seem to have experienced a vague but widespread feeling that their children could 'do better' if there were fewer of them to feed, clothe, and educate. And certainly increasing knowledge of birth control was a factor; in the words of François Bédarida it led to 'the fading of that age-old fatalism, which meant that all children were accepted passively as "sent by God"'. In particular, the trial in 1877 of Charles Bradlaugh and Annie Besant, accused of obscenity because they had reprinted an old pamphlet about contraception, helped to publicise birth control methods, judging by the marked fall in the birth rate in many countries (including Britain) from that date onwards. Quite apart from this, the medical profession was by this time stressing the debilitating effects of too many children on a woman's health. One writer[13] stated that 'it is looked upon as supremely ridiculous to have a great many [children]', and Dr Elizabeth Blackwell, in *How to Keep a Household in Health* (1870), went so far as to say: 'I do not consider, as it is so often stated, that the great object of marriage is to produce children; marriage has higher humanitarian objects.'

The numbers of children dropped perceptibly. Again we may see this from the children's writers themselves. Beatrix Potter, born in 1866, was one of two siblings. Kenneth Grahame, though he came from a large family, and A. A. Milne, though he had two brothers, were each to produce only one child when they married. They were not untypical. And the beginning and end of the period of the falling birth rate coincide almost to the years with the time during which the outstanding English children's books were being written.

Parents with small families inevitably tend to lavish closer attention on their offspring than do those with large broods,[14] and it is scarcely surprising that one literary result of the falling birth rate should be a sentimental idealisation of childhood, the creation (chiefly by lady writers) of such beings as Little Lord Fauntleroy (Frances Hodgson Burnett's novel was published in 1886). Any tendency towards a tougher attitude to children must moreover have been modified by the fact that there was no corresponding decline in the death rate of children before the beginning of the twentieth century. Despite a general increase in hygiene and continuing improvements in medicine, the young frequently fell victim to scarlet fever (the children's writer Mrs Molesworth lost a daughter because of it), or tuberculosis (Frances Hodgson Burnett lost a son through it), while others were sent to their grave by the continuing fondness of the medical profession for over-administering semi-poisonous medicines such as calomel

(Charles Kingsley and Louisa Alcott were among those overdosed with this).

One suspects too that the late Victorians tended to lavish more attention on their children because of the uncertainty of the adult, public world. It was a climate which must have encouraged people to turn inward to their own families, to obtain from their children the sense of security and stability which the outside world was not providing. In such conditions, the work of the great introspective children's writers was especially likely to be appreciated.

*

By the beginning of the 1860s, then, the conditions had been reached in which 'escapist' literature, aimed ostensibly at children, was likely to be written, and likely to find a sympathetic audience. And when the new movement in children's books began, it did so with a striking suddenness. Up to 1862, nothing had happened. But by the end of that year, two of the first wave of outstanding writers for children had their first stories composed, while a novel by a third of them was already being published in a magazine. It was called *The Water-Babies*.

PART ONE
Arrears of Destruction

Parson Lot takes a cold bath
Charles Kingsley and *The Water-Babies*

Kingsley's story appeared very modestly at first, making its bow in monthly parts without preamble or illustrations in the rather stodgy-looking pages of *Macmillan's Magazine*. In the issue for August 1862, and thereafter until the following March, it was printed under the heading *The Water-Babies: a Fairy Tale for a Land-Baby*, stated to be by 'The Rev. Professor Kingsley'. Then in May 1863 the whole story was reissued as a rather plain-looking green-covered book. The publishers, Macmillan again, thought fit to include only two complete illustrations, though there were decorations at the head of each chapter. Yet despite this rather self-effacing start in life, *The Water-Babies* was assured of public attention, for its author was already one of the most popular writers of the day.

Kingsley had made a big reputation in the fifteen years before it was published, first as a campaigner for social reform, then as a popular novelist, and later still as a writer on marine biology – and also, for good measure, as a reteller of classical myths for children. Clearly he was versatile, even a polymath; he was currently holding the Regius Professorship of Modern History at Cambridge. Yet even so, his public, which included Queen Victoria herself, could scarcely have expected such a curiosity as *The Water-Babies* to be the next production of his pen.

It was most curious, this tale of a North Country chimney-sweep's 'climbing boy' who, covered in soot and escaping across the moorland after a misunderstanding at a country house where his master has been employed, plunges himself into a stream to get cool and clean, and finds that he has turned into a tiny 'water-baby', less than four inches long and able to live an immortal existence beneath the surface of river and sea. Those who had read Kingsley's *Glaucus, or the Wonders of the Shore*, published seven years earlier and used in many nurseries, would not perhaps have been very surprised at Tom's encounters with salmon, lobster, and many smaller denizens of sea and river-bed; *Glaucus* was full of lively accounts of the habits of these creatures. But there had been nothing in Kingsley's writings – or for that matter in anyone else's – to prepare the reader for Tom's magical-cum-moral lessons at the hands of the maternal underwater fairies Mrs Bedonebyasyoudid and her sister Mrs Doasyouwouldbedoneby, or for his quest far across the ocean bed to find his old master Grimes and save him from his own hardness of heart.

Perceptive readers might recognise a touch of *The Pilgrim's Progress*, and its ancestors the old medieval romances, in these last chapters; others might catch a whiff of *Gulliver*, and those who knew their Hans Andersen might think that Kingsley had something of the Danish author's purpose and manner. But the book was really quite unprecedented. Nobody had ever before dared to mix together a fairy tale – and a completely invented one at that: there was nothing about water-babies in Grimm or Perrault or anyone else – with a touch of social comment about conditions of the working poor, a lot of specialist information about the habits of underwater creatures, and an almost Dantean account of a soul's moral and spiritual education in Purgatory; for Tom's experiences were quite clearly supposed to be those of a soul after death. To top it all, Kingsley had the nerve, as one reviewer spotted, to write the book chiefly in the style of Rabelais.[15]

It was quite different from anything else ever before written for children, and like all Kingsley's work it was both brilliant and a failure, self-contradictory, muddled, inspiring, sentimental, powerfully argumentative, irrationally prejudiced, superbly readable. In a small space it managed to discover and explore almost all the directions that children's books would take over the next hundred years. And in exploring them it usually fell flat on its face.

*

Charles Kingsley is a very puzzling figure to readers in the late twentieth century. In some respects we find him immensely congenial, a liberal in the modern style. Yet at a closer inspection the liberalism seems to crumble away, and we are left with something far more enigmatic, even distasteful.

He does not at first sight appear to have had in his personality the makings of an outstanding children's author. *The Water-Babies* seems an odd book to come from someone so active and extrovert, so concerned with public deeds, and apparently so little occupied with introspection. But again a closer investigation produces a different picture, and we find in him certain traits which we can discover in other great children's writers.

He was born at Holne in Devon in 1819, the same year of birth as

Queen Victoria – 'appropriate enough,' observes the best of his biographers, Susan Chitty, 'for one who combined in his person so many of the conflicts that racked the Victorian era'. He was the eldest of seven children of the Revd Charles Kingsley; his father had been brought up a country gentleman, but the family fortunes were squandered (first by guardians during his minority, then by himself), and, finding himself penniless at the age of thirty, he decided on the Church of England simply as a way of making a living. Once ordained, he moved with his wife from parish to parish as circumstances dictated; Holne was his second curacy, and only six weeks after Charles's birth the family had to shift again, this time to the Midlands. A couple of curacies later, with Charles aged five, they found themselves in the Fens, at Barnack in Northamptonshire, where they were at last able to make a settled home for a few years. Just as they arrived there, Charles's seven-month-old sister Louisa Mary died, an all too common event even in comfortably off English families at the time, largely thanks to that fondness of Victorian doctors for dosing babies with strong medicines at the slightest sign of illness. Charles tried to get his revenge in *The Water-Babies*, when Mrs Bedonebyasyoudid

> called up all the doctors, who give little children so much physic . . . and then she dosed them with calomel and jalap and salts and senna and brimstone and treacle; and horrible faces they made; and then she gave them a great emetic of mustard and water, and no basins; and began all over again; and that was the way she spent the morning.

And did the death of little Louisa Mary plant in his mind, even then in his early childhood, some notion of a paradise or purgatory peopled entirely by children who have died young?

He himself nearly followed his sister to an early grave, for the damp atmosphere of the Fens was thought to be making him ill, and he was heavily dosed with calomel. He survived both the illness and the treatment, but afterwards claimed that mercury poisoning from the calomel had inhibited the growth of his jaw, and so caused the stammer which was to afflict him in adult life.

He was a sturdily imaginative child; he delighted in stories of Button Cap, the ghost of a wicked old parson who was supposed to haunt the Rectory. And he liked to dress up in a pinafore for a surplice and preach sermons to the nursery chairs. His mother wrote down these sermons and showed them to the bishop, and she also preserved poems that he made up. She lavished a lot of attention on him, and throughout his life he felt especially close to her. He once wrote to his wife: 'I have nothing to care for in reality but my mother and you.'

His father was a remote, rather chilling figure who seems to have treated religion as a matter of business rather than spirituality, and who

discouraged any display of affection. Charles's most frequent contact
with him seems to have been when he went into the study to repeat his
lessons aloud, an experience which many nineteenth-century children
had to undergo till their brains seemed to turn to water, especially if
they were being crammed with the books of 'general information' that
became fashionable in the 1830s. Again, Charles got his revenge in *The
Water-Babies*, when Tom comes to the Isle of Tomtoddies, where the
people are turnips – all heads and no bodies – and worship the great idol
Examination:

> Then Tom stumbled on the hugest and softest nimble-comequick
> turnip you ever saw filling a hole in a crop of swedes, and it cried to
> him 'Can you tell me anything at all about anything you like?'
> 'About what?' says Tom.
> 'About anything you like; for as fast as I learn things I forget
> them again. So my mamma says that my intellect is not adapted
> for methodic science, and says that I must go in for general informa-
> tion.' . . .
> So he told him prettily enough, while the poor turnip listened very
> carefully; and the more he listened the more he forgot, and the more
> water ran out of him.

Charles Kingsley senior did allow his son one indulgence; he was a
sportsman and a naturalist, and he permitted young Charles to
accompany him on shooting expeditions in the Fens during the early
morning. Charles never forgot 'the shining meres, the golden reed-
beds, the countless water-fowl, the strange and gaudy insects', and it
was now that his own life as a naturalist began. But he had scarcely
begun to appreciate the Fenland landscape when the family moved once
more. They went west, back to Devon, and Charles to his delight found
that his new home was perched directly above the sea, in the spectacular
little port of Clovelly – a 'steep stair of houses clinging to the cliffs', he
called it in *Westward Ho!* The naval and fishing life of the Devon coast
entered deeply into his imagination; he had particular memories of
shipwreck seen from the cliffs, and of the British fleet sailing into
Plymouth after the Battle of Navarino. His father began to take him
and his brothers shell collecting, and Charles had his first contact with
what was to become his own especial private world, the microcosm of
the rock pool and sea shallows. 'Now that you have seen Clovelly,' he
wrote to his wife many years later, 'you know what was the inspiration
of my life before I met you.'

He was not sent to school until he was twelve. Then, after a year at a
preparatory establishment at Clifton (where he was stirred into some
sort of social awareness by a glimpse of the Bristol riots of 1831),
he became a pupil at Helston Grammar School, a good boarding

establishment on the south coast of Cornwall, where Coleridge's son Derwent was headmaster, and the assistant teachers included an expert naturalist who encouraged Kingsley to go botanising. Schooldays seem to have been generally happy for him, but they were marred by the death of his thirteen-year-old brother Herbert, also a pupil at the school. Herbert is known to have stolen a silver spoon, run away, sold it, and been caught after spending a night in the open. This is said to have given him rheumatic fever which led to heart failure; but there was a local tradition that he drowned himself in Looe Pool (a landlocked arm of the sea) and the fact that his grave in Helston churchyard bears only his initials suggests suicide.

And he put his poor hot sore feet into the water; and then his legs; and the farther he went in, the more the church-bells rang in his head . . . He was so hot and thirsty, and longed so to be clean for once, that he tumbled himself as quick as he could into the clear cool stream. And he had not been in it two minutes before he fell fast asleep, into the quietest, sunniest, cosiest sleep that ever he had in his life . . .

And, therefore, the keeper, and the groom, and Sir John made a great mistake, and were very unhappy . . . without any reason, when they found a black thing in the water, and said it was Tom's body, and that he had been drowned. They were utterly mistaken. Tom was quite alive, and cleaner, and merrier than he ever had been. The fairies had washed him, you see, in the swift river, so thoroughly, that not only his dirt, but his whole husk and shell had been washed quite off him, and the pretty little real Tom was washed out of the inside of it, and swam away . . .

If we knew for certain that Herbert Kingsley met his death by water (which we do not), we would surely be in no doubt as to why in *The Water-Babies* Kingsley fashioned the myth of the drowned child who was not really dead after all. Even if Herbert died in bed, we know that someone else close to Charles in boyhood met his end in the water: a Clovelly fisherman's son, who was the first of several close male friends in his life – 'my especial pet and bird's nesting companion, a little, delicate, precocious child'. The boy's corpse was found lashed to the rigging of his father's storm-wrecked boat.

The West Country was Charles's delight, and ever afterwards he thought of himself as one of its natives, retaining a Devon twang in his speech. But he was snatched away from it in his mid-teens, when his father became Rector of St Luke's, Chelsea, and he had to finish his schooling in London before going up to Magdalene College, Cambridge. The sense of this deprivation never left him; ever afterwards, when physically ill or (which was very often) suffering from a nervous collapse, he would decide that a Devon holiday was the only remedy, and would head West like a wounded animal seeking its burrow.

Cambridge introduced a new note into his life: dissipation and scepticism. He drank, hunted, rowed, kept a Scotch terrier, had fun with the local girls, and abandoned religious belief. He was soon feeling desperately guilty about it, even to the point of contemplating suicide. He also thought of taking to a 'wild prairie' life, chasing bison and grizzly bear in America like something out of Fenimore Cooper. Instead he was rescued from himself by the dark-haired Fanny Grenfell, youngest of four daughters of a Cornish tin magnate who, recently orphaned and left comfortably off, had formed themselves into an earnest sisterhood, reading the outpourings of the Oxford Movement and devoting themselves to virginity with the encourage-ment of Dr Pusey. Fanny soon took Charles's spiritual education in hand, just as Ellie does with Tom in *The Water-Babies*:

> And what did the little girl teach Tom? She taught him, first, what you have been taught ever since you said your first prayers at your mother's knees; but she taught him much more simply . . . And he jumped at her, and longed to hug and kiss her; but did not, remembering that she was a lady born; so he only jumped round and round her till he was quite tired.

After 'jumping round' Fanny Grenfell for a few years, much to the annoyance of her sisters, Charles won her, just as Tom finally wins Ellie. And in doing so he vowed himself to God and the Church with all the fervour of the newly converted. He would be a clergyman, and not just a tepid parson like his father. 'I am under a heavy debt to God,' he told Fanny, 'and how can I pay this better than by devoting myself to the religion I have scorned, making of the debauchee a preacher of purity and holiness, and of the destroyer of systems a weak though determined upholder of the only true system.'

For a little time he was attracted by Catholicism and the monastic life. But both of these soon came to repel him, and in any case he could not long keep his mind off Fanny's body, even before they were married and while he was being ordained. His love letters to her[16] certainly enlarge one's ideas of what a young bachelor parson might be thinking about and getting up to in the 1840s:

> When you go to bed tonight, forget that you ever wore a garment, and open your lips for my kisses and spread out each limb that I may lie between your breasts all night (Canticles I, 13) . . . [17]

> You shall come to me some morning when we can ensure solitude and secrecy, come as a penitent, barefoot, with dishevelled hair,

wearing one coarse garment only and then I will, in God's name solemnly absolve you. Afterwards I will bathe you from head to foot in kisses and fold you in my arms . . .

What can I do but write to my naughty baby who does not love me at all and who of course has forgotten me by this time? But I have not forgotten her, for my hands are perfumed with her delicious limbs, and I cannot wash off the scent, and every moment the thought comes across me of those mysterious recesses of beauty where my hands have been wandering . . . Only to acquire self-control and to keep under the happy body, to which God has permitted of late such exceeding liberty and bliss . . .

The first quotation refers to the 'festival nights' that Charles and Fanny kept on Thursdays, before their marriage, when, each in their separate homes, they were to imagine that they were lying together in sexual bliss. The second shows how for Kingsley, sexuality was bound up with the idea of penance; and indeed on Friday nights they agreed to behave as penitents. Charles stripped himself naked in his cottage bedroom and scourged himself. He also fasted, dressed 'as scantily as possible with decency', slept on the floor one night a week and rose at three o'clock to pray, and on one occasion 'went into the woods at night and lay naked upon thorns and when I came home my body was torn from head to foot'. His conscious reason for doing such things was not Manichean: he did not despise the flesh or want to mortify it, but regarded it as 'awful, glorious matter', and wished to 'purify' himself and Fanny so that they would eventually be fit for the 'religious ceremonies' of connubial sex. As a final penance they were to remain chaste for the first month of marriage, with Fanny 'a virgin bride, a sister only', before they came at last to the great moment of consummation. This final test, he told her, would

give us more perfect delight when we lie naked in each other's arms, clasped together toying with each other's limbs, buried in each other's bodies, struggling, panting, dying for a moment. Shall we not feel, even then, that there is more in store for us, that those thrilling writhings are but dim shadows of a union which shall be perfect?

Heaven, in other words, would consist of something very like perpetual copulation.

In fact, even after their marriage Charles could not get the ideas of penance and physical suffering out of his head when he thought about sex. For a wedding present he gave Fanny an illustrated manuscript he had begun to write about St Elizabeth of Hungary, which would describe how she died at the hands of a monkish torturer. He never got far with the text, but he made plenty of drawings of naked women being tortured. Other sketches by him, also given to Fanny, show the two of them naked or scantily clothed in poses which are at once religious and highly erotic. One depicts them having intercourse as they lie tied to a cross which floats across the sea. In another, again copulating, they are flying up to heaven on wings.

In all these drawings Fanny is depicted as slim and delicately built. But such portraits and photographs as survive show her to have been in reality distinctly plump, if not positively fat, a matron rather than a nymph, Mrs Doasyouwouldbedoneby rather than Ellie:

> When Sunday morning came, sure enough, Mrs Doasyouwouldbe-doneby came, too . . . She took Tom in her arms, and laid him in the softest place of all, and kissed him, and patted him, and talked to him, tenderly and low, such things as he had never heard before in his life; and Tom looked up into her eyes, and loved her, and loved, till he fell fast asleep from pure love.

Perhaps, for all his outpourings to Fanny about 'thrilling writhings', it was a motherly embrace which remained Kingsley's sexual ideal. And was he really so aggressively heterosexual as the letters to Fanny would suggest? We know that his brother Henry – in his time almost as popular a novelist as Charles – was bisexual if not entirely homosexual (he lived for a time with a close male friend, before beginning a childless marriage), and several people in Charles's lifetime and since have remarked on a vaguely feminine streak in him – a streak which seems to have led him to fear and hate the same thing in other people. He disliked Ruskin because he said you could tell from the man's face that his marriage hadn't been consummated, and he castigated John Henry Newman for 'a fastidious, maundering die-away effeminacy'. He even claimed, at the height of his half-crazy fear and hatred of Roman Catholicism, that the adoration of the Virgin was effeminate.

Any modern critic of *The Water-Babies* is inclined to make much of its sexual symbolism. It begins, after all, with something that hints at rape, a boy working his way down a chimney into a girl's bedroom; and Ellie's room, incidentally, is pure white, the colour of virginity.[18] It is after this quasi-sexual encounter that Tom runs away (no very coherent reason is given for his flight), and plunges himself into the stream (again Kingsley gives no very convincing motive for this). The notion strongly suggests itself that he is running away from sex, which he fears because it has made him impure, and is plunging himself into something that will both purify him and give him a kind of compensation for sex: cold water.

Kingsley had what can only be described as an obsession with washing and cold water. In the love letter quoted above he speaks of the attempt to 'wash off the scent' of Fanny's 'delicious limbs', and it is recorded that he could not bear even a speck of dirt on his clothes. And once he had become a social campaigner and was concerned to improve living conditions for the urban poor, he emphasised again and again the need for clean cold water, not just to drink, but to bathe in. 'Not for nothing,' he told a gathering at a Mechanics' Institute,

> was baptism chosen by the old Easterns as the sign of a new life. That morning cold bath, which foreigners consider as Young England's strangest superstition, has done as much, believe me, to abolish drunkenness, as any other cause whatsoever. With a clean skin and nerves and muscles braced by a sudden shock, men do not crave artificial stimulants. I have found that, *ceteris paribus*, a man's sobriety is in direct proportion to his cleanliness.[19]

*

He became Rector of Eversley, a village not far from Aldershot in Hampshire, and was to remain its parish priest for the rest of his life, living there with Fanny and the four children she bore him. He did his job well, attending energetically to the education and physical welfare of his poorer parishioners as well as their spiritual health. But Eversley could not long contain him. Among the books which Fanny had used to convert him back to religion was *The Kingdom of Christ* by Frederick Denison Maurice, himself a recent convert to the Church of England – his father was a Unitarian minister, and he had worked in literary journalism before turning to the church. Maurice was trying to make peace between the warring Evangelicals and the Oxford Movement by taking a kind of liberal middle road. In doing so he in effect set up a third faction in Victorian England's already divided religious life. It was described by its sympathisers as Christian Socialism, on account of the close interest its adherents took in Chartism, the rights of the poor, and social welfare. Those rather less sympathetic, observing the pugilistic nature of many of the beefy young men who clustered round Maurice, dubbed it 'Muscular Christianity'. Maurice's disciples claimed to abhor this label; actually they seem to have been rather flattered by it.

Kingsley attached himself to them, and when the Chartist movement came to the boil in April 1848 he rushed up to London and persuaded several other Muscular Christians that they should paper the metropolis with a poster he had written, addressed to the Chartists who at that moment were petitioning Parliament for universal male suffrage and other reforms that would benefit working men. Kingsley's poster was signed 'A Working Parson'. It expressed sympathy with the 'shameful filth and darkness' in which the working class had to live, but exhorted the Chartists to 'turn back from the precipice of riot, which ends in the gulf of universal distrust, stagnation, starvation', and argued that getting the vote would be valueless without a new spiritual and moral way of life: 'There will be no true freedom without virtue, no true science without religion, no true industry without the fear of God, and love to your fellow-citizens.'

Understandably this made no impression at all on the Chartists, or on anyone else, but Kingsley felt he had an immensely important message, and as soon as he had finished bill-posting he got his fellow Muscular Christians to start a periodical called *Politics for the People*, which was aimed at Chartists and other working-class readers who were eager for reform or revolution. Kingsley wrote for it under the name 'Parson Lot', which he chose because he thought of himself as Lot contemplating Sodom and Gomorrah. His first piece in the paper reiterated what he had said on the poster:

> I think you have fallen into the same mistake as the rich of whom you complain . . . the mistake of fancying that legislative reform is social reform, or that men's hearts can be changed by Act of Parliament . . . God will only reform society on condition of our reforming every man his own self . . . Too many of you are trying to do God's work with the devil's tools . . . What spirit is there but the devil's spirit, in bloodthirsty threats of *revenge*?[20]

Having made his message clear – don't start a revolution, he was telling the Chartists, just reform yourselves spiritually and God will do the rest – he turned in subsequent numbers of *Politics for the People* to writing chatty little pieces on how good it was for working men to visit the National Gallery and the British Museum, so that they could refresh their eyes 'when they are wearied with dull bricks and mortar'.

His position, then, was anti-revolutionary, almost plain reactionary. But even this milk-and-water socialism was enough to make him unpopular with the landowning classes – with the result that Fanny begged him to stop it, because she knew it was damaging his chances of preferment in the church. But he would not stop. He began to write a story called *Yeast*, which was serialised during 1848 in *Fraser's*, a magazine published by a friend of his. *Yeast* describes how a young man much like Kingsley himself is reconverted to Christianity and sets about investigating the living conditions of the poor. Among its characters is a socialist gamekeeper called Tregarva who writes a ballad about the iniquities of landowners:

> There's blood on your new foreign shrubs, squire;
> There's blood on your pointer's feet;
> There's blood on the game you sell, squire,
> And there's blood on the game you eat!

You have sold the labouring man, squire,
  Body and soul to shame,
To pay for your seat in the House, squire,
  And to pay for the feed of your game.

In the story this ballad causes the squire who reads it to have a stroke, and it seems to have had much the same effect on readers of *Fraser's*, who cancelled their subscriptions in droves, with the result that Kingsley was instructed to bring the story to an abrupt end. (Thus truncated, it was published in book form the next year.) But really the ballad was the only radical thing in *Yeast*. Most of the plot was concerned with the hero Lancelot Smith's infatuation with the squire's daughter, Argemone Lavington, with whom he enters into 'eye-wedlock' at the moment he first beholds her, coming out of a moorland chapel where she has been doing penance. Kingsley had meant to show how, once married, she and Lancelot become ideal landlords – social improvement being achieved not through revolution but by benevolent paternalism. When told to finish the story at the double, he killed off Argemone with typhus germs caught from visiting an agricultural labourer's hovel. She dies babbling of clean water.

Argemone, of course, was a portrait of Fanny, who loved *Yeast* so much she wanted to be buried with it. On the other hand, one of the Muscular Christians, J. M. Ludlow, who was the nominal editor of *Politics for the People*, thought it so awful that he begged Kingsley never to write another work of fiction. But Kingsley had now discovered about the horrible sanitary conditions on Jacob's Island, a notorious East End district where Bill Sikes meets his death in *Oliver Twist*, and this set him off on a second novel. It was called *Alton Locke, Tailor and Poet*, and its hero was based on Thomas Cooper, a Chartist Cockney poet who became a Christian convert through his friendship with Kingsley. The best part of the book, or at least the most lurid, describes Jacob's Island and a suicide plunging into the horrible water surrounding it:

> Locke rushed out on the balcony after him. The light of the policeman's lantern glared over the ghastly scene – along the double row of miserable house-backs, which lined the sides of the open tidal ditch . . . over bubbles of poisonous gas, and bloated carcasses of dogs and lumps of offal, floating in the stagnant olive green hell-broth, over the slow sullen rows of oily ripples which were dying away in the darkness beyond, sending up, as they stirred, hot breaths of miasma, – the only sign that a spark of humanity, after years of foul life, had quenched itself at last in that foul death.

Apart from this spectacularly smelly drowning, *Alton Locke* is chiefly concerned with the vicissitudes of its hero's relationship with smart society. At one moment he is the eloquent voice of the suffering working class, at the next he has willingly expunged all revolutionary sentiments from his poems at the behest of the dean of a Cambridge college, with whose daughter (Fanny again, of course) he is in love. There is a good deal of veiled autobiography. Finally Kingsley abandons the attempt to make anything rational out of all this, packs Alton off on a ship bound for America, and kills him during the voyage – typhus again.

Alton Locke came out soon after *Yeast*, but Kingsley was already drifting away from the Christian Socialists. His third novel, *Hypatia* (1853), ducked out of contemporary social issues entirely. It was set in classical times and its story, about a martyred female philosopher, appealed to that side of Kingsley which had made drawings of St Elizabeth being tortured. Next he gratified himself by writing a long poem on the Andromeda myth – doubly pleasing to him, because in this case the maiden was not merely chained naked to a rock but was being doused with sea water – and another, called 'Santa Maura', about a naked female saint dying on a cross. Meanwhile, he wrote to Tom Hughes, a fellow disciple of F. D. Maurice, that he now felt his involvement with the Christian Socialists had been a mistake: 'I have seen that the world was not going to be set right in any such rose-pink way . . . and that there are heavy arrears of *destruction* to be made up, before *construction* can ever begin.'[21] An odd remark, though at least one critic has observed that Kingsley's intellect was characterised largely by a fondness for destroying. Thomas Byrom writes in a 1969 introduction to the Everyman *Alton Locke*: 'We cannot help being shaken somewhat [in Kingsley's treatment of religion] by the almost total absence of positive convictions of a clear doctrinal nature, and by the pervasiveness of a destructive temper. At best Kingsley feels distaste and distrust, and at worst, hatred and fear.'

He was certainly a far better attacker than defender. Gerard Manley Hopkins once compared him to 'a man bouncing up from table with mouth full of bread and cheese and saying that he meant to stand no blasted nonsense'.[22] *The Water-Babies* is at its most eloquent when it is on the attack against one or other of Kingsley's favourite dislikes, whether it be evangelical novels for children or the incompetence of doctors. Quite what its positive moral is, Kingsley himself found hard to say. At the end of the book he writes: 'And now, my dear little man, what should we learn from this parable? We should learn thirty-seven or thirty-nine things, I am not exactly sure which . . . and if I am not quite right, still you will be, at long as you stick to hard work and cold water.'

Actually his opinions, such as they were, steadily drifted more and more towards the conservative. He wrote *Westward Ho!* in the mid-

1850s hoping to inject an 'Armada spirit' into England's conduct of the Crimean War, and he scribbled a pamphlet for the soldiers at the front telling them that they were fighting on God's side. He grumbled to Tom Hughes and J. M. Ludlow that Prince Albert was trying to stop the British army doing its job in the Crimea because the war would have a disastrous effect on his fellow German princelings. Yet only a few years later he was delighted to accept an appointment as a royal preacher at Windsor, and was using his court connections in the hope of getting himself some nice canonry or even deanery, in a manner more like Mr Slope than Parson Lot.

Eventually he got to be a Canon of Westminster. But the first thing that resulted from the royal favour was a Regius Professorship at Cambridge, in Modern History. He knew almost nothing about the subject – he had read Classics and Mathematics as an undergraduate – and one professional historian at the time remarked that they might as well send Kingsley to command the Channel Fleet as make him a Professor of History. His lectures were popular with the under-graduates, who cheered at his patriotic sentiments, but he contributed nothing whatever to the subject. The fact that he accepted the chair at all shows how, by the end of the 1850s, he had completely lost direction.

He had written himself out as an adult novelist. *Westward Ho!* was followed by an oddity called *Two Years Ago* (1857), chiefly devoted to ridiculing one of its characters, an opium-addict poet called Elsley Vavasour. (Tennyson mistakenly thought it was a portrait of him and took offence.) After this, almost everything Kingsley tried to write dried up after a few pages. It says something for him that he showed no jealousy when Tom Hughes asked him to look through a manuscript he had written entitled *Tom Brown's Schooldays*. Kingsley was enthusiastic, and told Hughes to get it into print at once, declaring that 'It will be a very great hit.'

He himself had in fact made some impact on the juvenile book market. *Westward Ho!* had a lot of child readers, and *Glaucus, or the Wonders of the Shore*, published the same year (1855), was enjoyed by children, though it was really addressed to adults and had no illustrations. It took its title from the Greek fable of the fisherman Glaucus, who eats a magic herb which allows him to follow the fish under the waves, and become 'for ever a companion of the fair semi-human forms . . . feeding his "silent flocks" far below . . . or basking with them on the sunny ledges in the summer noon, or wandering in the still bays on sultry nights amid the choir of Aphititre and her sea-nymphs'. The year after *Glaucus* appeared, Kingsley tackled a whole set of Greek myths, retelling them for children under the title *The Heroes*. The book was inspired by his irritation with Nathaniel Hawthorne's recently published *Wonder-Book*, in which the New Englander had cosified and prettified the myths, giving Midas a daughter called Marygold and portraying a lot of the adult characters as children. Kingsley's versions were closer to the originals, but rather cold and lifeless.

The Heroes was written for the immediate audience of his own children. Rose, the eldest, was twelve by the time it came out; Maurice (named after F. D. Maurice) was three years younger; and Mary was four when *The Heroes* got into print. Two years later the fourth and last child was born, a boy christened Grenville after Fanny's Grenfell ancestors, who included Sir Richard Grenville of *Westward Ho!* Rose was always her father's favourite – hence the luscious Rose Salterne in *Westward Ho!* – but he was a kind parent to them all, erring only on the side of over-indulgence. Yet the idea of writing stories for them does not seem to have occurred to him for a long while.

By the late 1850s he was in a very low state, suffering minor nervous breakdown after minor nervous breakdown, running off to Devon whenever he could, bickering with Fanny, who had become entirely stay-at-home, and feeling his religious faith, never secure at the best of times, to be slipping away from him. To F. D. Maurice he admitted being in 'a period of collapse. I live in dark nameless dissatisfaction and dread . . . Everything seems to me not worth working at.'[23] It was in this state of mind that he wrote *The Water-Babies*.

*

Fanny afterwards described how her husband had begun the book:

> Sitting at breakfast at the Rectory one spring morning this year [1862], the father was reminded of an old promise, 'Rose, Maurice, and Mary have got their book [*The Heroes*], and baby must have his.' He made no answer, but got up at once and went into the study, locking the door. In half an hour he returned with the story of little Tom. This was the first chapter of *The Water-Babies*, written off without a correction.[24]

Even allowing for the obvious exaggeration – the first chapter is far too long to have been written in half an hour – Fanny was obviously struck by the uncharacteristic fluency with which the story tumbled out of Charles. She observed that 'the rest of the book . . . was composed with the same quickness and ease as the first chapter – if indeed what was so purely an inspiration could be called composing, for the whole thing seemed to flow naturally out of his brain and heart, lightening both of a burden without exhausting either; and the copy went up to the printer's without a flaw.'[25]

This is a perceptive analysis of what *The Water-Babies* was doing for Kingsley: lightening him of a burden. As a writer for adults he had been a destroyer rather than a creator, a critic of society who had no idea how to set it right and perhaps scarcely cared, a sexual sadist (in imagination if not fact) who delighted in the destruction of women's bodies. Even his most popular book, *Westward Ho!*, was marked by violence done to its romantic heroine and hero – Rose dies at the hands of the Inquisition and Amyas Leigh is struck blind by lightning. Kingsley had dried up as an adult writer because this path of destruction in the end led to nothing, and he had no positive creed to offer. His personal beliefs, political and religious, had come to pieces, and there was nothing to fill their place except his scarcely rational ideas about sexuality and cold water. In *The Water-Babies* he was able to begin his task all over again, punching down most of the ideas which had supported children's literature up to this time; and now he could actually offer something positive to replace them, for his notions about human bodies and cold water could be worked into a children's story far more effectively than into an adult novel. In doing this he was the first writer in England, perhaps the first in the world with the exception of Hans Andersen, to discover that a children's book can be the perfect vehicle for an adult's most personal and private concerns.

Judging from the shape of the book, he seems to have had little idea where the narrative would lead him. The motive for the beginning was simple enough: he had been reading a government report on child labour, and seems to have talked to a sweep's boy himself – one James Seaward of Wokingham, who helped to sweep the chimneys at Eversley Rectory, used to declare that he was the original of Tom. It is said that *The Water-Babies* helped to make the use of boys for this purpose illegal; certainly the Act of Parliament forbidding it was passed within a year of the story's publication. But Kingsley's treatment of this social abuse in *The Water-Babies* is as flimsy as his handling of similar issues in *Yeast* and *Alton Locke*. He gives no account of the agonies undergone by such boys; James Seaward himself used to come down the flues not merely filthy but streaming with blood from torn knees, and boys often died from suffocation or from being trapped for hours in narrow flues. All this is left out of Kingsley's story; on the contrary, we are given the impression that Tom rather enjoyed his work. He is said to be 'as much at home in a chimney as a mole is underground', and he looks forward to the day when he can become a master sweep like Grimes and maltreat other boys in his turn. In fact, Kingsley apparently rather approves of the system; his only harsh words are reserved, as they were in *Politics for the People*, for the spiritual unhealthiness of the working class. We are told that Tom 'had never been taught to say his prayers. He had never heard of God, or of Christ, except in words which you have never heard, and which it would have been well if he had never heard.' Even Grimes, whom we might expect to be a die-hard villain, is painted with a certain sympathy. He has a proper admiration for Sir John Harthover, the squire who is employing him on the morning that Tom runs away; he has a pleasant man-to-man conversation with Sir John's gamekeeper; and near the end of the book he is reduced to tears (thereby saving himself from the Dantean punishment of being stuck permanently in a chimney pot) by the news that his mother has died: "'So my old mother's gone, and I never there to speak to her! Ah! a good woman she was . . . and now it's too late–too late!'"

The Water-Babies, then, is not a social parable. At times it seems like a prospectus for future genres of children's fiction. A few pages into the tale, as Tom springs from the window at Harthover and sets off across the fells, we find ourselves in something very much like an adventure story, in which Alan Breck Stewart or even Richard Hannay might be just around the corner.[26] Two chapters later we might be beneath the sea with Captain Nemo, in 'a deep, still reach' where Tom 'saw the water-forests'. Later still, Kingsley takes Tom off on one of those fantastic quests that have delighted twentieth-century writers; there are hints here of the voyage of the Dawn Treader, or even of Frodo's journey to Mordor. It is like a plan of things to come; but it remains only a plan, because Kingsley no sooner tries out one mode than he is drawn aside into another, so that the second half of the book in particular becomes, as Gillian Avery has said, an 'inchoate mass'. And everywhere there are contradictions and intellectual muddles.

The second chapter is largely a tirade against 'Cousin Cramchild of Boston U.S.' for writing books of instruction and not believing in fairies. This is a thin disguise for Peter Parley, a pseudonym first used by a Bostonian editor and publisher named Goodrich, who churned out books of facts from the late 1820s onwards; these flooded England as well as America, and were soon being imitated by British pedagogic hacks. Goodrich and his imitators deplored fairy stories and worshipped factual information. But what is Kingsley himself doing in *The Water-Babies* but swamping his child readers with substantial and scrupulously accurate facts about marine life? Later in the story, when Tom comes to the country where all the bad children's books are written, Kingsley takes a swipe at three American evangelical novels that were the rage at that time on both sides of the Atlantic, *The Wide Wide World* and *Queechy* by 'Elizabeth Wetherell' (Susan Bogert Warner), which he calls 'The Narrow Narrow World' and 'Squeeky', and *The Lamplighter* by Maria Susanna Cummins, which he mocks as 'The Pump-lighter'. And yet the central part of *The Water-Babies*, with the waif Tom being taught the Christian religion, itself resembles a whole host of evangelical conversion stories that were being produced for children in the mid-nineteenth century.

The Water-Babies has often been judged a failure because it achieves nothing fully. Tom himself never develops into anything; he remains in effect a baby (though nominally he grows up at the end), and he is charged with none of the meaning that may be found in his counterpart, Peter Pan. Even a contemporary reviewer who liked the book a good deal observed that his adventures are over far too quickly:

> Children . . . demand why his travels had need to come to an end when there was the Kraken to be visited, and the awful Maelstrom, and the whales, and the coral island manufacturers, and the tunnels under the deep, whereby the volcanoes are joined together.[27]

But as usual Kingsley was much less concerned to invent than to destroy. In *The Water-Babies* he was making up some of the 'heavy arrears of destruction' he felt to be due within children's literature, and was only incidentally interested in telling a story.

And yet it is this very urge to destroy which gives the book its life, and explains why, despite its faults, it has been regarded as a classic since its first appearance and is still read with enjoyment even though much of its subject matter is now obscure. Kingsley, 'bouncing up . . . and saying that he meant to stand no blasted nonsense', is an oddly attractive figure because of the force and eloquence of his anger. He himself is really the principal character in the book: the authorial voice is far more in evidence than the personality of Tom or even the underwater maternal fairies, and it is invariably an attractive voice. It is prejudiced, certainly, but the prejudices are those which the modern reader is almost bound to share – a hatred of pedants who cram children with facts, and of doctors who overdose them, and other such Victorian irritants which have not entirely disappeared from the world. And perhaps more important than this, the authorial voice is often very funny. Kingsley's Rabelaisian lists, which crop up in all contexts, such as the doctors' attempts to cure a professor's madness, induced by 'a very terrible old fairy' because he would not believe in water-babies:

> Now, the doctors had it all their own way; and to work they went in earnest, and they gave the poor professor divers and sundry medicines, as prescribed by the ancients and moderns from Hippocrates to Feuchtersleben . . . But they found that a great deal too much trouble . . . and so had recourse to . . .
>
>> Bezoar stone.
>> Diamargaritum.
>> A ram's brain boiled in spice.
>> Oil of wormwood.
>> Water of Nile.
>> Capers.
>> Good wine (but there was none to be got).
>> The water of a smith's forge.
>> Hops.

Ambergris.
Mandrake pillows.
Dormouse fat . . .
Champagne and turtle.
Red herrings and Soda water.
Good advice.
Gardening.
Croquet.
Musical soirées.
Aunt Sally.
Mild Tobacco.
The Saturday Review.
A carriage with outriders, etc. etc. . ..

And if he had but been a convict lunatic, and had shot at the Queen, killed his creditors to avoid paying them, or indulged in any other little amiable eccentricity of that kind, they would have given him in addition –

The healthiest situation in England, on Easthampstead Plain.
Free run of Windsor Forest.
The Times every morning.
A double-barrelled gun and pointers, and leave
to shoot three Wellington College boys a week (not more) in case black game was scarce . . .

Not surprisingly, some publishers of *The Water-Babies* have omitted these extraordinary digressions and have issued abridged editions containing only what may be strictly regarded as the story. In so doing they have removed the most vital and characteristic element in the book. And the few moments at which the book triumphantly succeeds on all counts are those where ferocious argument on some contemporary issue is expressed in narrative form – most notably the history of the nation of Doasyoulikes, who evolve *backwards* from man into ape because of their mental and moral laziness. This is at once a simple parable and a sarcastic piece of rhetoric in support of Darwin, to whose theory of evolution Kingsley subscribed energetically.

Fanny Kingsley recorded that her husband was 'quite unprepared' for the popular success of *The Water-Babies*. Every indication is that he wrote it as a *jeu d'esprit* which he did not expect to have a long life. There are private jokes – about local people at Eversley, and about Wellington College where Maurice Kingsley was a pupil – and endless contemporary references which Kingsley, had he thought about it, must have realised would date within a few years. There is also a kind of holiday cheerfulness about it all, most obviously in Kingsley's resolute refusal in his concluding 'Moral' to find any sort of message in the story. It is true that several times in the narrative he states the moral to be that 'your soul makes your body, just as a snail makes its shell', but this idea is not really pursued; apart from Tom growing prickles on his skin when he steals sweets and the Doasyoulikes turning into apes, nobody's appearance actually demonstrates their spiritual character. Kingsley wrote to F. D. Maurice that the book was intended 'to make children and grown folks understand that there is a quite miraculous and divine element underlying all physical nature', but whereas this may explain Tom's transformation into a water-baby it has comparatively little to do with the rest of the story. However, he went on to tell Maurice that he also wanted to emphasise 'that nobody knows anything about anything', and something much the same is said in the last sentence in the book:

> But remember always, as I told you at first, that this is all a fairy tale, and only fun and pretence; and, therefore, you are not to believe a word of it, even if it is true.

Kingsley himself did not believe a word of his fairy tale, and yet he must have felt it all to be 'true', so full was it of his personal convictions, his destructive hatred of the wrong-headedness of children's authors, and his obsession with maternal-sexual female figures and the purifying, regenerative power of cold water. What he had done was to show that 'untrue' stories, despised, ever since the days of John Locke,[28] by those who regarded themselves as the guardians and censors of English children's literature, could be deeply true, and therefore of inestimable value.

The Water-Babies was predominantly a work of destruction rather than construction, written at a time when its author's religious faith had nearly crumbled. One has a sense that in the book he was trying to remedy that loss of faith, was fumbling towards the creation of some kind of alternative religion, which was made up of things that really mattered to him. Mrs Bedonebyasyoudid and Mrs Doasyouwouldbe-doneby seem to be sketches towards that new religion. Of course, God and Christ are mentioned explicitly in the story, and at the end of the book Tom's reward, being allowed 'home' with Ellie on Sundays, hints at his admission to the Christian heaven. Yet *The Water-Babies* is not really an account of his education in Christianity. Kingsley tells us at the outset that Tom knows nothing of God and Christ, and Ellie certainly teaches him to say his prayers, yet one does not really feel at the end of the book that he has been initiated into conventional religion. Instead he seems to have learnt a parallel creed, in which maternal fairies take the place of the love of Christ, and the angelic hierarchy includes such unchristian figures as the mysterious Mother Carey, who 'sits making old beasts into new', and 'the old gentleman in the grey great-coat, who looks after the big copper boiler in the gulf of Mexico'. It is an odd religion, with both comic and sexual overtones, but it is curiously persuasive and numinous.

It is striking that Tom's initiation into it takes the form of a series of quests, attempts to reach some alluring or mysterious place set apart from his present existence. The first such journey is to Harthover, the great house to which he and Grimes set out in the early morning; their travels across the moor are described in such lyrical terms that Kingsley clearly feels the journey to be charged with meaning. Tom is already in search of a Good Place. But Harthover proves a false goal: he sullies it with his grime, and is soon off over the fells to the little cottage he can see at the bottom of Lewthwaite Crag. This cottage, in Vendale, seems to offer real peace. (He keeps hearing church bells in his head during his vertical climb down the Crag, an indication, of course, that he is ill with exhaustion, but a suggestion too of the quasi-religious nature of his quest.) In the cottage he seems to find real contentment as he contemplates its stone-flagged kitchen – 'a shiny clean stone floor, and curious old prints on the walls, and an old black oak sideboard full of bright pewter and brass dishes'. But this symbol of simple domesticity is not sufficient, and he quickly abandons it for the coolness of the stream. Even the regenerating and purifying cold water is not an end in itself, and soon he is journeying down the river in search of the great sea, surely the ultimate Good Place for him and for Kingsley. Yet scarcely has he reached it than he is sent off yet again, to the Other-end-of-Nowhere, to effect the salvation of Grimes and so reach a state of grace himself. And beyond that is yet another goal, the permission to go 'home' with Ellie on Sundays. This element in the book is no more than lightly sketched in, but its presence suggests that Kingsley was exploring the notion of the quest for an Enchanted Place where all shall be well.

*

Though he was only in his mid-forties when *The Water-Babies* appeared, he began to decline physically not long after its publication. He wrote his final novel, *Hereward the Wake*, which for its time was a good piece of historical romance, but lacked the old Kingsley fire and bombast; he had completed his work of destruction in *The Water-Babies*, and now had little to say. He visited the West Indies and America, developed a chest complaint, perhaps brought on by the heavy pipe-smoking in which he had indulged since undergraduate days, and died at Eversley in the cold months of 1875, aged fifty-five. Fanny survived him by many years and produced a massive biography of him in which almost all trace of the great conflicts of his life, both inner and outer, was covered up. By the time she herself died in 1891 *The Water-Babies* was reaching the height of its popularity in England and America, and could be seen to have cut away the undergrowth, so that a whole new wave of imaginative writing for children could germinate and grow. Kingsley's destructiveness had in this sense produced constructive results. And yet in other ways, as his two outstanding immediate successors in the genre seem to have realised, destructiveness itself had a lure to the imaginative writer, and there was much more that could be mocked and pulled to pieces before determined rebuilding could really begin.

2

Alice and the mockery of God

On 4 July 1862, a month before *The Water-Babies* began to be serialised in *Macmillan's*, Charles Lutwidge Dodgson, a thirty-year-old mathematics tutor at Christ Church, Oxford, went on a river trip with Lorina, Alice, and Edith Liddell, daughters of the Dean of that college, and told them the story which he later developed into *Alice's Adventures in Wonderland*, which was eventually published in November 1865, with the author named as 'Lewis Carroll'. Whereas *The Water-Babies* tends to be regarded nowadays as something of an antiquarian curiosity, *Alice* and its sequel *Through the Looking-Glass* stand at the centre of a still growing Lewis Carroll industry. To date at least seven full-length biographies of him have been published, and there are also two lives of Alice Liddell herself. There are also published editions of Dodgson's diaries and of selections from his voluminous correspondence, not to mention bibliographies and a whole substratum of enthusiasts' publications. Yet it would be rash to suppose that this intensive study has produced a clear picture of Dodgson–Carroll and of precisely why he wrote the *Alice* books.

The more the details of his life and works are raked over, the more confusing they become. The inquirer very quickly loses sight of the personality from which *Alice* emerged, and instead becomes distracted by C. L. Dodgson, diarist, letter writer, cultivator of child friends, photographer, literary lion hunter, mathematician, puzzle concocter, Oxford don, and author of a great deal of sentimental rubbish. The ruthlessly humorous mind that created the creatures of Wonderland and the Looking-Glass world is scarcely glimpsed, and after a time one wonders whether it ever existed. It is surprising indeed that no one has ever posited a Baconian theory about the composition of Alice, suggesting that it was really the work of, say, some brilliant Oxford figure such as Benjamin Jowett, or even John Henry Newman. The Victorian age was full of minds more obviously capable of turning out such stuff than was an obscure Christ Church mathematics lecturer. But the fact remains, indisputably, that Dodgson wrote *Alice*, and we are left with the enigma of this work of literature emerging from the pen of a man apparently temperamentally unsuited to liking such stuff, let alone writing it himself.

To be fair, the problem does not begin at the outset of Dodgson's life. His early years seem a credible prelude to his writing *Alice*. He was the son of the Revd Charles Dodgson, who had himself studied at Christ Church – he took a double First Class in Classics and Mathematics – and who taught there briefly before marrying and taking charge of one of the college's parishes, Daresbury in Cheshire. Later, when Charles Lutwidge was eleven, the family moved to a more lucrative living and a larger house, Croft Rectory in Yorkshire. Later still Mr Dodgson senior became a Canon of Ripon and Archdeacon of Richmond; some of his sermons were printed, and he also published a translation of Tertullian. He was as solid a Victorian father as might be imagined, and Lewis Carroll's first biographer, S. D. Collingwood, tells us that Mr Dodgson senior's 'reverence for sacred things was so great that he was never known to relate a story which included a jest upon words from the Bible'. And yet he had an ebullient sense of humour.

We know this from a letter he sent Charles in 1840, when the boy was approaching his eighth birthday. Mr Dodgson had to be away from Daresbury, and he wrote to reassure Charles that he would not forget to buy several things the boy had asked for. 'As soon as I get to Leeds,' he told him,

> I shall scream out in the middle of the street, *Ironmongers, Ironmongers*. Six hundred men will rush out of their shops in a moment – fly, fly, in all directions – ring the bells, call the constables, set the Town on fire. I WILL have a file and a screw driver and a ring, and if they are not brought directly, in forty seconds, I will leave nothing but one small cat alive in the whole Town of Leeds, and I shall only leave that, because I am afraid I shall not have time to kill it.[29]

And the fantasy goes on. What a howling there will be, he tells Charles – 'old women rushing up the chimneys and cows after them – ducks hiding themselves in coffee-cups, and fat geese trying to squeeze themselves into pencil cases', while the Mayor of Leeds will be found trying to disguise himself as a sponge cake, 'that he may escape the dreadful destruction of the Town'.

This is not merely nonsense, but Nonsense, the very art form of which Lewis Carroll was to become master: a simple idea pursued with a ruthless comic literalness to its very end. It is, perhaps, slightly less disciplined than anything in *Alice*, and in its final sentences the letter passes from Nonsense proper into surrealism, which is quite a different thing; the Mayor's wife is found not merely cowering in her own pincushion, but with 'all her dear little children, seventy-eight poor helpless infants, crammed into her mouth, and hiding themselves behind her double teeth'; there is also a brief appearance by a man who has tried to hide his donkey by cramming it up his nose. But if Mr Dodgson senior was not quite sure of the rules of the Nonsense game, he was evidently very glad to play it when the occasion seemed suitable.

He also seems to have encouraged Charles to go in for the same sort of thing, for at about the age of fourteen the boy started the first of what proved to be a whole series of 'family magazines', edited by himself for the amusement of his brothers and sisters, and chiefly consisting of comic squibs of one kind or another. The last of these, *The Rectory Umbrella*, was eventually put into print in the Lewis Carroll centenary year, 1932. Very little in it will raise a smile now; it is only apprentice stuff, but it does seem to be the product of a happy, tolerant household.

And yet one has the feeling that some essential fact about that family has not been told. Charles was one of eleven children; seven were girls, and he was the eldest of four brothers. Eleven was not an unusually large family for those days, though it was comparatively uncommon that all should survive into adult life, as the Dodgsons did. (Indeed Charles himself was the first to die, by some years; all except him lived into their seventies, and one reached ninety.) Yet of the eleven no less than eight remained unmarried: six of the sisters and two of the brothers – Charles himself, and his youngest brother Edwin, who became a missionary. We also know that there was a common family affliction, stammering. Charles himself suffered from it, and on one occasion he revealed to a specialist who had tried to cure him that six of his sisters stammered too:

> The state of the case regarding my sisters is this. There are 7 in all.
>   1 does not stammer.
>   2 stammer very slightly (of these one is such an invalid, you are not likely ever to see her).
>   2 stammer to a moderate amount (of these one is married and lives in the north of England – you will never see *her*).
>   2 stammer rather badly . . .
>   I hope they will come to you 2 or 3 at a time, as I am pretty sure they are all alike, and need the same rules.[30]

He says nothing about his brothers.

One of the many Lewis Carroll biographers, Derek Hudson, tried to find a way out of the maze of his subject's personality by showing specimens of his subject's handwriting to a graphologist. This person declared that Charles Dodgson's script at the age of twelve showed him to be 'impressionable and open to stimulation', also 'outstanding in maturity, tenderness, and sensitivity'. But the handwriting at the age of twenty 'shows clearly that he is now rigidly set in his ways . . . with decreased sensitivity and openness to events and people'. Mr Hudson concludes from this, and from his study of other evidence in general, that 'something fundamentally disturbing . . . must have occurred to upset Charles Dodgson's development between twelve and twenty'. He judges it to have been the 'chastening experience' of several years at a tough public school, followed by the death of his mother, which occurred when he was nineteen. This, Mr Hudson concludes, 'left a wound which healed very slowly, and never healed completely'. To strengthen his argument he cites the poem 'Solitude', written two years after the mother's death and printed in the magazine *The Train* in 1856 – it was one of the first pieces to bear the author's name 'Lewis Carroll':

> Here may the silent tears I weep
> Lull the vexed spirit into rest,
> As infants sob themselves to sleep
> Upon a mother's breast.[31]

But the most striking thing about the poem, of which there are seven stanzas in all, is not the strength of its emotion but its complete falsity of tone. It is merely a string of 'poetic' clichés. Like all the sentimental outpourings Dodgson was to produce during the next forty years, it just does not ring true.

In fact, it is very striking how little impression Dodgson's mother's death seems to have made on him. A letter written from Oxford to his sister Mary in March 1851, only a little over a month after it happened, makes absolutely no reference to it at all, and is extraordinarily bouncy and self-possessed:

> Many very happy returns of your birthday . . . I hope you will 'keep' it very happily on the Monday, and will imagine my presence when the health is drunk . . . Give Elizabeth my best thanks for her letter: I am tired of saying 'nice long', so let it be always understood in future.

There follows a facetious, nonsensical derivation of the word 'kakography', then an account of a dog-fight in the Christ Church quadrangle, then some gossipy news, and finally a grumble that he has 'left all my silk handkerchiefs at home' – would she send them? He concludes:

> I think this is one of the most magnificently long letters I have ever written. With best love to all, I remain
>
> Your very affectionate Brother
Charles Lutwidge Dodgson.[32]

This scarcely suggests somebody suffering from a six-week-old psychological wound. By contrast, when Dodgson's father died seventeen years later, his diary broke off abruptly, and when it resumed it did so with expressions of deep sorrow. He also remarked in a letter, some time after this, that his father's death had been 'the greatest blow that has ever fallen on my life'.[33]

And if his mother's death does not appear to have been a traumatic event, what about what Hudson calls the 'chastening experience' of public school? Here too we need to be careful. Charles Dodgson went to Rugby School in 1846, four years after the death of Dr Arnold had terminated the *Tom Brown's Schooldays* era. Dr Tait, headmaster in Dodgson's day, was no Arnold, but Dodgson seems to have found him quite tolerable, and took the trouble to get him to sit for a portrait photograph many years later, when Tait was Archbishop of Canterbury. The evidence that Dodgson hated Rugby is based on two entries in his diary, the first probably made about four years after he left the school:[34]

> During my stay I made I suppose some progress in learning of various kinds, but none of it was done *con amore*, and I spent an incalculable time in writing out impositions – this last I consider one of the chief faults of Rugby School. I made some friends there . . . but I cannot say that I look back upon my life at a Public School with any sensations of pleasure, or that any earthly considerations would induce me to go through my three years again.

Surely the tone here is not that of someone who has suffered a psychological trauma; rather, a languid undergraduate is looking back with a feeling of superiority to the days when he was a mere schoolboy. And the truth is that Dodgson made a good deal of academic progress while at Rugby, whether or not it was *con amore*. He won prizes in Classics, composition, divinity, history, and mathematics, and was recognised by the mathematical teacher as having outstanding ability.

The second diary entry, written while Dodgson was a young don at Christ Church, compares Rugby unfavourably to Radley, a public school near Oxford, chiefly because at Radley 'every boy has a snug little bedroom secured to himself, where he is free from interruption and annoyance'. Such privacy, Dodgson observes, would have been a great benefit to small boys at Rugby,

> as being a kind of counterbalance to any bullying they may suffer during the day . . . If I could have been secure from annoyance at night, the hardships of the daily life would have been comparative trifles to bear.[35]

This 'annoyance at night' may have been sexual advances from other boys; it may simply have been a continuation of the daytime bullying. But he is specifically talking about 'little boys' who have recently entered the school, and the surviving letters that he sent home to his sister Elizabeth from Rugby show that by the time he reached the sixth form he was getting a good deal of fun out of life there, going on long walks with friends to explore the remains of a Roman camp, having tea with one master, and wine and figs with another, and reading avidly ('I have read the 1st number of Dickens' new tale, "Davy Copperfield" . . . it seems a poor plot, but some of the characters and scenes are very good'). No doubt he had been really unhappy at Rugby at first; his stammer cannot have helped, and somebody wrote 'C. L. Dodgson is a muff' (slang for 'no good at games') in one of his school books. But to suggest that he began his undergraduate years at Oxford with more than a young man's usual mixed feelings about his schooldays seems unjustified in view of the evidence.

Charles Dodgson at twenty seems to have been as ebullient as at twelve. Letters home give lively descriptions of Commemoration at Oxford, of a visit to the Great Exhibition, and of a ridiculously incompetent performance by a professional conjurer. Entries in the diary he was now keeping suggest that his only conscious problem was how to cram his growing number of enthusiasms – literature, the theatre, sketching, and much else – into the available time. He was reading Classics as well as Mathematics, and he only got a Second Class in Classical Moderations and a Third in 'Greats' (Philosophy and Ancient History); but he managed a First in Mathematics Moderations and in the final examination in that subject, announcing this last success jubilantly to his sisters: 'I feel at present very like a child with a new toy, but I daresay I shall be tired of it soon, and wish to be Pope of Rome next . . . I have just given my Scout a bottle of wine to drink to my First.'

If we are to put a finger on the point at which this energetic young man began to change into the temperamentally very different C. L. Dodgson of later years, we might choose the moment at which there was procured for him, by no less a person than Dr Pusey of the Oxford Movement (an old friend of his father), a Studentship of Christ Church. This misleadingly named Studentship consisted, under the old statutes of the college then still in force, of twenty-five pounds a year and the right to remain in residence at the college for the rest of the holder's life, providing he proceeded in due course to being ordained as a clergyman, and remained unmarried.

This, then, may seem to us the slamming of the door, for certainly Dodgson was to remain at Christ Church for the rest of his life, unmarried. Yet his acceptance of the Studentship carried no such commitment; the majority of Students remained at the College only a few years before marrying and pursuing careers in the world outside –

as Dodgson's own father had done. Certainly Dodgson was tying himself more firmly to Christ Church when he began to tutor undergraduates in mathematics, and, a little later, became Sub-Librarian of the college; but these were simply ways of making a living, and his diary makes it clear that his chief goal at the time was financial independence from his father. In later years Christ Church definitely became his protective shell, but while he was in his twenties one may suspect that he still looked on it as a possible springboard to the world outside.

One way in which he hoped to impress that outside world was as a comic writer. In 1855 he began to contribute to the *Comic Times*, which was set up that year as a rival to *Punch*. He sent it several pieces of the sort he had written for the family magazines, most of them parodies, and when the *Comic Times* folded after a few issues he became a contributor to its successor *The Train*, here using for the first time the pseudonym Lewis Carroll, derived from his Christian names. Some of his *Train* contributions were sentimental verses, among them 'Solitude' quoted earlier, but for the most part they were contrived humorous pieces of the *Punch* school. Typical of these was a short story, resoundingly unfunny, about a man who thinks he has seen a shop advertising 'Romancement', but discovers it to be 'Roman Cement'. Actually this strain of facetious writing never left Dodgson, and quite late in life it led him to produce such stuff as the long poem 'Phantasmagoria', about a conversation between a ghost and the man whom he has been sent to haunt. He did such things as this well enough, but they are funny only in the urbane, contrived manner of the C. S. Calverley school of light verse, which is quite different from the furious comedy of *Alice*:

> Then, peering round with curious eyes,
>   He muttered 'Goodness gracious!'
> And so went on to criticize –
> 'Your room's an inconvenient size:
>   It's neither snug nor spacious.
>
> 'That narrow window, I expect,
>   Serves but to let the dusk in – '
> 'But please,' said I, 'to recollect
> 'Twas fashioned by an architect
>   Who pinned his faith on Ruskin!'[36]

Oddly, one may feel that the first chill note in Dodgson's early years at Christ Church is struck when he takes up photography. It seems an innocent enough pastime, and he was quickly to become one of the masters of the Victorian camera, at least where portraits were concerned.

And yet one cannot help feeling from the beginning that he went in for photography with such energy because it was a kind of substitute for real personal relationships, at least where adults were concerned; it allowed him to be an observer without having to participate. Certainly once he had become technically accomplished he went in search of the famous, using his camera as a kind of butterfly net to trap specimens:

> Only Mrs Tennyson was at home, and I sent in my card . . . I was most kindly received and spent nearly an hour there . . . She even seemed to think it was not hopeless that Tennyson might sit [for his photograph].[37]

He duly got his Tennyson picture, and the Laureate proved to be only the first of a whole gallery of distinguished persons – the Rossettis, Thackeray, Ruskin, Lord Salisbury, Prince Leopold and his family. And it is also obvious that Dodgson practised photography largely because it gave him a respectable way of picking up little girls.

This is crudely stated, but there seems to be no other way of describing something so blatant:

> Dear Sir,
>
>   I travelled from Thirsk about a month ago with a family party, father and 2 children, and have been wishing to find them again in order to procure, if I could, photographs of the children, as I am a great collector of those works of art, and an amateur photographer myself. My travelling companion said he had been many years in Darlington, and it has been suggested to me that perhaps you were he. If this is not so, excuse my having troubled you to no purpose.
>
> Faithfully yours,
C. L. Dodgson[38]

'Procure . . . I am a great collector . . .' The choice of phrase may be unfortunate, but it is all too accurate. Helmut Gernsheim, author of *Lewis Carroll: Photographer* (1950), judges Dodgson to have been 'the most outstanding photographer of children in the nineteenth century'; but then he had every opportunity to be, considering that he took pains to acquire pictures – and elaborately posed pictures at that – of virtually every beautiful female child he came across, even if the original encounter had only been very brief. At first, up to about the mid 1860s, he was shy of making a direct approach, and would try to discover the child's name by some roundabout route. But a few years later he had built up a whole repertoire of ways of introducing himself. 'He was waiting for a train to Oxford,' recalled one of his child-friends of their first meeting, in the gardens near Reading station, 'and we went and sat on the same seat. He began to talk to us, and showed us puzzles and the

tiniest of tiny scissors, which fascinated me, I remember, and which he
kept in his pocket book. He made us write our names and address and
then hurried off to catch his train.'[39] A few days later the girls received a
copy of *Alice* (this was 1869) and an invitation to Christ Church to be
photographed. Such was the usual pattern.

Dodgson's biographers have on the whole tried to make light of this
aspect of his life, emphasising the benefits his child-friends derived
from the relationship (and there were plenty of these: good teas,
expeditions, presents, photographs, amusing stories and puzzles)
rather than attempting to explain the precise nature of Dodgson's
feelings for the children. Derek Hudson seems to have been responsible
for the notion, quite widely held, that he liked little girls because he
stammered less in their company: 'As the stammerer begins to make his
way into adult society the barrier between him and the rest of the world
becomes increasingly formidable . . . it is a curious fact that he is often at
his happiest in the company of children. He can talk to them, he finds,
quite naturally and freely . . .' Mr Hudson's hypothetical stammerer
may find this, but there is no clear evidence that Dodgson did.
Certainly the brother of one of his child-friends recalled that he was
'affected with a slight stutter in the presence of grown-ups', which
seems to imply that the stammer vanished in the company of children;
on the other hand, Princess Alice, Countess of Athlone, records[40] of a
meeting with him: 'When I was only five I offended him once when, at a
children's party at Hatfield, he was telling a story. He was a stammerer
and being unable to follow what he was saying I suddenly asked in a
loud voice, "Why does he waggle his mouth like that?" I was hastily
removed by the lady-in-waiting.'

Even Florence Becker Lennon, who of all Lewis Carroll biographers
is most inclined to indulge in psychological analysis, accepts the not-
stammering-with-children theory, and talks of Dodgson's relationship
with little girls as 'spiritualized'. It was left to Anne Clark in her 1979
life of Dodgson, and to the editors of *The Letters of Lewis Carroll*,
published in the same year, to suggest that Charles Dodgson was not
the only member of his family to be attracted by members of the
opposite sex who were very much younger than himself. The genealo-
gical table at the beginning of *The Letters of Lewis Carroll* shows that
the only two Dodgson brothers who married, Skeffington and Wilfred,
both chose brides about a dozen years their juniors, and Anne Clark
has pointed out that an entry in Dodgson's diaries shows that Wilfred
was pursuing his future wife, one Alice Donkin, when she was only
fourteen – possibly even earlier, for Charles himself had discovered and
photographed her when she was eleven. Alice Donkin and Wilfred
Dodgson had a long and apparently happy marriage, begun when she
was twenty, producing a large number of children of whom Charles
warmly approved ('Alice has somehow managed to make these

children combine the high spirits of children with the good manners of grown-up people', he told Wilfred in the 1880s). Such opposition as was made to the relationship between Wilfred and Alice in its early days was apparently less on the grounds of her age than of Wilfred's lack of financial security – he eventually became agent to a big Shropshire landowner, but at this time had no 'prospects' – and Charles merely advised Wilfred to keep away from the fourteen-year-old Alice 'for a couple of years' rather than abandon her completely.

At the time that the Alice Donkin matter was being noted in his diary, in October 1865, Charles's relationship with his own Alice had in effect come to an end. But is it absurd to suppose that things could have gone otherwise, and that Alice Liddell, like Alice Donkin, might have spent her adult years as Mrs Dodgson?

*

Alice Liddell has been popularly regarded as Beatrice to Lewis Carroll's Dante at least since 1932, when as an old lady in her eighties she emerged briefly into the limelight to participate in the centenary of Dodgson's birth, and to publish her recollections (brief and uninformative) of the genesis of *Alice* and her friendship with its author. Nothing that has appeared in print since then has told us anything more of importance about her, either as Muse or child; Anne Clark's misleadingly titled *The Real Alice* suggests, if anything, that she was a rather disagreeable adult, and Colin Gordon's life of her is really a discursive history of her family and her in-laws (in 1880 she married a man named Hargreaves). Dodgson's biographers have really discovered nothing about his relationship with Alice; *The Letters of Lewis Carroll* tell us nothing; and crucial parts of Dodgson's diaries are missing.

This last, of course, is a fact of some interest. It seems a little unlikely that anyone bothered to suppress the four whole volumes which have vanished, especially as we know that Dodgson's nephew and first biographer, Collingwood, had them, and quoted from them; the diary as a whole is too bland for anyone to have been likely to find it embarrassing. Two of the missing volumes cover the years 1854-5, when Dodgson was finishing his undergraduate studies and beginning life as a don; the later two cover the years 1858-62, the period in which his friendship with the Liddell sisters was ripening, and, naturally, his biographers have fretted at being deprived of them. Fortunately the next surviving volume happens to include the summer months of 1862, when the story of *Alice* was being told to the children. One can hardly imagine that the missing parts, were they to turn up, would reveal anything very striking: merely the usual tea-parties and jaunts which marked the progress of Dodgson's child-friendships. But a missing page in one of the surviving volumes, that covering the summer of 1863, is rather a different matter.

The page has been removed after an entry for 25 June, when Mrs Liddell, Alice's mother, rather uncharacteristically allowed Dodgson to take Lorina, Alice, and Edith back to Oxford by train, unchaperoned, after a trip down river in which the whole Liddell family had participated (the rest of them went back by road). The absence of a chaperone was notable because Lorina, the eldest, was now old enough for one to be required by the etiquette of the age. The day ended happily, but then something seems to have happened which caused a breach between Dodgson and the Liddells which was never properly healed. It is here that the page has been removed, and after it there are few references to the Liddells or Alice. Such as do appear contain clear indications that there has been a breach; on 5 December, Dodgson records of some Christ Church theatricals: 'Mrs Liddell and the children were there – but I held aloof from them as I have done all this term.' He spent a little time with the girls at the Deanery a few weeks later, but there was no resumption of the old friendship, and when in May 1864 he asked Mrs Liddell's permission to take the younger children on the river he found that 'Mrs Liddell will not let *any* come in future – rather superfluous caution'. After this, even though he was living a hundred yards or so from her family house, he scarcely saw Alice again for six years, when a 'wonderful thing' occurred, and Mrs Liddell brought Alice to be photographed. Then came an even longer interval, and his final encounter with Alice, in 1888, was when she was a married woman of thirty-five.

It is impossible not to speculate that Dodgson's cold-shouldering by Mrs Liddell in the summer of 1863 happened because she suspected that he wanted to marry one of her daughters, or that his feelings towards them were not simply those of avuncular friendship. According to Anne Clark's life of Dodgson, there is a tradition among Alice's descendants that Dodgson actually made an offer of marriage, and that it was rejected; on the other hand, Alice's son Caryl Hargreaves told Derek Hudson: 'I do not think that Dodgson was ever "in love" with my mother . . . that is to say, contemplated marriage.' If Mrs Liddell did harbour such a suspicion, she would have been hostile to the idea not necessarily because of the age difference (see the case of Wilfred Dodgson and Alice Donkin) but because Dodgson was a very poor matrimonial catch. Mrs Liddell was in fact notorious in Christ Church as a matchmaker, thought to be on the look-out for husbands for her daughters among the titled undergraduates; so much so that this was the subject of a verse satire, *Cakeless*, written by one of the undergraduates and printed in 1874. (The book was suppressed, and the author rusticated from the university.) Dodgson's feelings for the Liddell girls were apparently the subject of jokes in the college, for in *Cakeless* he appears in thin disguise under the name 'Kraftsohn', and is seen at the daughters' wedding, 'biting his nails'. Even Dodgson's cautious and discreet first biographer, Collingwood, speculated (in an unpublished letter) that the 'shadow of some disappointment' which he felt hung over his uncle's life might have been the result of 'Alice's marriage to Hargreaves', which, he suggested, 'may have seemed to him the greatest tragedy of his life'.

So it may; and then again it may have made no difference to him. Certainly in later years he did not usually try to keep up any sort of intimacy with his child-friends after they had reached puberty. The end he had in view, unconsciously, may not have been a marriage like his brother Wilfred's, but the sort of gratification he presumably got from photographing small girls in the nude. He tried this briefly in 1879, but gave it up abruptly a year later, and indeed abandoned all forms of photography along with it, as if the experience had been altogether too disturbing.

We simply do not know, even given the great mass of evidence, exactly what were his feelings for his child-friends in general, and for Alice Liddell in particular. And, to tell the truth, it hardly matters, for *Alice's Adventures in Wonderland* is not about Alice Liddell at all.

*

Lewis Carroll did not invent Nonsense. One may find suggestions of it, for instance, in Shakespeare's fools and jesters, and in the *lugenmärchen* or 'lying tales' that the Grimms and other folklorists discovered throughout Europe.

> Last Sunday morning at six o'clock in the evening as I was sailing over the tops of the mountains in my little boat, I met two men on horseback riding on one mare: so I asked them, 'Could they tell me whether the little old woman was dead yet who was hanged last Saturday week for drowning herself in a shower of feathers?' They said they could not positively inform me, but if I went to Sir Gammer Vans he could tell me all about it. 'But how am I to know the house?' said I. 'Ho, 'tis easy enough,' said they, 'for 'tis a brick house, built entirely of flints, standing alone by itself in the middle of sixty or seventy others just like it.[41]

This is an English example, recorded by the nineteenth-century collector Joseph Jacobs, and one suspects that the celebrated eighteenth-century piece of nonsense, 'The Great Panjandrum', is traditional too, though it has been ascribed to various wits and authors:

> So she went into the garden to cut a cabbage-leaf, to make an apple-pie; and at the same time a great she-bear, coming up the street, pops its head into the shop. 'What! no soap?' So he died, and she very

imprudently married the barber; and there were present the Picnin-
nies, and the Joblillies, and the Garyalies, and the great Panjandrum
himself, with the little round button at top, and they all fell to playing
the game of catch as catch can, till the gun powder ran out at the heels
of their boots.[42]

A grotesquely comic little chapbook, *The World Turned Upside Down*,
which was in circulation at the beginning of the nineteenth century,
gets near pure Nonsense when it describes such curiosities as a man
trying to jump down his own throat.

Charles Dodgson would have known 'The Great Panjandrum': it
was printed in one of Maria Edgeworth's *Harry and Lucy* stories, and
he was given her books to read in childhood. He knew too the
'Nonsensical Story about Giants and Fairies' which forms an interlude
in Catherine Sinclair's *Holiday House* (1839), the book he gave to the
Liddell sisters for Christmas 1861; this story, told by the naughty
children's indulgent uncle, includes a giant so tall that 'he was obliged
to climb up a ladder to comb his own hair'. And we may confidently
assume that Dodgson was well acquainted with Edward Lear's *Book of
Nonsense*; several editions of it were in circulation by the time he came
to write *Alice*, and it was a favourite in a large number of middle-class
households.

His own first attempts at Nonsense, in the family magazines and the
pages of *The Comic Times* and *The Train* were largely parodies, and in
general they neither had the skill nor were aimed at the sensitive targets
of the parodies in *Alice*. A rather different kind of Nonsense begins to
appear in his letters to children just before the creation of *Alice*,
however. For example, in January 1862 he writes to Tennyson's son
Hallam:

> I am glad you liked the knife, and I think it a pity you should not be
> allowed to use it 'till you are older'. However, as you *are* older now,
> perhaps you have begun to use it by this time: if you were allowed to
> cut your finger with it, once a week, just a little, you know, till it
> began to bleed, and a good deep cut every birthday, I should think
> that would be enough, and it would last a long time so. Only I hope
> that if Lionel ever wants to have *his* fingers cut with it, you will be
> kind to your brother, and hurt him as much as he likes.[43]

This is the real thing, the ruthless pursuit of a single idea on purely
logical grounds, to an absurd and horrific conclusion. With such
materials, *Alice* was built.

It was not built quickly. We do not know exactly what Dodgson told
Alice, Lorina, and Edith Liddell in their rowing boat on the Thames at
Oxford on 4 July 1862, for the 'headings' of the story that he wrote out

the next morning (while travelling on a train to London) do not survive. Apparently the narrative was left unfinished on that first occasion, for a month later, on another river trip with the Liddells on 6 August, Dodgson found himself obliged to 'go on with my interminable fairy-tale of *Alice's Adventures*'. He did not begin to write the narrative out fully until 13 November, and he was still at work on the manuscript the following March, when he borrowed a book of natural history from the Deanery to help with the pictures he was drawing of some of the animals. Alice Liddell was not presented with the finished manuscript until November 1864, and probably she was not the first child to see it. It was lent in the spring of 1863 to the family of George MacDonald, with whom (as we shall see) Dodgson was on warm terms, and it appears that other children were shown it, for, when approaching John Tenniel to get illustrations for the published version, Dodgson explained that 'it has been read and liked by so many children, and I have been so often asked to publish it, that I have decided on doing so'. It seems that Alice Liddell may have been almost the only one of his child-friends not to be consulted during the later stages of composition.

Alice's Adventures in Wonderland and *Through the Looking-Glass* are so well known that trying to re-examine them with a fresh eye is rather like attempting to make a new estimate of the Bible or Shakespeare. It is difficult to find a yardstick by which to measure them; there seems, at first sight, to be no other work of literature like them. Yet they did inspire a number of imitations, which began to appear a few years after the publication of *Wonderland*, and continued in a trickle up to the last decade of the nineteenth century, by which time it seems to have been universally discovered that no one could successfully copy Lewis Carroll. Indeed they could not, but the very failure of the imitations provides clear evidence of what *Alice* achieved. Set against them, the characteristics of Lewis Carroll stand out very clearly.

Several of the imitations were so far from *Alice* in character and intention that they tell us little. These are books which blend Carroll-like fantasy with moral earnestness. Christina Rossetti's *Speaking Likenesses* (1874) is one such – a book which its author admitted had been written 'in the Alice style with an eye to the market'. It is about Flora, who escapes from a disastrous birthday party into a fantasy world where all the unpleasant characteristics of selfish children are personified in 'speaking likenesses'. Alice Corkran's *Down the Snow Stairs* (1887) is even more earnest, resembling an evangelical novel in its tale of Kitty, who is taken off by a snowman to a magical land where she is cured of selfish behaviour, and returns resolving to behave better towards her crippled brother. Somewhat closer in spirit to *Alice* is one of the first imitations to appear, *Mopsa the Fairy* (1869) by Jean Ingelow. This is a dream story, in which the boy Jack discovers a nest of fairies in a tree, and is taken off to fairyland on the back of an albatross named Jenny. *Mopsa*, though not without charm, seems almost like a drug-induced hallucination in the way that the characters or scenes change without warning or pattern. It shows us that Alice is by comparison very tightly organised; even the dreamlike transitions in *Through the Looking-Glass* are carefully planned moves from one square of the chessboard to another.

We are in territory much closer to *Alice* with a handful of comic fantasies without moral purpose, which were written in the Lewis Carroll style, or as near to it as the authors could get. The best of these is *The Wallypug of Why* (1895) by G. E. Farrow.[44] This is the story of Girlie, who is taken off by her doll Dumpsey Deazil 'to the land of Why, where all the questions and answers come from'. On the way she meets such people as a Doctor-in-law, who gives 'professional advice' without being asked for it and then demands a large fee, and a Fish who is 'fishing for compliments'. The Wallypug himself is a 'kind of king', who is governed by his people instead of governing them, and has to address them all as 'Your Majesty'.

It is not that *The Wallypug of Why* fails to equal Lewis Carroll's fertility of imagination; rather the opposite. It is too full of invention. Farrow presents us with crazy character after crazy character – a Crocodile who is nursing a cup of tea because it is 'weak tea' and must therefore be poorly, and a Sea who sends Girlie a letter – the letter C ('That's a letter isn't it, stupid?'). By comparison, *Alice* is strikingly restrained, classical rather than romantic in its disciplined organisation. (This makes Tenniel, really a very stiff and formal artist compared to most comic draughtsmen of his day, peculiarly suitable as an illustrator.) Carroll-Dodgson has not tried to produce a gallery of comic characters as Farrow has. He has not even tried to invent 'characters' at all; he deals in types, pared down to their barest essentials. The Duchess is not, say, 'the Funny Old Duchess of Wonderland', or 'Duchess Thingmebob', as she might be in the hands of a lesser writer. She is simply The Duchess.

> The Duchess was sitting on a three-legged stool in the middle, nursing a baby: the cook was leaning over the fire, stirring a large cauldron which seemed to be full of soup.

The Duchess, *the* cook, and in effect *the* baby – they are all types rather than characters. And there are remarkably few of them: the Duchess and the Queen of Hearts are really one and the same person, as are the Mad Hatter and the March Hare, the several Kings, Tweedledum and Tweedledee, of course, and possibly Humpty Dumpty and the Cheshire Cat. Other 'doublings' may be worked out; Carroll has not set out to invent a multitude of funny people at all, but has worked with as small a palate as possible.

So if his intention was not, as it seems, to amuse by fertility of imagination, what was he up to? Consciously or half-consciously, as is generally well known, he was making a lot of mathematical and logical jokes. Dodgson himself noted, with evident approval, that the critic in *John Bull* had observed 'that the book furnishes evidence that Mathematics are not inconsistent with writing works of the imagination'. Nearly a century later, Martin Gardner demonstrated this in his *Annotated Alice* (1960), which supplies *Wonderland* and *Through the Looking-Glass* with notes identifying, and in some cases solving, the paradoxes buried in the texts. Francis Huxley's *The Raven and the Writing-Desk* (1976), undoubtedly brilliant but certainly incomprehensible to most people, takes this further and explores in truly Carrollian terms the mathematical and logical roots of the stories, and of *The Hunting of the Snark*, the only other product of Dodgson's pen which may be called 'true Lewis Carroll'. For those disinclined to turn to Huxley or even Gardner, all that need be said is that the study of mathematics is closely related to the invention of Nonsense, for each depends on being literal-minded – on taking numbers and words exactly at their face value.

> 'How old did you say you were?'
> Alice made a short calculation, and said 'Seven years and six months.'
> 'Wrong!' Humpty Dumpty exclaimed triumphantly. 'You never said a word like it.'

At the same time, mathematicians are able, when making calculations, to adopt whatever word or symbol they like as representative of the things they are dealing with. Einstein was under no obligation to express his theory of relativity as $E=mc^2$; he might just as well have said, had he chosen different symbols, that 'Cheese=Jam Mustard^2'. A mathematician sees the truth in Humpty Dumpty's statement that 'when I use a word, it means just what I choose it to mean – neither more nor less'.[45]

The realisation that the *Alice* books are so deeply rooted in mathematics has occupied readers 'and critics' attention in recent years, to the extent that the assumption has perhaps grown up that they are *only* a series of mathematical or logical jokes. But a glance, again, at some of the *Alice* imitations shows us that this is not so, and that *Alice* itself has a characteristic that is lacking from all of them, something which underlies the mathematical-logical comedy, and operates on a deeper level than it.

Before we identify it, we need to turn back for a moment to Lewis Carroll's distinguished predecessor in the field of Nonsense. Edward Lear's limericks, as we have observed, are chiefly about eccentricity and the alienation of the eccentric from society:

> There was an Old Man of Whitehaven,
> Who danced a quadrille with a Raven;
> But they said – 'It's absurd, to encourage this bird!'
> So they smashed that Old Man of Whitehaven.

'Alienation' is, indeed, too mild a word for what happens to many of Lear's Old Men and Old Women. Some of them, the lucky ones, are allowed to conduct their odd lives unmolested ('He tore off his boots, and subsisted on roots, / That borascible person of Bangor'). Others, less fortunate, endure mockery ('But they said, It ain't pleasant, to see you at present, / You stupid Old Man of Melrose'). But many come to an abrupt end: 'They threw some large stones, which broke most of his bones, / And displeased that old person of Chester.' (What modern children's writer could get away with such stuff, without arousing outraged cries from librarians and teachers about 'unacceptable levels of violence'?)

Lear, in fact, was substituting for the rather feeble drolleries of the early limerick books46 something much more grotesque. He was the first person to realise that Nonsense is inextricably associated with violence, destruction, annihilation, and that any Nonsensical proposition, if pursued logically to its conclusion, must end in Nothing. And this realisation underlies *Alice*:

> 'And how many hours a day did you do lessons?' said Alice, in a hurry to change the subject.
> 'Ten hours the first day,' said the Mock Turtle: 'nine the next, and so on.'
> 'What a curious plan!' exclaimed Alice.
> 'That's the reason they're called lessons,' the Gryphon remarked: 'because they lessen from day to day.'
> This was quite a new idea to Alice, and she thought it over a little before she made her next remark. 'Then the eleventh day must have been a holiday?'
> 'Of course it was,' said the Mock Turtle.
> 'And how did you manage on the twelfth?' Alice went on eagerly.
> 'That's enough about lessons,' the Gryphon interrupted in a very decided tone. 'Tell her something about the games now.'

The state of Nothingness or Not Being, which at the very least is death and at its worst is something more frightening, lies just around every corner in both *Wonderland* and *Through the Looking-Glass*; and it is this that gives the books a driving purpose, even a sense of desperate urgency, that is utterly lacking from the bland *Alice* imitations by other writers. Alice begins her adventures by falling an apparently endless fall, and, as William Empson noted long ago,[47] this brings in the first of the death jokes: '"Well," thought Alice to herself, "after such a fall as this . . . I wouldn't say anything about it, even if I fell off the top of the house!" (which was very likely true).' The fall itself should, properly, end in annihilation, but its apparently harmless conclusion ('down she came upon a heap of sticks and dry leaves') is a false comfort, for soon Alice is in an even more perilous situation, 'shutting up like a telescope', and wondering if the shrinking will end 'in my going out altogether, like a candle'. Shortly after, she is suffering a complete crisis of identity ('I'm sure I'm not Ada . . . for her hair goes in such long ringlets, and mine doesn't go in ringlets at all . . .'), is drowning in her own tears, and is hearing the Mouse recite a tale of slaughter ('I'll be judge, I'll be jury, said cunning old Fury, I'll try the whole cause and condemn you to death'). Next, she has grown too big for the White Rabbit's house, so that 'there seemed to be no sort of chance of her ever getting out of the room again'. After nearly murdering Bill the Lizard by kicking him up the chimney, she escapes from the house, tiny again, to find herself faced by 'an enormous puppy' which 'would be very likely to eat her up'. Faced by the Caterpillar, she is unable to answer the question 'Who are *You*?', and soon afterwards finds herself in the Duchess's kitchen, which seems to be a temple positively dedicated to the cause of violence and destruction ('a constant howling and sneezing, and every now and then a great crash'). At the conclusion of this episode a baby completely ceases to be a human being at all ('It makes rather a handsome pig, I think'), and Alice's next port of call is the Mad Tea-Party, which explores another possible form of Nothingness – the time is always six o'clock, and the Hatter and Hare are condemned to the endless repetition of their tea-party, setting riddles that have no answer as they move slowly around the table, with something worse in store for them:

'Then you keep moving round, I suppose?' said Alice.
'Exactly so,' said the Hatter: 'as the things get used up.'
'But what happens when you come to the beginning again?' Alice ventured to ask.
'Suppose we change the subject,' the March Hare interrupted, yawning.

The subject is *always* changed at such moments. Only the Cheshire Cat seems immune to the threat of extinction; it must be regarded as the only free individual in the *Alice* books, having command over its own non-existence ('This time it vanished quite slowly, beginning with the

end of the tail, and ending with the grin'). Humpty Dumpty, one feels,
ought to have the same power in *Through the Looking-Glass*; he seems
to be an equally detached commentator on the action (Alice consults
him about the meaning of 'Jabberwocky'), who claims ultimate power
– words mean just what he chooses them to mean. But *Through the
Looking-Glass* is an even more ruthless book than *Wonderland*, and
Humpty Dumpty is not spared:

> Alice . . . said 'Good-bye!' once more, and, getting no answer to this,
> she quietly walked away . . . At this moment a heavy crash shook the
> forest from end to end.

And, though nothing further is said about it, we know that all the king's
horses and all the king's men, who rush past Alice the next moment,
will not be able to piece together the shattered remnants of Humpty
Dumpty.

Children, it may be objected, do not perceive much of this. Possibly
not – though the Queen of Hearts' reiteration of 'Off with his head!' is
deeply alarming to very young readers, and many adults retain vague
memories of being somehow frightened by the *Alice* books in
childhood, to the extent of positively disliking them.[48] And in any case,
Alice is not (beyond a certain point) a children's book at all, in the sense
that it is not what it purports to be, the adventures of a child called
Alice. The Alice figure is presented in the form of a child because it is
required that this figure should ask innocent, unsophisticated questions
of the persons encountered. She is certainly not a portrait of Alice
Liddell – one should note that even in Dodgson's original manuscript
Alice's Adventures Underground, his drawings do not portray Alice
herself, who had short hair. He drew a picture of her on the last page
(afterwards covering it with a photograph), but this is very different
from the nondescript long-haired child who appears in his own
illustrations to the story itself (which were, of course, replaced by John
Tenniel's pictures in the published book). Alice is Everyman.

That the *Alice* books should consist, on their deepest level, of an
exploration of violence, death, and Nothingness is not in itself very
surprising. Comedy tends to lead in that direction. What is especially
striking about *Alice*, given what we know about Charles Lutwidge
Dodgson, is that he does not stop simply at the exploration of
Nothingness, but creates something that is specifically a mockery of
Christian belief.

*

This is most obviously true of the verse parodies which are such a
feature of the *Alice* books. These parodies are not strictly necessary to
the story, but they strike a recurrent note in it. They are, in many

instances, not merely parodies of serious poems, but of verses whose message is specifically Christian.[49] The first to appear in the story,

> How doth the little crocodile
>   Improve his shining tail,
> And pour the waters of the Nile
>   On every golden scale!

parodies Isaac Watts's poem 'Against Idleness and Mischief', one of the best known pieces in his *Divine Songs* (1715):

> How doth the little busy bee
>   Improve each shining hour,
> And gather honey all the day
>   From every opening flower!
>
> In works of labour or of skill,
>   I would be busy too;
> For Satan finds some mischief still
>   For idle hands to do.

Alice's next attempt at recitation, in the company of the Caterpillar, produces similar results. 'You are old, father William' is a send-up of Southey's didactic poem 'The Old Man's Comforts and How He Gained Them', which has a markedly Christian message:

> 'I am cheerful, young man,' father William replied,
>   'Let the cause thy attention engage;
> In the days of my youth I remember'd my God!
>   And He hath not forgotten my age.'

Similarly ''Tis the voice of the Lobster' parodies Isaac Watts's ''Tis the voice of the sluggard', whose subject is reproved because 'he scarce reads his Bible', while the White Knight's song in *Through the Looking-Glass* is modelled on Wordsworth's 'Resolution and Independence', which concludes:

> 'God,' said I, 'be my help and stay secure;
> I'll think of the Leech-gatherer on the lonely moor!'

It is something of a shock to realise that it was, again and again, implicitly religious material that Dodgson was twisting into his own nonsensical, violent shapes. Southey's pious Father William becomes crafty, tough, and furious-tempered ('Be off, or I'll kick you down stairs'); the 'little busy bee' of Watts's Sunday School verse turns into a 'little crocodile', quick to consume all around it 'with gently smiling jaws'; the same poet's object lesson about the Sluggard's neglect of his religion turns into a sinister fable about an Owl and a Panther, made all the nastier because the reader is left to work out the end:

> When the pie was all finished, the Owl, as a boon,
> Was kindly permitted to pocket the spoon:
> While the Panther received knife and fork with a growl,
> And concluded the banquet by –

The astonishing thing is that the man who wrote these parodies spent much of the latter part of his life protesting against such things. Like his father, he abhorred reference to sacred things. He refused to take some child-friends to a stage play based on *The Water-Babies*[50] because there had been interpolated into it a parody of a Salvation Army hymn. If ever he heard the word 'Damn' spoken or said on stage (and he was a frequent theatre-goer, delighting in the company of theatrical children), he would write to the performers or the management, objecting in the strongest possible terms – *HMS Pinafore*, with its reiteration of 'He said Damn me!' came in for an especially strong attack from him. He wrote at length, in more than one context, on the subject of Irreverence:

> No type of anecdote seems so sure to amuse the social circle as that which turns some familiar Bible-phrase into a grotesque parody. Sometimes the wretched jest is retailed, half-apologetically, as said by a child, 'and, of course,' it is added, 'the *child* meant no harm!' Possibly: but does the *grown man* mean no harm, who thus degrades what he ought to treat with reverence, just to raise a laugh?[51]

Can this really be the author who turned the pious sentiments of Watts and Southey into comic grotesqueries?

At first sight the contradiction between Lewis Carroll the parodist and Charles Dodgson the defender of Reverence seems to be, like the Hatter's raven-and-writing-desk conundrum, a riddle with no answer. The solution, if there is one, is surely that proposed by Elisabeth Sewell in *The Field of Nonsense* (1952): that both the parodies and the anguished piety spring from the same thing, the fact that Dodgson's religious beliefs were utterly insecure.

Such insecurity would certainly explain both the willingness, in one mode of his mind (the Lewis Carroll mode) to mock religious sentiments, and the horror with which the more conscious, rational part of him viewed any attempt to shake the presumably wobbly structure of his religion.[52] And indeed we find a distinct suggestion of insecurity in religion in his refusal to proceed fully into Holy Orders.

When Dr Pusey put Dodgson's name up for a Studentship of Christ

Church, he told him that he 'had made a rule to nominate only those who were going to take Holy Orders. I told him that was my intention, & he nominated me.' But when the time came to be ordained, Dodgson said he 'had changed my mind'. He had become established as Mathematical Lecturer, and had 'no sort of inclination to give it up & take parochial work'. He consulted Samuel Wilberforce, Bishop of Oxford, and also Henry Parry Liddon of Christ Church, a leading figure in the Oxford Movement, and the conclusion was reached that Dodgson should take Deacon's Orders 'as a sort of experiment, which would enable me to try how the occupation of a clergyman suited me, & *then* decide whether I would take full Orders'; meanwhile he was free to regard himself 'as *practically* a layman'; so 'I took Deacon's Orders in that spirit'.[53]

This might be interpreted as simply an excess of conscience – Dodgson was uneasy at retaining his academic job while accepting clerical orders – were it not that in every Oxford college at this time there were dons who were nominally priests of the Church of England but spent almost all their time in academic work. Possibly he was simply being more scrupulous than them. Yet his considerable conscience-searching on the subject combined with his fear of irreverence towards religion on one side, and the parodies of religious poetry in *Alice* on the other, do add up to the suggestion that, in the most private areas of his mind, religion was something about which he had no certainty whatever.

He took Deacon's Orders in 1861, the year before the creation of *Alice*, and never did proceed to the priesthood. He tried to avoid taking any kind of service, which he said was an ordeal – allegedly on account of his stammer; but why should reading a service be more painful to a stammerer than giving a lecture, something that he did hundreds of times without complaint?

*

Is it fanciful, too, to suggest that the parodies of Isaac Watts, Southey, and Wordsworth in *Alice* are not the only element in it of religious mockery? Is not the story's very structure a parody of religion?

Its opening and closing passages provide a frame to the narrative which identifies it as a dream; but not just any kind of dream. 'Alice was beginning to get very tired of sitting by her sister on the bank . . . the hot day made her feel very sleepy and stupid . . .' It is in such fashion that some of the great visionary poems of the medieval world begin, among them the Middle English *Pearl* and *Piers Plowman* (whose dreamer lies down on the hillside 'In a somer seson when soft was the sonne'), and the *Roman de la Rose*. *Alice*, one is perhaps being told, is going to be some such vision. And a moment later, when the White Rabbit leads

Alice down the rabbit hole, is there not a faint suggestion of Dante's passage through the gate of Hell with Virgil as guide? Certainly it is to a Dantean underworld that Alice comes, where many of the inhabitants are condemned to a punitive repetition of their tasks – the Duchess perpetually enduring the pepper and flying pots and pans of the Cook, the Mock Turtle and Gryphon for ever sighing by the sea, the Mad Hatter and March Hare endlessly moving round the tea table while time stands still. Alice has had a glimpse of Paradise, a vision of 'the loveliest garden you ever saw'. But when she finally reaches the rose garden it is not Paradise, not an Enchanted Place, but a cruel parody of Heaven where divine justice takes the form of the Queen of Hearts forever screaming 'Off with her head!' Moreover, Alice's attempts to get into the garden introduce into the story another element of religious parody.

> Tied round the neck of the bottle was a paper label with the words 'DRINK ME' beautifully printed on it in large letters . . . she found . . . a very small cake, on which the words 'EAT ME' were beautifully marked in currants.

The choice of words here is very striking. Carroll could so easily have labelled the bottle and the cake 'Drink this' or 'Eat this', or some such. The use of the word 'Me' contains one particular echo:

> . . . and when he had given thanks, he brake it, and gave it to his disciples, saying, Take, eat; this is my Body which is given for you . . . Drink ye all of this; for this is my Blood . . .

Are not the 'very small cake' and the delicious liquid which Alice eats and drinks the elements of Holy Communion, Christ's body and blood?

Dodgson would have known the Thirty-Nine Articles of the Church of England very well – the more so, perhaps, since he had considered very carefully the question of ordination. Article XXVIII, 'Of the Lord's Supper', states that Holy Communion is to be regarded as 'a sign of the love that Christians ought to have among themselves one to another' as well as 'a Sacrament of our Redemption by Christ's death'. It brings the Christian into closer fellowship with his fellow men, and links him to God as a created being. But Alice's eating and drinking of what might be called her anti-Communion has precisely the opposite effect. When she eats and drinks she changes size abruptly, and in consequence alienates herself utterly from the occupants of Wonderland, and even from her own person. She becomes huge and terrifies the White Rabbit and his servants; she becomes tiny and nearly drowns in her own tears. Moreover, these changes are a denial of her status as a created being fashioned by God; she has no identity, nothing of her remains the same. In both *Wonderland* and *Looking-Glass* she is uncertain even of her name. All this is a negation of the Christian concept of the nature of human beings. Alice is the victim of a mindless, Godless universe. C. N. Manlove has observed[54] of fantasy literature that it 'exhibits [an] insistence on and celebration of the separate identities of created things'. If that is so, *Alice* is an anti-fantasy, and its heroine's progress towards the secret garden that is her goal is a discovery that created things do *not* have separate identities. The baby turns into a pig. The dormouse becomes an object to be stuffed into a teapot. The court turns into a pack of cards. The Cheshire Cat fades into a grin. It is a world that is constantly uncreating itself. No wonder that Charles Dodgson turned his back on it.

*

That he did turn his back on it it is obvious from a reading of *The Letters of Lewis Carroll*. That book is misnamed; it should be called *The Letters of C. L. Dodgson*, for it is almost impossible to detect the spirit of Lewis Carroll anywhere in it. The few flashes of brilliant nonsense in early letters to children are soon overwhelmed by a mass of fussy, sentimental, tiresome characteristics, while the nonsense itself is replaced by acrostics and puzzles. More than this, Dodgson has evidently rewritten *Alice* itself in his own mind. He never discusses the story itself, or any of its characters, but talks of it as if it were some sickly Sunday School story all about the conversion of dying waifs: his 'pleasantest thought' about *Alice*, he says to one correspondent, is that it has 'given real and innocent pleasure . . . to sick and suffering children'. It was this spirit which led him to compose the unbelievably sentimental 'Easter Greeting to Every Child Who Loves *Alice*', an effusion (attached to later editions of the book) which could not be more foreign to the spirit of *Alice* if it tried:

> 'Dear Child,
>   Please to fancy, if you can, that you are reading a real letter, from a real friend whom you have seen, and whose voice you can seem to yourself to hear, wishing you, as I do now with all my heart, a happy Easter.'

What would the Mad Hatter have said to that?

It is, perhaps, no surprise that C. L. Dodgson, having peered into the abyss of Nothingness and Anti-Religion in *Alice's Adventures in Wonderland* should have shuddered at the sight, stepped back hastily, and turned his mind to safer stuff. The next thing he wrote after *Wonderland* was 'Bruno's Revenge', a saccharine little tale about a fairy boy who is taught by the narrator (C. L. Dodgson in person) not to spoil his sister's garden out of wicked motives of revenge; it was printed in *Aunt Judy's Magazine* in 1867, and eventually formed the kernel of Dodgson's last book, *Sylvie and Bruno* (1889, with a second volume in 1893). *Sylvie and Bruno* is one of the most muddled, sentimental, drearily pious works ever produced in the Victorian age, but one can see why Dodgson wrote it. Having made up his 'arrears of destruction' in the *Alice* stories, he naturally wanted to reconstruct. But, like Kingsley, he found rebuilding far harder than knocking down. *Sylvie and Bruno* contains a number of seriously intentioned, carefully reasoned discussions of religion, such as one might read in the pages of Charlotte M. Yonge. They are quite unobjectionable, but they are not the work of the mind that created *Alice*. That mind had annihilated itself after the creation of *Through the Looking-Glass* (1871) and *The Hunting of the Snark* (1876). The *Snark*, indeed, is a record of its annihilation, for it ends with a soft and silent vanishing. With that vanishing, the mockery of religion vanished too, and the pious Mr Dodgson remained in sole command of his strange personality for the eventless remainder of his life. His deep fear of irreverence as he got older was surely a terror that the God-mocking Lewis Carroll might one day return.

*

Alice was not much liked by children when it first came out. It made no impact at all compared, say, to *The Boy's Own Paper*, which was an instant success when it began publication a little over a decade later. In a survey of children's reading habits conducted in 1888,[55] *Alice* does not feature at all in the popularity polls. Nor did adults take to it at once. A large number of the original reviews were dismissive, regarding it either as nothing remarkable or 'stiff, overwrought' (*The Athenaeum*); most of those who liked it were keener to praise Tenniel's drawings than Dodgson's text.[56] Yet by the time *Through the Looking-Glass* came out six years later the original book had become universally known and loved. 'Of course everyone knows who Alice is,' observed the *Spectator*, reviewing the sequel. By the time Dodgson died, in 1898, Sir Walter Besant felt himself able to declare that *Alice's Adventures in Wonderland* was 'a book of that extremely rare kind which will belong to all the generations to come until the language becomes obsolete'. The Victorians had discovered that they needed Lewis Carroll. Presumably, therefore, they needed his Anti-Religion, his act of destruction. It is often said that *Alice* cleared away the dead wood in children's literature, and marked the arrival (in Harvey Darton's words) of 'liberty of thought in children's books'. But it did far more than this. It provided a whole language, albeit a covert, coded one, for the much needed rejection of the old secure system of beliefs. It was published just as the two great religious spearheads of the nineteenth century, the Evangelicals and the Oxford Movement, were losing their original force, and in its anti-religious sentiments it heralded the coming of an era of scepticism. Moreover, in its exploration of Nothingness and Not Being it denied the old certainties about the physical world, just then being shaken in another fashion by Darwin, whose *Origin of Species* appeared six years before *Alice*. (The baby, surely, is *evolving* into a pig.) *Alice* was, therefore, far more than its author realised, a tract for the times.

3

George MacDonald and the tender grandmother

On 9 July 1862 Charles Dodgson wrote in his diary: 'To Tudor Lodge, where I met Mr MacDonald coming out. I walked a mile or so with him, on his way to a publisher, with the MS. of his fairy tale "The Light Princess" in which he showed me some exquisite drawings by Hughes.'

It is a rather striking coincidence that Dodgson, who only a few days earlier had told the story of *Alice* to the Liddell children, should happen to call on George MacDonald at his London home on the morning when MacDonald was taking to the publisher the short story that began his career as a children's writer. Charles Kingsley, meanwhile, was writing *The Water-Babies*. In other words, these three men began to make their contributions to children's literature within weeks of each other. Moreover, all three were ministers of religion – if of very different types – and all three had intense scientific or mathematical interests. A pattern begins to emerge, particularly when we realise that religious uncertainty, a thread which seems to run through *The Water-Babies* and *Alice*, played a central part in the life of George MacDonald.

*

He was born at Huntly in Aberdeenshire in 1824, and claimed descent from a MacDonald who escaped the massacre of the clan by the Campbells at Glencoe in 1692. His great-grandfather was a piper in the 1745 rebellion, and fought at Culloden. The piper's son, George's grandfather, founded a spinning factory and bleaching business at Huntly, on the River Bogie – an appropriate setting for the childhood of a boy whose writings were largely to concern water and bogeys.[57] But by the time George was born, the Industrial Revolution had made the family businesses obsolete and unprofitable, and his father had become a tenant farmer. The family was conscious of its social position: George and his three brothers were not allowed to speak the Aberdeenshire dialect at table or before their elders, although among themselves and with social inferiors they would lapse into the vernacular. Mac-Donald's novels would, in time, help to establish what has been called the 'Kailyard' school of literature, with their homely picture of Scottish village and small-town life. But he can scarcely be called a deeply Scottish writer: he wrote for the English public, and when he included Scottish dialect in his books he did so self-consciously. When writing from the depths of his imagination, in his fantasies, he inhabited a country of the mind which had nothing to do with Scotland – except with regard to the religious and spiritual questions which hung over it. His paternal grandmother had left the parish church and taken herself to the ferociously Calvinistic 'Missionar Kirk', and Calvinism was the *datum* of George's religious experience.

His mother, invalided for many years with tuberculosis, died when he was eight, and at least one critic[58] has used this fact to interpret all MacDonald's fiction. Certainly mother-figures haunt his stories, and one cannot doubt that the loss affected him deeply: all his life he treasured a letter written by her, in which she described her regret at having to wean him when he was only a few weeks old. But one should not press this Freudian interpretation of his imagination too hard, at least not to the point of deducing that he hated and feared his father. The very opposite seems to have been true: the father, not apparently a stern Calvinist in character, seems to have run a happy home after his wife's death, allowing the four boys (of whom George was the second) to run about the place as they wished; and when he eventually remarried, seven years later, he chose a wife who is reported to have been unfailingly kind and loving to the boys. George said that he 'had never asked his father for anything . . . but it was given', and there are strikingly lovable fathers in his stories: Diamond's kindly father, Joseph, in *At the Back of the North Wind*; and, in the Curdie books, Peter the miner (Curdie's own father) and Irene's 'King-papa', who is seen more than once stooping down from his great white horse to enfold his child in his arms, a memorable image of strong and loving fatherhood. There is a similarly loving father in MacDonald's near-autobiographical novel *Ranald Bannerman's Boyhood*.

In fact, in the childhood years after the death of his mother, George seems to have been full of high spirits. At about the age of twelve he wrote to his father that

> tho' I would be sorry to displease you in any way, yet I must tell you that the sea is my delight and that I wish to go to it as soon as possible, and I hope that you will not use your parental authority to prevent me, as you undoubtedly can.[59]

We know almost nothing about his childhood reading matter, but perhaps the urge to leave home and travel was fostered by *The Pilgrim's*

Progress, a favourite book all his life, and one which profoundly influenced his fantasy writing.

He won a bursary to King's College, Aberdeen, where he found himself particularly drawn into the study of natural science, and for a time thought of becoming a chemist or a doctor. He was attracted less by scientific knowledge itself than by its metaphysical implications. One may assume there is autobiography in the passage in his fantasy novel *Lilith* where the narrator says of his obsession with scientific studies:

> It was chiefly the wonder they woke that drew me. I was constantly seeing, and on the outlook to see, strange analogies, not only between the facts of different sciences of the same order, or between physical and metaphysical facts, but between physical hypotheses and suggestions glimmering out of the metaphysical dreams into which I was in the habit of falling. I was at the same time much given to a premature indulgence of the impulse to turn hypothesis into theory.

This sounds like a description of the mind of a writer of science fiction, and indeed many of MacDonald's stories border on that genre or actually cross into it. *Lilith* itself, for example, touches on the notion of several different worlds or time zones co-existing on the same physical plane; when first published (in 1895) it was read with great interest by H. G. Wells, who had simultaneously explored the same notion in *The Time Machine*, published the same year.

MacDonald's absorption in metaphysical speculation perhaps dates from, and was certainly encouraged by, a vacation from his studies at Aberdeen, when he took a job cataloguing a neglected library in some great mansion or castle in the far north of Scotland. This place has never been identified, but it became a permanent feature of his imagination, and was undoubtedly the original of Princess Irene's home in *The Princess and the Goblin*, 'a large house, half castle, half farmhouse, on the side of [a] mountain, about halfway between its base and its peak'. Such a house becomes a symbol, in this novel and in others of MacDonald's tales, for the universe itself – too large to be explored thoroughly by anyone, containing forgotten stairs and turrets and distant, dusty rooms, not to mention dark unknowable cellars; both frightening and, in its middle regions, homelike and comforting. The image of the library-within-a-castle recurs too; in *Lilith*, the story into which, at the end of his life, MacDonald tried to pack all his metaphysical obsessions, the character of Adam himself, the first man, takes the form of Mr Raven, a librarian in a castle.

What MacDonald found in that library galvanised his imagination. It was there that he read many of the English poets for the first time, but he also knew German, and the library's owner had stocked the shelves with the German Romantic writers of the late eighteenth and early nineteenth centuries. This led him to discover E. T. A. Hoffmann, author of many ornate fairy stories, such as the tale of Coppelia, the doll who comes alive; La Motte Fouqué, whose tale of Undine the water sprite MacDonald thought 'the most beautiful' of all fairy stories; and 'Novalis', the poet Friedrich von Hardenberg, whose own life was as tragically romantic as his verse – at the age of twenty-two he fell in love with a twelve-year-old girl, who not long afterwards died of tuberculosis. Of these three writers, Novalis was the one who exercised the most powerful attraction to MacDonald. He set himself to making translations of Novalis' poems, and his own first prose works, *Phantastes*, was a practical demonstration of Novalis' principle of fantasy writing, itself quoted as an epigraph to MacDonald's book:

> . . . narratives without coherence but rather with association like dreams . . . [which] can at best have an allegorical meaning in general, and an indirect effect like music.

Very probably within the same library MacDonald found the works of Swedenborg, which were certainly to influence his metaphysical-scientific speculations. Possibly it was now too that he first read the writings of the late sixteenth-century German mystic Jacob Boehme, from whom he was to derive many ideas found in his fantasy stories: among them, that of water as 'the primordial principal of nature', and the notion of a perpetual state of evolution within the created universe, so that creatures may evolve upwards towards God, or downwards. So, in MacDonald's stories, we have the air-fish in 'The Golden Key' which, as a reward for goodness, is cooked and eaten but in the process becomes a higher being, 'a lovely little creature in human shape, with large white wings'; and the red worm in *Lilith*, which Mr Raven plucks from the ground and tosses in the air: 'It spread great wings, gorgeous in red and black, and soared aloft.' And there are also the Uglies in *The Princess and Curdie*, human beings relegated to the shapes of grotesque beasts as a punishment, and, in *The Princess and the Goblin*, the goblins themselves, who were once 'very like other people', but in consequence of spiritual corruption have become 'ludicrously grotesque both in face and form'. MacDonald, in other words, explored the idea that Kingsley had touched on in *The Water-Babies* – that souls make bodies, and outward appearances indicate inward spiritual states. It was an ingenious answer of the imagination to Darwin.

Alongside such discoveries as Novalis and Boehme, the English poets may have seemed a little tame to someone of MacDonald's turn of mind, though one can see from *Phantasies* that he digested Spenser eagerly enough. And Blake made a deep mark on him; in later years there hung in his study an engraving, taken from Blake, of an aged man entering a tomb, and the same man emerging from it young, vigorous, and radiant. He adapted the same picture for his bookplate, and the notion of death not as an end but as a process of cleansing and revitalising runs through his stories. Anodos and Mr Vane, heroes of *Phantasies* and *Lilith*, both die to rise again, and Diamond's death at the end of *At the Back of the North Wind* is obviously a prelude to his return to the North Wind's mysterious country (Purgatory). The cleansing fire of roses in the Curdie books, administered by the old Princess, who is the nearest MacDonald came to a representation of God, is similarly purgatorial. Here, of course, we are in Dante's territory, and MacDonald absorbed the *Divine Comedy* deeply. It provides much of the structure of *Lilith* and *The Golden Key*, and is referred to openly in *At the Back of the North Wind*.

Inevitably, the young George MacDonald, having discovered this rich literary hoard in the castle library, began to write poetry. His son Greville describes his father's first efforts as 'so weird and obscure that it is difficult to detect their motive'; we know that the dominant mood of them was that of gothic gloom and a romanticised death-wish – a contemporary at Aberdeen speaks of MacDonald walking up and down the seashore, 'addressing the sea and the waves and the storm', and he was in the habit of saying, 'I wish we were all dead.' There are hints here of the destructiveness that was eventually to dominate his writing. But he also got on efficiently with the business of earning a living.

*

He went south and took a tutorship with a Congregationalist family in London, and soon afterwards became engaged to a girl whose family were of the same religious persuasion – Louisa Powell, daughter of a leather merchant. He was to make what seems to have been a very happy marriage with her, but one cannot help speculating about his romantic-sexual nature. Love plays a strikingly large part in his fantasy stories – striking because it is by no means an essential element in the genre (for example, Tolkien and C. S. Lewis, in many respects close to MacDonald, managed almost entirely without it in their books). It is usually one of two kinds: the love of a child or childlike person for a maternal figure (Diamond for the North Wind, Irene and Curdie for the old princess, and many similar instances in the shorter fairy stories), or – and this is just as striking – the love of child for child. MacDonald is one of the very few children's authors who make a success of portraying romantic feelings between a boy and a girl. Irene and Curdie are strongly attracted to each other from their first meeting in *The Princess and the Goblin*, and MacDonald's unselfconscious description of this is paralleled by many instances in his other tales: Tangle and Mossy's love for each other in 'The Golden Key', Colin's love for a girl stolen by the fairies in 'The Carasoyn', Diamond's affection for the crossing-sweeper Nanny in *At the Back of the North Wind*, to cite just a few. Even more striking is the love of the adult hero, Mr Vane, for the motherly child Lona in *Lilith*.

> Her hair was much longer, and she was become almost a woman, but not one beauty of childhood had she outgrown. When first we met after our long separation, she laid down her infant, put her arms round my neck, and clung to me silent, her face glowing with gladness; the child whimpered; she sprang to him, and had him in her bosom instantly. To see her with any thoughtless, obstinate, or irritable little one, was to think of a tender grandmother. I seemed to have known her for ages – for always – from before time began! I hardly remembered my mother, but in my mind's eye she now looked like Lona; and if I imagined sister or child, invariably she had the face of Lona! My every imagination flew to her; she was my heart's wife!

'A tender grandmother': not 'a tender mother'. The difference may seem slight, almost casual, but it is not. Again and again the women who dominate MacDonald's books are not mother-figures so much as grandmother-figures. His very first work of prose fiction, *Phantasies*, opens with its hero discovering in a locked drawer of an old desk a tiny fairy-figure who grows in a moment into a beautiful full-sized woman; he is drawn to her beauty 'by an attraction as irresistible as incomprehensible', but she warns him:

> 'Foolish boy, if you could touch me, I should hurt you. Besides, I was two hundred and thirty-seven years old, last Midsummer eve; and a man must not fall in love with his grandmother, you know.'

This grandmother-fairy is the first of a long line of such beings in MacDonald's stories, the two most notable being the old Princess in the Curdie books, and the North Wind. Each is aged, indeed timeless; each can shrink to child-size, and the next moment stand giantlike and terrible. Within the terms of the stories such beings are expressions of the nature of God or Providence, but one cannot help supposing that the grandmother-figure who can also become a child had a private psychological meaning for MacDonald. It seems impossible to guess what that was; one can only note that his wife was two years older than him, and seems to have treated him largely with amused maternal (even grand-maternal) tolerance; that he was especially deeply attached to his daughter Lilia,[60] and – perhaps most striking – that in 1872 he arranged for John Ruskin to meet the adolescent Rose La Touche secretly at the MacDonald house, despite the fact that Rose's parents had forbidden such a meeting, and that most people considered Ruskin to be sexually abnormal. Did he share something of Ruskin's (and Dodgson's, and Novalis') obsession with the beauty of young girls? Was this one of the poles of his romantic-sexual feelings, and was the other a need for a grandmotherly love?

*

Soon after arriving in London he decided that he should become a Congregational minister; not, apparently, because he had a firm religious faith but because this seemed a way of finding one. He spoke of himself, in a letter to his father, as 'always searching for faith in place of contemplating the truths of the gospel which produce faith', and in this respect he remained entirely Protestant throughout his life. In other ways, though, he had a more Catholic, sacramental imagination. His stories deal with spiritual transformations achieved through sacramental means (baptismal immersions in water, cleansing fires, and suchlike), and bread and wine feature often in them; Curdie, who in *The Princess and Curdie* has become somewhat Christ-like, cures the weak and poisoned king with a diet of fresh bread and good wine (as opposed to the adulterated wine the corrupt court has been giving him). The one religious state of mind MacDonald never experienced was secure orthodoxy; his books show how he was constantly in search of some new spiritual experience which would test him, and the few references in them to conventional religion are chiefly contemptuous. The preacher in *The Princess and Curdie* is described as a 'sermon-pump', devoted to upholding the rottenness of the secular state; and one may find a similar notion in *Lilith*, where there is a description of the Bags, a race of grotesque giants, worshipping 'the biggest and fattest of them',

> so proud that nobody can see him; and the giants go to his house at certain times, and call out to him, and tell him how fat he is, and beg him to make them strong and eat more and grow fat like him.

One can find the same sort of contempt for official or organised religion in MacDonald's realistic adult novels; for example the preacher to the London congregation in *David Elginbrod* is portrayed as chiefly interested in keeping his rich parishioners happy.

MacDonald's chief religious difficulty has usually been represented, by those who have written about him, as an inability to accept the Calvinist doctrine that only the elect will achieve salvation, while the rest of humanity will be damned. MacDonald, it is said, was fretting at the Calvinist chains of his childhood. Certainly this is true as far as it goes, and his failure as a minister was due most obviously to this doctrinal problem. He was appointed to a Congregational chapel at Arundel in Sussex, but was soon in trouble with his hearers for expressing the opinion that the heathen might find salvation, and even that animals might go to heaven. His differences with them eventually led him to resign, and he and his family thereafter lived in various parts of England, sometimes supported by the charity of rich benefactors, while MacDonald made what he could by lecturing on science and literature, and by preaching where he could hire a hall. In the end he gave up being a nonconformist minister altogether, settled in London, and found some sort of sanctuary in the Church of England, among the congregation of Charles Kingsley's mentor F. D. Maurice. But whereas Kingsley had embraced Maurice's teaching because of its liberalism and social concern, MacDonald apparently found it acceptable to him because it approached his own view of the nature of good and evil.

He portrayed Maurice under thin disguise in *David Elginbrod*, where he said of him: 'He believes entirely that God loves, yea *is* love, and, therefore, that hell itself must be subservient to that love, and but an embodiment of it.' The notion of hell, and indeed of all evil, as an embodiment of God is pervasive in MacDonald's writing. Among the children's books, one may perceive it in *At the Back of the North Wind*, where North Wind performs an apparently evil action – sinking a ship – as part of the larger divine plan. It is the central notion in *The Wise Woman*, a children's novella written by MacDonald in the interval between his two Curdie books, which describes the sufferings imposed upon two selfish little girls by a 'wise woman' who clearly represents God. The Curdie stories themselves, on the other hand, seem to deal with embodiments of evil which cannot be workings of the divine plan – the goblins beneath the mountain in *The Princess and the Goblin*, and the wicked courtiers in *The Princess and Curdie*. But both the goblins and courtiers are stagey, ridiculous villains, necessities of a rather crude plot rather than serious characterisations of evil. There must *be* villains, so that Curdie and Irene are in peril; but the point of the story is their reaction to that peril, and the trust and love that they come to put in the Godlike old princess, who is never there when they go and look for her, but always appears when she is least expected and most needed. By the end of MacDonald's life and *Lilith*, this notion that God is everything and everything is God (which he very probably first acquired from Boehme) had become explicit. Lilith herself, the demon creature who according to Jewish folklore was Adam's first wife, is in MacDonald's story both devil and god, temptress and eternal mother. There is no evil; and the reader of *Lilith* may feel that there is no good either.[61]

Yet we should not suppose that MacDonald, turning his back on

Calvinist theology and embracing a universe where 'good' and 'evil' were not true distinctions, had rejected the idea of the wicked receiving punishment. In fact the castigation of evil-doers plays a large part in his fiction. At times, indeed, he bears a resemblance to one of his wife's aunts, of whom it was said that 'she could never lie comfortable in bed if she might not believe in hellfire and everlasting pains'. Perhaps this element of Calvinism ran too deep in MacDonald to be eradicated by his changes of religious opinion; perhaps he simply had what we would now call a sadistic streak. At any rate he presents us in one story[62] with a little girl who declares: 'If I was a man, I would kill all the wicked people in the world', and this clearly has the author's approval. The old princess in the Curdie books, Godlike and all-loving as she is, nevertheless remarks that 'There are plenty of bad things that want killing', and the punishments she metes out to the evil courtiers who have tried to poison Irene's king-father are about as unpleasant as anything in children's literature: one has his leg bitten to pieces, another has a finger twisted off, and MacDonald hints that even worse is going on. 'The terrors of the imagination were fast yielding to those of sensuous experience,' he says; a sentence that seems to relish physical pain. Even the saintly Curdie kills dogs by hitting them through the brain with his mattock, and disables the palace cook with the same instrument. *Lilith* and the short story 'The Cruel Painter' contain a great deal of practical detail about vampirism, while the latter describes an artist whose delight is to depict terrible tortures on his canvases. The suspicion grows that this may be a portrait of MacDonald himself. Perhaps nastiest of all, because of the simplicity and apparent innocence of its style, is 'The Giant's Heart', a short story about two children (the nauseatingly named Buffy-Bob and Tricksey-Wee) who torture a giant by squeezing drops of 'spider-juice' on to his heart:

> The giant had given an awful roar of pain the moment they anointed his heart, and had fallen down in a fit . . . The first words he uttered were, –
> 'Oh, my heart! my heart! . . .'
> Here he fainted again; for Tricksey-Wee, finding the heart beginning to swell a little, had given it the least touch of spider-juice . . .

* * *

MacDonald began to make his name as a writer by publishing *Within and Without* (1855), a blank verse play describing the attempts of one Count Julian, a former monk, to reconcile earthly with heavenly love. Charles Kingsley was among its admirers. Next, in 1857, MacDonald spent a mere two months writing 'a kind of fairy tale . . . in the hope that it will pay me better than the more evidently serious work'. This was

Phantasies, which did not prove a money-spinner, but was an act of self-discovery. In it, with astonishing sureness and fluency, he mapped out the imaginative territory which he would explore in closer detail in his later fantasy stories.

Phantasies is nowadays best known as the book which introduced C. S. Lewis to MacDonald's writings, and set him on his own course as a writer of fantasy. Lewis's admirers, coming to it hopefully, are often puzzled by its extraordinary style and content. Lewis spoke of it as 'baptising' his imagination, which implies that it is a holy book. It is actually very unholy, but reading it is rather like experiencing some sort of total immersion, so that the baptismal metaphor is not entirely inappropriate.

A modern reader may suppose the book to be largely about sexuality, and in fact *Phantasies*, unlike most of MacDonald's writings, may be interpreted almost entirely in sexual terms. The hero Anodos, whose name is Greek for 'pathless', is on his twenty-first birthday initiated by a fairy mother-(or grandmother-) figure into a Fairyland whose features and events seem to stand for sexual experience and a child's or young man's reactions to it. He is menaced by the masculine, perhaps father-like, Ash tree, but is saved by the maternal Beech ('"Why, you baby!" said she, and kissed me with the sweetest kiss of winds and odours'). The experience of lying in her arms leaves him feeling 'as if new-born'. But he is tricked into the arms of the Maid of the Alder, who he has been told 'will smother you with her web of hair, if you let her near you at night'; and this and subsequent experiences with other female inhabitants of Fairyland give Anodos a sense of guilt and pollution which seem to be symbolic of a young man's guilty reaction to sexuality. Later he comes to a strange palace, where, in a library (the library-in-the-castle), he reads of a land where children are born without conception and there is no physical love between the sexes; he also reads of a young man who can only see the woman he loves by means of a mirror. In the palace he discovers a womblike hall to which he returns again and again; later, he brings a female statue to life by chanting a startlingly erotic ballad to it, commanding each part of her body to come to life, from her feet gradually upwards:

> Rise the limbs, sedately sloping,
>   Strong and gentle, full and free;
> Soft and slow, like certain hoping,
>   Drawing nigh the broad firm knee . . .
> Temple columns, close combining,
>   Lift a holy mystery . . .

The whole of *Phantastes*, indeed, may be interpreted as being about the 'holy mystery' of sex – with the possible exception of the climactic scene, where Anodos dies in the act of exposing a false religion whose god devours its worshippers; this would appear to be autobiography of a different sort, and may refer to MacDonald's resignation from his Arundel ministry.

In fact *Phantastes* is many things, and an exclusively sexual interpretation ignores many other layers of meaning – or at least, layers of implied meaning, for MacDonald was not usually an allegorist. He denied that *Phantasies* was an allegory, called it simply a 'fairy tale', and elsewhere asserted that fairy stories such as he wrote did not have one specific meaning. He continued: 'Everyone, however, who feels the story, will read its meaning after his own nature and development ... A genuine work of art must mean many things; the truer its art, the more things it will mean.'[63] MacDonald, in other words, wished to be a myth-maker rather than an allegorist. C. S. Lewis judged him to have succeeded in this more than any other modern writer, and indeed it is hard to think of any other nineteenth or twentieth-century author who excelled him in sheer fertility of mythic imagination.

Not surprisingly, after *Phantastes*, which appeared in print in 1858, MacDonald found himself uncertain what to do next. He had poured everything into the book; where could he go next, and how could he make a living as a writer? No immediate answer was apparent, and he tried his hand at several projects which failed. Meanwhile *Phantastes* brought him a number of admirers. We do not know what C. L. Dodgson thought of it, but it was in the year after its publication that he first met MacDonald, and the book's reputation probably encouraged him to get to know its author. Though the two men had little in common as writers, there were points of correspondence. Was the original idea of *Through the Looking-Glass* possibly suggested by the lover-in-the-mirror story in *Phantastes*? (The young man in this story looks into the mirror and sees that the room reflected in it is his own room – and yet not his own.) MacDonald apparently had Lewis Carroll in mind when he wrote the short story 'Cross Purposes' (1867), a rambling dreamlike tale about two children who wander into a very Wonderland-like fairy world – one of them is even called Alice. And did he take the mirror idea back again from Lewis Carroll in *Lilith*, where Vane the hero passes more than once from one world to another by means of a looking-glass? But such points of connection are slight, and Dodgson had more interest in the MacDonald children, particularly Lilia, than in their father's writings. He showed them the manuscript of *Alice's Adventures Underground* at quite an early stage in its composition – the spring of 1863 – and asked if they thought it worth publishing. His son, Greville, declared that he 'wished there were 60,000 volumes of it', and the family's enthusiasm played a large part in encouraging 'Uncle Dodgson' to put it into print. Later, Dodgson delighted in watching the public performances of *Pilgrim's*

Progress for which the family became celebrated, Lilia playing Christiana and MacDonald himself Mr Greatheart, a role for which his bearded, increasingly patriarchal appearance was entirely suited.

MacDonald's next full-length work of fiction after *Phantasies* was *David Elginbrod* (1863), a partly autobiographical novel about a young Scot coming south, which descends at times to gothic hack-writing – there is a mesmerist in it called Funkelstein, who has an evil power over the hero's beloved, Euphrasia Cameron. It was the first of many 'realistic' works of fiction by MacDonald, dealing with the theological worries of young Scotsmen, or based on memories of his childhood. The adult novels are now entirely forgotten; several of the realistic novels for children, or about them, have survived on the shelves of public libraries.[64] None of them contains the essential MacDonald.

However, by the time that *David Elginbrod* was published he had begun to discover an outlet for his fantasy imagination in the form of short stories for children. The first of these seems to have been 'The Light Princess', the tale that Dodgson accompanied on its travels to the printer. It is MacDonald's most cheerful, and therefore least characteristic, fairy story – a pun on the word 'gravity', for the princess has no *gravitas* (she is perpetually laughing) and also no physical gravity; eventually she acquires both after a prince has nearly sacrificed himself for her. Among the next to be written were 'The Giant's Heart' (the sadistic piece about the spider-juice) and 'The Castle', which seems like an early sketch for *The Princess and the Goblin* with its account of a family of children inhabiting an enormous castle.[65] Macdonald does not seem to have known what to do with these stories at first, for he printed them in *Adela Cathcart* (1864), a loosely knit novel for adults with a good deal of fireside story-telling in it. This, no doubt, was partly because he always liked the story-within-a-story method: there is scarcely a full-length book of his that does not contain at least one secondary story within it, told by one of the characters. But it was also because his short fantasy stories were not exclusively for children; along with 'The Light Princess', 'The Giant's Heart', and 'The Castle', *Adela Cathcart* contained 'The Cruel Painter', the grisly story about the artist who delights in painting pictures of torture. Indeed for the rest of his life MacDonald had a habit of producing Poe-like grotesque tales that sit oddly alongside his fairy stories. There was a blackness in his imagination which could not be contained in his writings for children.[66]

His first specifically children's book was *Dealings with the Fairies* (1867), in which 'The Light Princess' and 'The Giant's Heart' were reprinted alongside 'Cross Purposes' (his *Alice* imitation), 'The Shadows' (an early sketch for *At the Back of the North Wind*), and 'The Golden Key'.[67] This last-named story has been called MacDonald's masterpiece, and is certainly his most perfectly crafted piece of work, a

miniature *Phantasies* for children. It is at once very simple and very
complicated: the tale of a boy and a girl, Mossy and Tangle, and their
pilgrimage through life to the grave and beyond, all told in richly
symbolic terms, as they go beneath sea and land, and visit the elements
of the earth before passing out of this world.

Again, sexual symbolism pervades the narrative, but this is only one
level of its meaning. 'The Golden Key' is the pure essence of
MacDonald; but it is, perhaps, the nucleus of a great story rather than
one which itself achieves greatness. Like *Phantasies* it is too dense, too
symbolic, and too lacking in ordinary, comprehensible events to
communicate much at a first or even a second reading. Few children are
likely to be moved by it.

MacDonald might, indeed, have remained merely an interesting
footnote to children's literature had he not, in his search for an adequate
income, begun to write for a children's magazine, *Good Words for the
Young*, published in London by a fellow Scot, Alexander Strahan. His
involvement with this magazine (which he actually edited himself for a
few months) made him begin something he had not attempted before, a
full-length children's fantasy. *At the Back of the North Wind* appeared
in the pages of *Good Words for the Young* in 1868, and Strahan
published it as a book three years later, by which time MacDonald had
produced another serial for the paper, *The Princess and the Goblin*.

These are the two books by which MacDonald is now chiefly
remembered. They are both compromises between the 'essential'
MacDonald – the author of *Phantasies, Lilith*, and 'The Golden Key' –
and the writer with eleven children who had to earn a living. They were
obviously written in a hurry, without much revision, and both are
rambling and repetitive. *At the Back of the North Wind* owes rather a
lot – too much for present day taste – to the sentimental evangelical
novels for children which had been popular since the 1850s; Diamond,
the poor illiterate half-invalid boy who is befriended by North Wind,
would not be out of place in the pages of Hesba Stretton's *Jessica's First
Prayer* or other mid-Victorian Sunday School diehards; and 'Good
Words for the Young' might not be a bad subtitle for the whole book.
MacDonald the Congregationalist preacher has temporarily taken over
from MacDonald the myth-maker, as he was inclined to do when a
story was being written to make money. But even this diluted form of
the MacDonald imagination has a powerful appeal, and no one who has
read the story in early childhood will forget the account of the land 'at
the back of the North Wind', a place of utter stillness where 'nothing
went wrong . . . neither was anything quite right . . . but everything was
going to be right some day'. *At the Back of the North Wind* is no less
than a rewriting of the *Purgatorio* for children.

The Princess and the Goblin is as rambling as *At the Back of the
North Wind*. Its scene shifts with almost monotonous predictability

between the mines, where Curdie the miner's boy is struggling to discover what horrid plot the goblins are hatching, and the turret room in the castle – the room where little Princess Irene meets and is amazed by her great-great-grandmother, who sits for ever spinning, has a great white globe like the moon, and a flock of pigeons that come and go at her command.[68] But now there is nothing out of key, not a whiff of the Sunday School; instead, the story is redolent of Grimm and Perrault. It was in fact the first original British children's book to make an utterly confident, fresh use of such traditional materials as an old fairy spinning in a tower, and a race of wicked dwarfs beneath a mountain – or rather, beneath the castle itself; for MacDonald uses the stuff of folklore to construct a parable about the Christian universe. There are demons down below gnawing at the foundations; a precarious security within the main rooms; and a divine being high above who sometimes holds aloof from events, sometimes intervenes dramatically. Really, *The Princess and the Goblin* is as powerful a piece of religious teaching as ever came the way of a Sunday School child.

MacDonald was doing what Kingsley had tried to do but largely failed, and what Dodgson had refused to do: creating an alternative religious landscape which a child's mind could explore and which could offer spiritual nourishment. It was a positive achievement, not an act of destruction, and MacDonald was almost unique in it. Hans Andersen had done something of the same, but, despite MacDonald's example, almost no British writer for children seemed prepared to face the challenge until C. S. Lewis, an avowed disciple of MacDonald, began his Narnia cycle nearly eighty years later.[69]

In fact, MacDonald himself quickly lost the touch for it, and began to become a destroyer rather than a creator. Something went wrong between the two Curdie books. *The Wise Woman*, which emerged in 1875 (after *The Princess and the Goblin* and before *The Princess and Curdie*) is a very unpleasant book.[70] Where there should be lightness of touch in the story of the Wise Woman's handling of the two selfish girls, there is something closer to horror. She abducts them both without telling their parents what has happened to them, and subjects them to treatment which is not only frightening and unpleasant, but keeps failing to cure them. Finally she blinds two of the parents and puts a third into a coma. If this is a parable about God, as clearly it is, then MacDonald's view of the Creator seems to have become black and despairing.

The Princess and Curdie, written as a serial in 1877, confirms that this is so. A disproportionate amount of the book – about the first third – is taken up once again with Irene's great-great-grandmother, the old princess, as if MacDonald needs to reassure himself that the benevolent God of the first Curdie book is still there. It is evident that she is not, or at least that she is changed. She now tends to appear not as a beautiful maiden, but as 'a small withered creature . . . like a long-legged spider holding up its own web'. Even when rejuvenating herself and standing up to her full height she is still 'plainly very old'. Eventually she reappears as young and beautiful, but by this time we have been told that the miners regard her as a witch, 'an old hating witch, whose delight was to do mischief'. They call her Old Mother Wotherwop, and associate her with calamities in the mine. Curdie rejects these stories, but it seems that the miners are not entirely wrong; she tells him: 'It is one thing what you or your father may think about me, and quite another what a foolish or bad man may see in me.' She is not so very far, perhaps, from Lilith.

The second Curdie book is largely a parable about appearances and how they may deceive – Curdie is given the power of detecting the beast-natures which lurk in apparently good people – and also a reworking of the story of Christ. Curdie is 'one who is come to set things right in the king's house', like Christ coming into the world, and his purging of the evil courtiers in the palace is preceded by a servant-girl telling her fellows, John-the-Baptist-like, 'If you do not repent of your bad ways, you are going to be punished – all turned out of the palace together.' But MacDonald will not allow them to repent; he prefers that they should wallow in their iniquities, and so be punished by physical torture (mauling by the dreadful beasts whom Curdie has brought with him), and even when this is complete he will not let humanity alone. Curdie and Irene duly marry and become king and queen, but they have no children, and the kingdom passes into bad hands after their death; its foundations are undermined by the greedy populace, eager for gold and jewels from the mines, and 'one day at noon, when life was at its highest, the whole city fell with a roaring crash. The cries of men and the shrieks of women went up with its dust, and then there was a great silence'. The parable is, of course, being followed through to its end; this is the Last Judgement. But it is a very strange Last Judgement: no one is saved. In fact the conclusion of *The Princess and Curdie* is reminiscent not of the book of Revelation but of the fall of Sodom and Gomorrah.

With the destruction of the city at the end of *The Princess and Curdie*, MacDonald's writing for children in effect came to an end. Almost all the books he was to produce for the remainder of his life were for adults. That he should stop regarding himself as a children's author is not in itself surprising; he had never indeed really done so, declaring that, 'I do not write for children, but for the childlike, whether of five, or fifty, or seventy-five.' What is striking is the increasingly pessimistic, even sinister, character of his spiritual vision. That pessimism is all too clear in *A Rough Shaking* (1891), his one remaining book for young readers, which is a nightmarish account of the maltreatment of a boy who has lost his mother in an earthquake. At the very end of his life as a writer, in *Lilith*, which was published in 1895, the old visionary power returned, but with more disturbing results than ever; for this final fantasy, with its vision of evil-as-good and good-as-evil, its wild, uncontrolled symbolism, and its hotchpotch of gnostic religions and sinister folklore, is evidence of a mind in disintegration. One is not surprised to learn that, soon after *Lilith* was published, MacDonald withdrew into total silence, not speaking even to members of his family. He died in 1905, at the age of eighty-one.

Like Lewis Carroll, he had looked over the brink, and had examined the darkness which lay beyond the religious beliefs of his day. Like Kingsley, his writing for children was largely a search for a positive religious experience that could replace conventional Christianity. At first he found that experience in *At the Back of the North Wind* (though really that book scarcely departs from the normal Christian world-view), and in *The Princess and the Goblin*, with its marvellous image of the all-powerful grandmother presiding over the rambling, half-known, mysterious mansion – an image that is at once Arcadian in its suggestion of a paradisial landscape set apart from the real world, and also a clever parable for the whole universe. But MacDonald's visionary power would not let him stop there, and, like Kingsley, he found that destruction of the old certainties was easier than the creation of new ones.

He did, however, leave one positive trail that may have been discovered by a later author for children, a fellow Scot and an exponent of the Kailyard school of novels. In *Lilith*, Mr Vane finds himself in a country inhabited by children who have not grown up. Lona, whom Vane loves and who is eventually killed by Lilith, is one of these. The children are full of pranks and quite unafraid of anything – except the possibility that some of them after all may begin to grow. One of them is called Peter. We do not know whether J. M. Barrie read *Lilith*, but *Peter Pan*, an outstanding piece of quasi-religious myth-making for children, began to form itself in his imagination no more than six years after it was published.

4
Louisa Alcott and the happy family

For the first ninety years of children's fiction in England and America, no one questioned the nature of the family. Home life was where the children were to get their religious and moral education. The rationalist authors of the moral tales which poured from the presses in the second half of the eighteenth century portrayed a home circle where the parents knew beyond doubt what was right and wrong, and passed on their certainties effortlessly to their offspring. Children often erred – thereby providing the authors with some sort of plot – but there was never any doubt as to where the path of righteousness lay. Such stones naturally accepted that family headship belonged to the father, and if he was not always much in evidence, that was simply because there were more important calls on his time than childish things. When he did appear, his authority was nothing less than God-like. Mr Fairchild in Mary Martha Sherwood's *The Fairchild Family* (1818), that most celebrated of hellfire evangelical novels for children, says to one of his sons: 'I stand in the place of God to you whilst you are a child', and he seems himself to have the power of deciding his children's salvation or damnation, as he warns them of the judgement that awaits sinners.

As it turned out, Mr Fairchild was one of the last of his species. The very evangelical fervour that had helped to create Mrs Sherwood's story undermined the notion of the family as the seat of moral and spiritual authority. Evangelical religion deals with the conversion of the individual, and writers of this persuasion soon discovered that children had plot-value not just as material for conversion but as the agents of that conversion. The discovery was made, indeed, by James Janeway in the 1670s with his *Token for Children* and its accounts of holy deaths of the very young. By the mid-nineteenth century it was a commonplace of evangelical fiction for a child, initially converted by some God-fearing adult, to go on to convert other grown people by a mixture of winsomeness, piety, and pathos. Hesba Stretton's *Jessica's First Prayer* (1867) and Mrs O. F. Walton's *Christie's Old Organ*

(1875), two of the best-known books of this type, describe urban waifs encountering religion and then themselves bringing about the conversion of others. Quite apart from this, the old faith in the father-dominated family as the source of moral wisdom seems to have become shaky by about 1850, judging from the fact that the stream of moral tales for the young dried up in the 1830s. Its end was marked in 1830 by Catherine Sinclair's *Holiday House* (Lewis Carroll's 1861 Christmas present to the Liddells), a book which is about parentless children on the rampage, with the substitute parent (a jolly uncle) abdicating responsibility: the only piece of advice he gives the children is 'never crack nuts with your teeth'.

A few writers, notably Charlotte M. Yonge, continued to regard the family as the source of moral wisdom, and did not question this role. But elsewhere there were plenty of hints that a change of attitude was taking place. Lewis Carroll had nothing to say about parenthood, other than his depiction of the Duchess throwing her baby casually across the kitchen to Alice; but Kingsley and MacDonald are more explicit. Both have a striking interest in mothers or mother-figures, rather than fathers, as the moral arbiter Mrs Doasyouwouldbedoneby, North Wind, and so on – and both allow children to convert their elders: Tom the water-baby softens the hard heart of Grimes, and Diamond in *At the Back of the North Wind* reforms a drunken cabman. Kingsley has almost nothing to say about fathers, but MacDonald pays a good deal of attention to them, and though he generally paints them as kindly they are not the stern upholders of authority. Peter, Curdie's father, is his son's helper rather than his leader, ready to follow the boy's wisdom and judgement in matters of importance, and when the Princess Irene's 'king-papa' really comes on to the stage in *The Princess and Curdie*, we see an ailing old man, the dupe of his courtiers, who has to be nursed back to strength and wisdom by his daughter and Curdie. Even when healthy again he remains childlike; his greatest pleasure is to let the housekeeper's small grand-daughter play with his crown, using it as a pretend porridge-pot.

This subversive attitude to the old structure of the family was not portrayed in any nineteenth-century 'realistic' novel for children written in England. But in the work of an American, Louisa M. Alcott, we see clearly the questioning of parental authority which is hinted at by the English fantasy writers. Alcott was driven to write in this fashion about home life because of the extraordinary nature of her own family.

*

We know that she was brought up, in her own nursery days, on the moral tales of Maria Edgeworth, the most accomplished of the old rational school of English lady writers for children. But the secure, placid world of Miss Edgeworth's *Harry and Lucy* stories must surely have highlighted for Louisa Alcott the instability of the home in which she found herself. She was the daughter of Bronson Alcott, who, depending on one's outlook, was either a major American thinker and educationalist, or a lazy good-for-nothing with a command of humbug equalling that of the Wizard of Oz. Amos Alcox (to give him his original name) had begun adult life as a travelling salesman, peddling fancy goods around his native Connecticut and further afield. He quickly developed a talent for making no money whatsoever and accumulating large debts – a characteristic that was to remain with him for the rest of his life, and was quite unaccompanied by bad conscience. He also changed his surname from Alcox to Alcott, apparently to avoid dirty jokes, and called himself by his second baptismal name. Under this new label, Bronson Alcott, he soon came to believe that he had a personal mission from God to set up schools on Transcendental principles. Quite what were those principles was hard to say, since a feature of Transcendentalism, as practised by Alcox/Alcott and other Americans of the same persuasion around the early 1830s, was a refusal to define ideas. Bronson Alcott's 'teaching method', if it can be called that, was to let idealistic talk pour from what one of his pupils called his 'dreamy brain', and hold Conversations with the children, so as to draw out of them talents which he believed were already there. Nothing was to be forced in – which was just as well, since Alcott's own store of education had been scanty, and he really had little *to* force in.

While trying to run a school on this basis in the city of Boston, he took on as 'female assistant' the sister of a preacher, a lady named Abigail May. The school was not much of a success, but he married her. Then they set off together to Philadelphia to run another, and it was there that she gave birth to their first two children. Anna, born in 1831, was a docile blonde whose gentle nature harmonised from the first with her father's dreaminess; Louisa May, born two years later, was quite different. Unlike her father and elder sister she was dark in hair and complexion (Alcott actually considered fair colouring a sign of grace); she had an angular, fretful personality, and was constantly chafing against the world.

Her father found it much harder to instil notions of right and wrong into her than into the placid Anna. On the other hand, Louisa was on much closer terms than Anna with their mother, whose rather pugnacious, masculine looks she had inherited. As an adult, her writing was to display both these characteristics – at one moment fretting against life for not allowing her to be as she wished, then turning with security to the protection and reassurance of maternal love.

The Philadelphia venture failed in due course, and Bronson Alcott opened his next school back in Boston, this time in the Masonic Temple, with a redoubtable spinster named Elizabeth Peabody (the original of Miss Birdseye in Henry James's *The Bostonians*) as his helper. The Alcotts named their third child Elizabeth (born in 1835) after her. But even Miss Peabody, who had a boundless appetite for good causes, found her patience and enthusiasm tried by Bronson, whom she said had a 'want of humility' and lacked a 'sober estimate of his own place among his fellows'. He published a volume of *Conversations on the Gospels*, based on talks he had with his pupils, but Boston society was offended by the way in which he had led the children on to ask, in connection with the birth of Christ, about such things as conception and circumcision. (One child remarked that babies were made 'out of the naughtiness of other people'.) Then he admitted a black child into his school – he was a committed Abolitionist – and this was too much for public opinion. The Temple School closed in 1840, and the Alcotts moved out to the small Massachusetts town of Concord, to be near Ralph Waldo Emerson, who liked and sympathised with Bronson and his ideas.

Concord was by now becoming a kind of Mecca of Transcendentalism, with writers and thinkers of like mind setting up home there. Alcott hopefully called it 'Concordia', and found a cottage at a low rent where he reckoned to be able to keep his family by growing vegetables for them. Meat, even if he could have afforded it, was in fact forbidden by the particular Transcendental code he had drawn up; a contemporary observed of him in verse:

Give him carrots, potatoes, squash, turnips and peas,
And a handful of crackers without any cheese,
And a cup of cold water to wash down all these,
And he'd prate of the spirit as long as you please.

'Prating of the spirit' was about the only activity (other than growing vegetables) in which Bronson Alcott was now willing to engage, since the world had rejected his educational ideas. He was perfectly happy to accept fees for holding public Conversations to expound his thought, but that was as far as wage-earning went. After a while, he and a number of fellow-Transcendentalists began an experiment in communal living on a run-down farm near 'Concordia' that they named Fruitlands. The place was soon crammed with dietary reformers and assorted cranks, including a nudist. Most of the work was done by Alcott's wife Abigail, always known as 'Abba' – an appropriate name, considering its Aramaic meaning, 'father'; for it was she who now carried the entire burden of providing for her family. She laboured at Fruitlands, doing all the chores and bringing up four children (the youngest, May, was born in 1840) while the men preoccupied themselves with idealism. Louisa, aged seven, observed the goings-on with a certain detached amusement – one member of the all-vegetarian community, she alleged, was sent packing for the sin of *eating a fish tail* at a neighbour's house.

The Fruitlands venture, unaptly named, collapsed after a few months, and there was nearly a break-up of the Alcott marriage, Abba having realised that her husband was no longer prepared to lift a finger for herself and the children. 'Anna and I cried in bed,' recorded Louisa in her journal, 'and I prayed to God to keep us all together.' She consoled herself by copying out the hymns from her favourite book, *The Pilgrim's Progress*. In fact the family stayed together, largely thanks to the charity of friends – Emerson would sometimes place a banknote under a book or behind a candlestick in the Alcott living room, 'when he thinks Father wants a little money, and no one will help him earn'. Abba was in a state of constant exhaustion and depression, but she managed to find the emotional energy to help and stimulate her second daughter – largely, no doubt, because she and Louisa were of the same physical and emotional type: dark, mannish-looking, full of nervous energy. When Louisa was in her early teens she wrote in her journal:

> I am old for my age, and don't care much for girls' things. People think I'm wild and queer; but Mother understands and helps me . . . Now I'm going to *work really*, for I feel a true desire to improve, and be a help and comfort, not a care, to my dear mother.[71]

She soon had her chance to carry out this resolution, for the family moved into Boston to try to make some money. Bronson did nothing more than encourage people to pay him for the privilege of listening to him talk, but Abba earned a small wage by distributing charity to the poor (the activity which, like Marmee in *Little Women*, she liked best), and she, Anna, and Louisa held reading and writing classes for black adults. The moment the girls were old enough to undertake paid work by themselves, they did so; Louisa took jobs as a teacher, a lady's companion, and lower down the social scale, as a seamstress, maid, or even washerwoman. 'Father idle,' she wrote laconically in her journal. She began to earn a little by authorship, writing melodramatic little pieces of fiction for the newspapers and magazines. This sort of thing came naturally to her, for she and her sisters had long had the private amusement of performing plays, which Louisa wrote, with such titles as *The Captives of Castille, or the Moorish Maiden's Vow*. But she only received a few dollars from the newspaper editors, and life continued to be very hard. Her younger sister Elizabeth became ill with scarlet fever, caught from a neighbour whom Abba had been nursing; not surprisingly, considering her family's never-ending state of struggle, Elizabeth lost the will to live, became half-deranged, and died at the age of twenty-three. Anna, the placid sister, found herself a dull but worthy insurance salesman named John Pratt as a husband; Louisa contemplated suicide, considering throwing herself off the Mill Dam into Boston's Back Bay, but she changed her mind, and soon afterwards started to make a lot more money, by pouring out dime-novel romances of an even more lurid kind.

Typical of these was *Pauline's Passion and Punishment*, one of many 'yellow-back' stories she produced pseudonymously or anonymously (her idealistic father was not let in on the secret) during the 1860s. Pauline is a sex-kitten (there is no other word for her) who has been jilted by her lover, and gets her revenge by marrying a handsome teenage Latin American and flaunting him in front of the lover and the woman he has wedded. The story ends with the jealous lover pushing Pauline's child-husband over a cliff, and the lover's wife (who has developed a passion for the boy) jumping after him.

Nothing could be further from *Little Women*, and one may be inclined to dismiss such stuff as merely a way to earn money fast – *Pauline's Passion and Punishment* got its creator a hundred dollar prize from a magazine. In fact this story, and others from what might be called the 'hidden years' of Louisa Alcott, says quite a lot about its author. For a start, the heroine is a protagonist and manipulator, whereas the stereotyped heroine of Gothic fiction is submissive and ultra-feminine, a victim.[72] And there is something else that Pauline, creature of dime-novel as she may be, has in common with her creator.

Louisa Alcott's adolescence was marked by an almost complete absence of love-affairs. Her only romantic feelings seem to have been for a man fifteen years older than herself, no less than Henry David Thoreau, who with his brother John was running a school in Concord which the Alcott girls attended. Louisa wrote devoted letters to him, which she never sent. From this, and from the fact that in the sequel to *Little Women* she makes Jo marry a German professor of advanced years, we may infer that she was capable of being attracted by men old enough to be her father. (Was she actually looking for a substitute father, her real one having failed to perform his role?) Yet, like the passionate Pauline, she seems also to have been susceptible, by the time she reached maturity, to adolescent boys. She is known to have been very fond, if only in a maternal way, of one Ladislas Wisniewski, an eighteen-year-old Pole whom she met on a trip to Europe (as paid companion to an invalid) when she was thirty-three, shortly before she wrote *Little Women*; she said he was one of the originals of Laurie in that book. It is also recorded that, at the age of twenty-eight, she liked to spend the time with Ralph Waldo Emerson's sixteen-year-old son Julian, and there are hints of other attachments to teenagers. Pauline's choice of a boy of nineteen for her husband, in that lurid story, seems to reflect this inclination.

One may surmise that Louisa liked to be mother to young boys – and in the later part of the *Little Women* saga her heroine Jo does just that, mothering a crowd of young males at the school she and her Professor Bhaer are running (on vaguely Bronson Alcott principles). By the time of *Jo's Boys*, the final book in the series, Jo has become not just 'Aunty Jo' or 'Mrs Jo' but 'Mother Bhaer'. Yet if she was mother, and if she sought for a father in her yearnings for Thoreau, she also liked to *be* the father.

In the family plays she wrote and performed with her sisters, Louisa always took the male roles, just as Jo does on similar occasions in *Little Women*. It was natural: she had inherited her mother's masculine features. But one has the suspicion that the plays were written largely so that she could play these roles. Like Jo, she seems to have felt most true to her own nature when she could put on doublet and boots.

> No gentlemen were admitted; so Jo played male parts to her heart's content, and took immense satisfaction in a pair of russet-leather boots given her by a friend. These boots, an old foil, and a slashed doublet once used by an artist for some picture, were Jo's chief treasures, and appeared on all occasions . . .

Louisa's elder sister Anna always played the leading ladies in these performances. Anna's counterpart in *Little Women* is Jo's sister Meg, and as the book progresses the reader is left in no doubt as to Jo's strength of feeling for her. 'She gets prettier each day, and I'm in love with her sometimes,' she tells her mother, in a letter signed 'Topsy-Turvy Jo'. When Meg gets engaged to John Brooke (who is almost as colourless as his real-life counterpart, Anna's husband John Pratt), Jo sighs: 'I just wish I could marry Meg myself, and keep her safe in the family.'

Anna Alcott's betrothal and marriage to John Pratt caused Louisa pain that seems, if anything, to have been deeper than that suffered by Jo. 'I moaned in private over my great loss, and said I'd never forgive J. for taking Anna from me,' she wrote in her journal. That entry, says one of her biographers, Martha Saxton, 'doesn't convey the violent anguish' the announcement of the engagement gave her. This was in the spring of 1858, when Louisa was twenty-six; her contemplation of suicide came about six months later. Was she really in love with her sister?

*

Not altogether surprisingly, she looked on the outbreak of the Civil War as offering, if not the solution to her difficulties, at least a break in the perpetual chain of her family's struggles to survive, and perhaps her private emotional-sexual sufferings too. She went as a nurse to a war hospital in Washington, found the conditions almost intolerable, caught typhoid, was heavily dosed with calomel, contracted mercury poisoning in consequence, and was sent home to her family in a broken-down state. Yet the experience seems to have been stimulating; she published a book about it, *Hospital Sketches* (1863), which made her a small reputation, and on the strength of this she found a publisher for a novel called *Moods* (1864), whose heroine has a romantic attachment to someone much like her beloved Thoreau. Its reception, however, was sufficiently poor for her to abandon any further plans for serious authorship for the time being, and turn back to 'rubbishy tales for they pay the best'. One of the pieces of hack-work she was asked to undertake was the editorship of a Boston children's magazine called *Merry's Museum*, whose founder had been the celebrated popular pedagogue Peter Parley. Simultaneously a publisher asked her to write 'a *girls'* story', this being a newly discovered type of popular fiction. She agreed to begin work on both. 'Didn't like either,' she wrote in her journal.

The editorship soon faded out, and the book was done quickly – twelve chapters in a month or so, and the remaining eleven in a few weeks more. It was not easy-going, compared to the sensational dime-novel stuff – 'I plod away', she said – and when the publisher (one Thomas Niles of Roberts Brothers in Boston) saw the first twelve chapters he was not enthusiastic. 'He thought it *dull*; so do I,' she wrote. 'But [I] work away and mean to try the experiment; for lively, simple books are very much needed for girls, and perhaps I can supply the need.'

Mr Niles and Louisa Alcott were not altogether wrong; *Little Women* really *is* dull, if read purely for narrative excitement. Almost nothing happens. The March girls (whose surname is a variant on that of Louisa's mother's surname, May, which Louisa herself bore as a second Christian name) manage to enjoy Christmas despite the absence of their father at the Civil War. They perform a play, meet a neighbour's grandson called Laurie, run a family magazine and a private post office, and have gentle flirtations. Beth nearly dies of scarlet fever, Meg becomes engaged to John Brooke, and Father comes home just in time to join the celebrations. The book seems at first glance to be no more than a series of sketches of life in a rather saccharinely portrayed but otherwise unremarkable family. The casual reader might suppose the Marches to be really quite conventional. Yet a second look shows that the story is a veiled account of all that Louisa had suffered, and at the same time a kind of celebration of the fact that she had survived. It castigates family life for imposing suffering, and yet asserts that only in the family can sanity be found.

She had a literary model, as well as her own experiences, to draw on. The genre of 'girls' stories' was new – indeed, had hardly established itself[73] – but in England, Charlotte M. Yonge had already produced one notable book about a girl's experiences within her family circle, *The Daisy Chain* (1856). Since Louisa Alcott was devoted to Miss Yonge's tear-jerking bestseller *The Heir of Redclyffe* (Jo in *Little Women* is seen weeping over it), we may suspect that she had read *The Daisy Chain* too. In it she would have found, on the very first page, a character to attract her sympathy: Ethel, one of the daughters of the house, 'a thin, lank, angular, sallow girl, just fifteen, trembling from head to foot with restrained eagerness as she tried to curb her tone into the requisite civility'. The book describes Ethel's struggles with conventional sex-roles: she learns Latin and Greek from a brother's books, and is full of energetic plans for setting the world to rights, but she is eventually persuaded to suppress her boyishness and concentrate on ladylike pursuits. Not only does she anticipate Jo March in *Little Women*; her family's surname is May.

The Daisy Chain takes its title from Ethel's father's nickname for his family; similarly *Little Women* is named after what Mr March would like his daughters to be. In the case of Jo, on whose personality *Little Women* hangs, the title is deeply ironic. She is neither little (she is 'very tall' and has 'big hands and feet'), nor womanly. She is 'rapidly shooting up into a woman' but 'didn't like it'. Masculinity is her guiding principle. 'I'm the man of the family now papa is away,' she tells her sisters at the beginning of the book, and the story is constructed to demonstrate the truth of this statement. She acts as brother, lover, and father to her sisters. She woos them in male costume during the Christmas play, earns money for them (by selling a story), and, in a revealing moment, has all her hair cut off:

'Your hair! Your beautiful hair!' 'Oh, Jo, how could you? Your one beauty.' 'My dear girl, there was no need of this.' 'She doesn't look like Jo any more, but I love her dearly for it!'
    As everyone exclaimed, and Beth hugged the cropped head tenderly, Jo assumed an indifferent air . . . 'It will do my brains good to have that mop taken off; my head feels deliciously light and cool, and the barber said I could soon have a curly crop, which will be boyish, becoming, and easy to keep in order. I'm satisfied; so please take the money, and let's have supper.'

She has done this ostensibly to get money (by selling the hair) to help her father, who is in hospital in Washington; but her action coincides with the departure from home of her mother, who up to then has been Jo's rival as father-figure. Meanwhile, the family's real father, Mr March, has to remain offstage for the entire drama, making his appearance only for the final tableau. It was not just that Louisa Alcott could not fit her own father into her Utopian fictional household (which clearly she could not); Mr March's absence is essential to Jo's exploration of the male role.

When *Little Women* was published, in the late summer of 1868, Louisa Alcott began to receive letters about the sequel she had promised to write if the book should prove popular: 'Girls write to ask who the little women marry, as if that was the only end and aim of a woman's life. I *won't* marry Jo to Laurie to please any one.' This was not just cussedness towards her readers. A marriage of Jo to Laurie, the archetypal boy-next-door, would have been out of the question, for deep-seated reasons. Laurie in fact *is* Jo, in another manifestation; tall, dark and coltish, notably effeminate for his sex just as she is masculine for hers. He has 'small hands and feet', cuts flowers for her in a ladylike fashion, plays the piano beautifully, is 'not very strong', and, to top it all, is known by a female nickname: 'My first name is Theodore, but I don't like it, for the fellows called me Dora, so I made them say Laurie instead.' Other than these characteristics, Laurie has very little personality. He is in fact quite unnecessary to the story as a separate character: Jo herself is the real boy-next-door. In the sequel, he is supposed to be in love with Jo, but this is scarcely convincing, and he is very quickly persuaded to change his mind and marry Jo's fluffily pretty little sister Amy instead – as Jo herself would surely have liked to do.[74]

Although *Little Women* describes Jo's assumption of the masculine role, it is not an account of a battle won. The Jo-Louisa character loses out in the end, not so much to real men as to her own sex – to Marmee, her mother, who once fought the same battle herself, and lost it. Marmee, we are told, was once as impetuous and hasty-tempered (that is, as masculine) as Jo, but she finally subdued her real nature to convention:

> 'Yes, I've learned to check the hasty words that rise to my lips; and when I feel that they mean to break out against my will, I just go away a minute, and give myself a little shake for being so weak and wicked,' answered Mrs March . . . 'Your father, Jo, . . . helped and comforted me, and showed me that I must try to practise all the virtues I would have my little girls possess, for I was their example.'

The 'pilgrimage' which Marmee encourages the girls to make throughout the story – suggested by *The Pilgrim's Progress*, which they are rereading – is not (for Jo) the spiritual journey it appears to be, but a quest, undertaken reluctantly enough, for a conventionally feminine sex-role. By the end of the book, in spite of all her masculine role-playing, in spite even of her shorn head, Jo has reached that goal, and is recognised by her father as a true 'little woman':

'In spite of the curly crop, I don't see the "son Jo" whom I left a year
ago,' said Mr March. 'I see a young lady who pins her collar straight,
laces her boots neatly, and neither whistles, talks slang, nor lies on
the rug as she used to do . . . I rather miss my wild girl; but if I get a
strong, helpful, tender-hearted woman in her place, I shall feel quite
satisfied.'

And if we doubt whether Louisa Alcott herself had, like Jo, lost that
particular battle, we need only turn to the pages of the Boston *Woman's
Journal*, to which she contributed frequently after *Little Women* had
made her famous. She has been represented as a feminist, but her
articles in this ladies' magazine are full of 'womanly' gush: 'The home-
making, the comfort, the sympathy, the grace and atmosphere that a
true woman can provide is the noble part, and embraces all that is
helpful for soul as well as body,' she writes in a piece about domestic
arts. It is, she says, a woman's 'fate to be called upon to lead a quiet self-
sacrificing life with peculiar trials, needs and joys, and it seems to me
that a very simple one is fitted to us whose hearts are usually more alive
than heads, and whose hands are tied in many ways.'[75] Jo March has
truly become Josephine.

Little Women, then, is a record of a struggle lost, and along the way it
communicates something of the misery that Louisa had felt during her
own battle. The turning-point in the novel comes when Amy, in
revenge for being left out of an expedition, destroys the manuscript of a
set of fairy stories which Jo has been working at for several years.[76]
Amy's behaviour seems to us quite outrageous, and Jo's anger – which
allows her to let Amy ice-skate in a dangerous place, and so have a
minor accident – is quite understandable, almost justifiable. But the
accident causes Jo terrible remorse, and it is from this moment on that,
with Marmee's encouragement, she tries to tame her masculine
aggression and to cultivate feminine self-control. The incident seems to
stand for something more than itself; Amy has, after all, symbolically
destroyed Jo's capacity as a wage-earner, and has attacked her deep
attachment to the life of the imagination, which throughout the book
goes hand in hand with her masculinity – she is constantly found
immersed in works of imaginative literature (*Undine, The Heir of
Redclyffe*, Dickens) which seem to offer an escape from the family
confines. Amy is cutting Jo off from all this, and bringing her back into
the family fold.

The story is about Jo's struggles with the concept of 'family' just as
much as it is about her sex-role battle. Near the beginning, she observes
to herself 'that keeping her temper at home was a much harder task than
facing a rebel or two down South', and for the first part of the book she
is reluctant to put herself second to the needs of the family. As Meg says
on the first page, 'we can make our little sacrifices, and ought to do it

gladly. But I am afraid I don't.' These words must reflect Louisa Alcott's own feelings during the years when she had to be seamstress, washerwoman, hired domestic, and drudge of every kind, simply to support the family. But after Amy's destruction of her manuscript, Jo abandons any thoughts of independence, and instead conducts a battle to keep the family together; the final chapters are largely concerned with her hopes of frustrating Meg's romance with John Brooke, because a marriage is going to break up the family – Brooke's sin is that he is making 'a hole in the family'.

Louisa Alcott, like Jo in the early stages of her 'pilgrimage', at first hated the burden of supporting her family. But as the years passed she came to welcome that burden, and to make it her emotional preoccupation. She had done so much for the family that it *must* all have been worthwhile. And so Marmee in *Little Women* gives her daughters an exhortation to 'Make this home happy, so that you may be fit for homes of your own if they are offered you, and contented here if they are not'; and the voice that speaks this platitude is really that of Louisa, whose family home *had* to be happy, since it was all that she possessed. *Little Women* had originated as a piece of subversion against the family and parental authority, but had ended up by declaring its support for those very institutions – by portraying the family as an Arcadia.

*

Louisa Alcott's platitude about the happy home was accepted by most of her readers as a simple, truthful statement – that family life was a good thing, and should be cultivated. In writing *Little Women* she gave birth to a new genre, the American family novel, and herself immediately set to work producing further examples of it. They, like the stories of most of her imitators, had almost nothing truthful to say about families. The second part of *Little Women*, published a few months after the first volume appeared, dealt – despite Louisa Alcott's reaction to her readers' letters – chiefly with the question of 'who the little women marry'. Strikingly, she did not know what to call this second volume, and it appeared merely as *Little Women, Part II*. Publishers, not content with this, tried out various titles when it was reissued or pirated: *Little Women Married, Little Women Wedded, Nice Wives, Little Wives*, and eventually *Good Wives*. Louisa had simply been trying to avoid the admission, which the title had to make, that marriage *was* the final goal of her little women.

It was not to be her own goal. Now in her mid-thirties, she took on more and more, in reality, the role Jo had preferred – that of 'father'. The financial success of *Little Women* and its sequels, and of the other nondescript girls' stories she churned out (*An Old-Fashioned Girl, Eight Cousins*, and *Rose in Bloom* were the best known of them), made her the all-provider of the Alcott family. When her sister Anna's husband died young, she wrote another 'March' book, *Little Men* (1871), simply to get money for the widow and her children, though in fact Anna had been left well off. Similarly, when her youngest sister May died after childbirth in Europe, Louisa had the baby sent to America and took over the task of being its father (the real father was Swiss) as well as mother. Meanwhile, her own father was only too willing to live off her literary income – though ironically her fame helped to make his own name, and his public Conversations became quite popular, especially those in which he talked about *Little Women* and its creator. Eventually, after Louisa's mother had died, he had a stroke which confined him to bed and made it necessary for him to eat with a bib. The irony of this second childhood, with Louisa fathering him, did not escape them both; the old man even sprouted a crop of new hair, baby-fashion, on a head that had been bald for years. Louisa went on writing, but her health, always bad since the calomel dosing of 1862, gradually broke down under the strain of being breadwinner for so many mouths. By the time she finished *Jo's Boys* (1886) she expressed a half-wish, at the end of the story, that the entire March clan might be engulfed in an earthquake. Her father died two years later, and she herself survived him by only forty-eight hours, there being no longer any need for her to go on living.

It might have been better for American popular fiction had the March family never existed, so many were the second-rate girls 'novels in the Alcott mode that followed the appearance of *Little Women*. A few, like Susan Coolidge's *What Katy Did* (1872), made some attempt to tackle the problems of sex-roles and family membership. Katy Carr, in the Coolidge book, is a Jo-like character who has to go through a chastening experience (an accident which invalids her) before she can learn to discipline her boyishness and be a little mother to the household – not a little father, for her own father is a strong presence in the book, and Katy really has none of the sexual ambiguity of Jo. Other writers avoided the issue by creating a kind of aggressive femininity, which allowed their heroines to charm hearts and get their own way without playing traitor to their sex. This produced the 'Pollyanna' or 'glad girl' school of writing, featuring girls of unbearable cheerfulness.[77] What all these books have in common is the belief, fundamental to so much American writing for children from *Little Women* to the pre-Vietnam era, that a Utopian life can be achieved, a Just City built, within the walls of the family home, in the real world.

Louisa Alcott had set out to be subversive, to describe her doubts about sexual stereotyping and the demands of family life, but she became a traitor to her destructive cause, and was in the end responsible for an act of construction, the creation of the Arcadian family novel. In England, meanwhile, construction had not yet been achieved.

Kingsley, Carroll, and MacDonald had shaken the foundations of faith and had exposed the hollowness of the old ideas upon which children's literature had been built; but they had scarcely managed to put anything in their place. They left that to a new generation of writers.

PART TWO
The Arcadians

Bevis, the Pioneer

During the 1870s and 1880s, English writers for children made some attempt to create new values in their fiction, to find something positive that could take the place of the old ideas that *Alice* (more obviously than any other book) had helped to sweep away. Three authors in particular engaged in valiant efforts, though none of them was really successful: Mrs Ewing, Mrs Molesworth, and Frances Hodgson Burnett.

Mrs Ewing, the first of them to get into print, was potentially the best. Her mother was a Yorkshire clergyman's wife who edited *Aunt Judy's Magazine* to eke out the clerical income, and Juliana Horatia Ewing herself was married to an impecunious army officer, an amateur musician who composed the hymn 'Jerusalem the Golden' and borrowed eighty pounds from his wife to buy a piano on which to play it. The Ewings had no children and she died young, but during the years of her marriage, while moving from one army posting to another, she produced a series of children's novellas which had an enthusiastic following (E. Nesbit and Kipling were among her admirers) and went some way towards finding a new mode of juvenile fiction. She wrote for children because she had always told stories to her brothers and sisters, and most of her books have well-crafted plots. But the one by which she most deserves to be remembered is notable not for its narrative but in a sense for its lack of narrative.

It is called *Mrs Overtheway's Remembrances*, and Mrs Ewing wrote it at the beginning of her literary career, in the 1860s.[78] It seemed to open the door to a new way of writing for, and about, children. 'Mrs Overtheway' is the name that Ida, a lonely small girl, gives to the old lady whose front door is opposite her nursery window, and who comes out each morning, prayer book in hand, to go to early service. Ida, an orphan living in her uncle's house, becomes obsessed with Mrs Overtheway, and determines to make contact with her. This she achieves by breaking bounds and picking a bunch of primroses for the old lady in a neighbouring wood. The old lady, enchanted with the flowers, comes to tea with Ida and tells stories of her own childhood. These stories are of the utmost simplicity. For the most part indeed they are scarcely stories at all, but slim, delicately textured recollections of the sensations and perceptions experienced in childhood. Mrs Overtheway tells how as a child she visited a grand personage in a manor house that has stood empty a long time; the visit is in a sense a disappointment in that the lady of the manor fails to come anywhere near the little girl's fairy tale expectations of her. But then the girl perceives the excitement that lies in the apparently ordinary drawing room: there are strange objects and pieces of furniture which both frighten and fascinate her, and her very disappointment with the grand lady is itself a memorable experience.

After this first tale told by Mrs Overtheway, the book begins to fall off; the amount of 'plot' steadily increases, and there is a trite and sentimental ending in which Ida's supposedly dead father returns alive from his shipwreck. Even so, *Mrs Overtheway's Remembrances* is a pioneer book in its portrayal of childhood as a state of perception, a special way of observing and reacting to ordinary surroundings. The child (it is suggested) has some special kind of vision that is denied to most adults, and is therefore perhaps the inhabitant of a kind of Arcadia. The grown-ups appear in the book as in general a rather hostile race, who are by no means certain how to treat children (for example, Mrs Overtheway remembers how she was invited to stay in a big house, then ignored by her hostess and most of the adults). Only a few adults, like Mrs Overtheway herself, still possess the vision of childhood, and have kept alive the child within them. It was no more than Wordsworth had said in 'Intimations of Immortality', but it was the first time that someone had tried to express it in a book for children.

Mrs Ewing's later books contain further hints of childhood itself as an Arcadia, but no more than hints. Most of them are contrived stories about orphans and foundlings, with dramatic deaths on the battlefield, contrived happy endings, and other devices of hack fiction. The best of her tales of this kind – *Lob Lie-by-the-Fire* (1874), *Jackanapes* (1883), and *Daddy Darwin's Dovecote* (1884) – have touches of *Silas Marner* and *Cranford*, and seem to be addressed chiefly to a grown-up audience. She sometimes tried to recapture her old vision; *A Great Emergency* (1877) begins in a manner that anticipates Nesbit's *The Treasure-Seekers*, with a boy narrator who resembles Oswald Bastable, while *Six to Sixteen* (1875) is supposedly the autobiography of the sixteen-year-old daughter of an army officer. But *A Great Emergency* peters out into a second-rate school-and-running-away story, and *Six to Sixteen* pays more attention to the adult characters than to its narrator, and is written in the style of an adult three-decker novel.

Mrs Mary Louisa Molesworth never came near the perceptions of Mrs Ewing in *Mrs Overtheway's Remembrances*, but she was certainly interested in developing a set of positive values for children's fiction in the wake of the devastation caused by *Alice*. Like Mrs Ewing she was the wife of an army officer, and was even more unlucky in her matrimonial choice: Captain Richard Molesworth had a piece of shrapnel in his head from the Crimean War, and it gave him a foul temper. His wife eventually left him, taking the children with her, though not before she had written several adult novels describing unhappy marriages. These sank without trace, and it was Sir Noel Paton, the original illustrator of *The Water-Babies*, who suggested that she might do better as a children's writer – 'Better do a small thing *well*,' he told her, 'than a great thing indifferently.' It is evident that she herself regarded children's books as in the end 'a small thing'; she rarely threw her whole self and experience into them, and they are almost always narrated by a grown-up, talking down. Moreover, the grown-up is often rather haughty at that; Mrs Molesworth herself was an awesome, brittle woman, of whom her grandchildren (and probably her children) were distinctly afraid.

Her first children's book, '*Carrots': Just a Little Boy* (1876), explores the notion suggested in *Mrs Overtheway's Remembrances* that childhood is a state of being set apart, a time of special perceptions. But it is crude and sugary where Mrs Ewing's book is subtle. 'Carrots', a small redhead (based on one of Mrs Molesworth's own sons), is an innocent entirely unsullied by the world, leading an existence that is placid and unruffled. He only experiences unhappiness when he misunderstands adults and so acts mistakenly. He knows that nurse has lost a half sovereign, but does not connect this with the 'yellow sixpence' he has found and hidden for safe-keeping, thereby incurring a charge of dishonesty. He is in fact morally faultless, and, once the reader has realised this, it is something of a shock to discover that he is no mere toddler but six years old. The narrator admits that he is 'in some ways a good deal of a baby for his age', and half suggests that his innocence is the naivety of a half-wit:

> He had a queer, babylike way of not seeming to take in quickly what was said to him, and staring up in your face with his great oxen-like eyes, that did a little excuse Maurice's [his elder brother's] way of laughing at him and telling him that he was 'half-witted'. But no one that really looked at those honest, sensible, tender eyes would for an instant have thought that there was any 'want' in their owner. It was all *there* – the root of all goodness, cleverness, and manliness – just as in the acorn there is the oak, but of course it had a great deal of *growing* before it . . . [and] would need all the care and watchful tenderness and wise directing that could be given it . . . Do you understand a little why it seems sometimes such a very, very solemn thing to have the charge of children?

There is no evidence that the narrator actually wants Carrots to grow up. By celebrating his half-wit innocence, she seems to suggest that adults would prefer him to remain exactly like this.

Quite apart from its ludicrous inaccuracy in describing a six-year-old (even a strictly brought up Victorian one), 'Carrots' is written exclusively from the mother's point of view and not the child's. Its portrayal of Carrots' world as blissful and Arcadian totally ignores the emotional ups and downs that real children experience from the hour of birth. But then Carrots is in no sense a real child; nor is he portrayed in the eighteenth-and early nineteenth-century fashion, as an adult-in-miniature. He is something quite different, a member of a totally different race of beings from adults. His perpetual goodness suggests that he belongs to some minor order of angels. On the other hand, his role about the house is that of a pet lap-dog, to be cossetted when the adults want something to stroke, and reproved occasionally when, in his innocence, he commits some minor fault. But there is never any question who is master: morally, we are back in the days of *The Fairchild Family*, with the parent playing the role of God.

Mrs Molesworth wrote another book in the 'Carrots' style, *The Adventures of Herr Baby* (1881), which purports to describe her family travelling round Europe, as they did in the years immediately after she had left her husband. Carrots had been made to speak in baby-talk, and his successor was no different:

'Oh, you stupid little goose,' she said . . .
Baby looked at her gravely. He had his own way of defending himself.
'Werry well. If him's a goose him won't talk to you, and him won't tell you somesing *werry* funny and dedful bootiful that him heard in the 'groind room.'

Mrs Molesworth was not the first person to represent the speech of small children in this glutinous fashion – Lewis Carroll had done it in 1867, in his short story 'Bruno's Revenge' – but no one before her seems to have realised its commercial potential. Once she had done it, the idea became immensely popular. Swinburne, whose peculiar emotional needs were for some reason satisfied by this sort of thing, compared her with George Eliot, and imitations by other authors began to appear.[79] Illustrators did their stuff at portraying the curly golden hair, big blue eyes, merry smiles, and rosy cheeks, and Kate Greenaway, publishing her first picture book *Under the Window* at Christmas 1879, soon after this fashion had begun, found the public only too ready for her own angelic little creatures.

Mrs Molesworth, meanwhile, widened her range, and produced nearly a hundred more books during the remainder of her life; she is now best remembered for *The Cuckoo Clock* (1877), *The Tapestry Room* (1879), and *The Carved Lions* (1895), stories which combine touches of fantasy (derived both from Carroll and MacDonald) with realistic accounts of children's relationships with adults. They are not without distinction, but they tend to be unimaginative as fantasy, while their 'realism' is only a little removed from the old-fashioned moral tale – Griselda, heroine of *The Cuckoo Clock*, ends the book by learning to 'do her duty'. *The Cuckoo Clock*, indeed, is largely a celebration of a stable social order; the book lovingly describes the Cranford-like characters of the two spinster aunts, Miss Grizzel and Miss Tabitha, with whom Griselda comes to live. Perhaps Mrs Molesworth set out as a children's writer by believing Arcadia to consist of the separate, very unadult-like world of childhood itself; but by the time she wrote *The Cuckoo Clock* her Arcadia seems instead to have been quiet middle-class adult society.[80] She had therefore really deserted the cause of children's books.

She was partly responsible for the cult of a figure which we may for convenience label the Beautiful Child. Carrots and Herr Baby are certainly young specimens of this creature, who is distinguished by his or her naivety (especially in contact with the adult world), by an almost heavenly innocence (which can spill over into sheer idiocy), and, of course, by radiant good looks. The Beautiful Child had been hovering on the edge of children's literature ever since its inception; there are shades of it in Wordsworth's and Blake's view of childhood, and even in seventeenth-century Puritan accounts of child deathbeds. But the late Victorians gave it commercial value. The first of them to popularise it was Florence Montgomery in *Misunderstood* (1869), a novel about two brothers, one delicate and the other sturdy and wild; their father is hostile towards the wild one, Humphrey, but it is he who falls into a mortal illness after the brothers have had an accident, and the book ends with the father's remorse. Like *Holiday House* it was a plea for parental approval of high spirits, but the sentimentality of the ending concentrated the reader's attention on the vulnerability of childhood, and the book undoubtedly contributed to the cult of the Beautiful Child. Among those to capitalise on that cult was Frances Hodgson Burnett.

Born Frances Hodgson in Manchester, she emigrated to America in her mid-teens after her ironmonger father had died; like Louisa Alcott she was soon supporting her family by writing cheap fiction for the popular magazines, and she developed an eye for making clichés about England into tasty fiction for the American mass-market. She began by churning out dialect stories about North Country working lasses; next, after she had married an American, Swan Burnett, and produced two sons, she wrote the best-known Beautiful Child story of all, *Little Lord Fauntleroy*.

Her marriage was no happier than Mrs Ewing's or Mrs Molesworth's – she despised her husband (a doctor) and soon edged him out of her life to make way for a young would-be-actor, with whom she made an equally unhappy second marriage. But she got plenty of emotional gratification from her sons, Lionel and Vivian, whom she actually brought up as Beautiful Children. They were dressed in velvet suits with lace collars (a fashion that was just beginning), and were encouraged to call their mother 'Dearest'. She delighted in any aspect of their behaviour that could be called winsome, and took great note of their childish conversations. The story of *Little Lord Fauntleroy* arose in her mind after Vivian, who regarded himself as entirely American, speculated as to what precisely an English duke might be. Hence the tale of Cedric Errol, the small American citizen who turns out to be heir to a British earldom, but has to melt the hard heart of his titled grandfather before his American mother is allowed into the ancestral halls. Cedric is the Beautiful Child *par excellence*, a Hollywood version of Carrots. He was born with 'a quantity of soft, fine, gold-coloured hair', 'never gave anyone trouble', 'seemed to feel that everyone was his friend', and has 'a very confiding nature and a kind little heart'.

Little Lord Fauntleroy swept across America like a plague when it was published in 1886, and thousands of small boys found themselves forced into velvet and lace, and were made to grow their hair in ringlets. The Beautiful Child became almost as much a national craze in Britain, too. Mrs Burnett might as well have stopped writing books after this, so much money did she make out of *Fauntleroy* in print and on the stage. Nevertheless, she went on to produce several children's books that were workmanlike and sober in comparison with *Fauntleroy*, and one, *The Secret Garden*, which is outstanding. But it was not published until 1911, and belongs to a later stage in the development of writing for children.

Mrs Ewing, Mrs Molesworth, and Mrs Burnett had tried to develop a new kind of children's literature by writing chiefly about childhood itself. Mrs Ewing might have managed it, but she lacked the conviction to continue with the experiment; the other two did not have any real understanding of children. Far more successful than '*Carrots*' or *Little Lord Fauntleroy* at portraying the emotions of childhood was Robert Louis Stevenson's *A Child's Garden of Verses* (1885), just as his *Treasure Island* (1883) beat all the contemporary boys' adventure writers at their own game. But *A Child's Garden* offers, quite rightly, only the merest sketch of childhood, while *Treasure Island* is a kind of oblique comment on adventure fiction rather than a new development in the genre. Like *The Hobbit* fifty years later, it is largely an anti-adventure story, with the supposed hero, Jim Hawkins, scarcely ever performing an act of physical courage and usually skulking in the background while the action is going on. The book's real hero is its villain, Long John Silver, who is not only more 'intelligent' (Jim Hawkins's own word for him) than anyone else in the story, but also the most adaptable and cheerful in the face of failure; he is the portrait of the perfect politician. By contrast the supposedly 'good' Squire

Trelawney is a greedy hot-head; Doctor Livesey contributes little of moral value to the Squire's party, and the only truly 'good' character is the steely professional seaman Smollett, by no means a superficially attractive personality, who nevertheless can measure up to Silver's courage and ingenuity. This is all very subtle, and it arises from Stevenson's contemplation of the moral blacks and whites and the cardboard characters of the adventure stories on which he had been brought up – the tales of Ballantyne and W. H. G. Kingston in particular.[81] Yet it is difficult to see how *Treasure Island* might offer a blueprint to any author hoping to build on what Stevenson had done. His own next work in the genre, *Kidnapped* (1886), is another exercise in moral ambiguity, this time to the extent that every character is made up of carefully chosen shades of grey. This is done less subtly than in *Treasure Island*, and it becomes faintly irritating. Meanwhile, Rider Haggard wrote *King Solomon's Mines* (1885) in a deliberate attempt to equal the popular success of *Treasure Island*, and he succeeded – though his story entirely lacks the moral subtlety of Stevenson's, and seems banal and predictable by comparison.

Treasure Island, then, was not a book that opened up a new path for others, any more than in America writers could use Mark Twain's *Adventures of Tom Sawyer* (1876) and *Adventures of Huckleberry Finn* (1884) as guideposts. Like Stevenson, Twain was chiefly concerned to hold up the moral values of other writers, and of society, to the light; *Huckleberry Finn* closely resembles *Treasure Island* in that its hero undergoes a moral education which shows him that society's values are really topsy-turvy, though, like Jim Hawkins, Huck scarcely realises what he has learnt. But any real step forward in children's literature would have to come not just from a questioning of existing values but a positing of new ones.

*

The beginnings of that positing of new values may be seen in an unlikely place, *Bevis: the Story of a Boy* (1882) by the English writer Richard Jefferies. This book is not often read now. It is over-long, becoming increasingly tedious after the early chapters. Yet the beginning is not merely a *tour de force* in its own right, but a blueprint for books that would be written a generation later. Together with *Wood Magic* (1881), Jefferies' first children's story, it contains the germ of the great Edwardian children's narratives.

Richard Jefferies belongs to a distinct movement in late nineteenth-century English writing, a movement that can be generally labelled 'ruralist', and which, though at first it had nothing to do with children's books, was soon to have a profound influence on them. The son of a Wiltshire gentleman farmer, he was brought up on the shore of Coate

Water at the foot of the Marlborough Downs. The lake is now swallowed up in suburban Swindon, but was then a true Arcadia, fringed with marshland and dotted with the cottages of labourers who would still tug their forelocks not merely at Mr Jefferies senior but at Dick and his brother too. Dick was born in 1848 and only had desultory schooling, spending most of his boyhood wandering around the farm and the meadows, exploring, boating, and making camps. He was adventurous beyond the norm, and the story is told that he and a cousin, when in their teens, ran away to France, vaguely hoping to get as far as Moscow. Finding their command of French unequal to the occasion, they changed direction, recrossed the Channel, and headed for Liverpool with a view to sailing to America. Their money ran out and they came back home.

Jefferies soon discovered that sufficient excitement could be found on his own doorstep, and began to contribute pieces about country life to local newspapers. He wrote some half-heartedly radical stuff about the living conditions of farm workers, but was far less interested in social matters than in the sheer charm of country life. One of his most readable books, *The Gamekeeper at Home* (1878), celebrates rustic philosophy with energy and delight, though it now seems rather condescending. In this and in his other rural writings, Jefferies owed something to the Romantic Movement's interest in country people and wild scenery, something to Gilbert White, and perhaps a little to George Borrow's travel books. At his best, Jefferies is a wonderful guide to the Wiltshire scenery. At his worst, he lapses into a kind of sub-Wordsworthian pantheism, communing with nature in purple prose.

He was a highly unlikely person to write children's books, and in a sense he did not. He merely turned, on two occasions, to reminiscences of his own childhood for further raw material for his musings about the countryside. Neither *Wood Magic* nor *Bevis* made much impact at the time of their publication, or after, and they contributed very little to his meagre income – he died young after enduring severe illness and extreme poverty. But they broke new ground in children's literature. Indeed, they broke too much of it at once to be successful books in themselves.

Wood Magic has as its central figure the boy Bevis, 'little "Sir" Bevis' as Jefferies calls him, referring to the old romance of *Sir Bevis of Hampton*, on which many generations of English children before Victoria's reign were brought up. Bevis is Jefferies himself, aged about six or seven, living on a farm that is recognisably Coate, and allowed to roam the fields and woods providing he does not disappear for too long, and does not fall foul of the Bailiff. His perpetual companion is his long-suffering spaniel Pan – no carelessly chosen name, for the pagan rural deity turns up again and again in late nineteenth-century English writings about the countryside. The book begins realistically, describing Bevis's idle wanderings and musings in the farmhouse garden on a hot summer day. There is an account of his disappearance, and of the whole household searching for him in panic; he is found fast asleep under an oak, and the Bailiff vents his irritation with the boy by thrashing Bevis's spaniel. (Animals and birds are always being thrashed, caught in traps, and shot in Jefferies' writings; there is no sentimentality towards them.) But after all this, *Wood Magic* slips into quite a different mode of writing.

Bevis has the power of understanding the speech of birds and animals, even of the trees and the wind, apparently just because he is a child, with his child's perception and vision still unfaded. First, he becomes the observer of the Machiavellian behaviour of the weasel, who plays every kind of trick on the other animals so as to get his bloodthirsty way. This is a prelude to the saga of Kapchack the magpie, king of all the woodland creatures, a terrible tyrant whose downfall is much desired by his subjects, but who, like the weasel, spins a web of intrigue so intricate that he seems inviolable. Finally, Kapchack is destroyed – not by the animals, but by a man to whom, by chance, he has done a great wrong – and a new monarch takes his place.

Bevis is party to all this; the animals, who address him as 'dear' or 'darling', take him into their confidence, yet discourage him from making any kind of intervention. His relationship to them has faint touches of Christopher Robin and much more of Mowgli; *Wood Magic*, indeed, anticipates the *Jungle Book* in its involvement of a human child with the internecine struggles of the animal kingdom. But 'little "Sir" Bevis' lacks the stature and energy of Mowgli, while among the animals there is no character to measure up to Shere Khan, Baloo, or Bagheera. Jefferies seems uncertain whether he is writing about individual animals, with names and personalities, such as Kapchack, Ki Ki the hawk, or Cloctaw the jackdaw, or simply about 'the squirrel', 'the weasel', 'the stoat', which is how he describes many of them. In other words, he is hovering between Aesop, who used the different species of animal to represent human types, and the full-blown modern animal story in which each creature is given a proper name and a differentiated personality.

Wood Magic fails to satisfy a modern reader because it falls between these stools, yet historically speaking it is important. It was a long time since animals had played any great part in English writing for children; in the late eighteenth and early nineteenth century there was a fashion for a type of moral tale in which an animal – generally a dog, a horse, or a household pet – narrated its 'memoirs', really a set of moralistic observations on human (especially child) behaviour. Anna Sewell's *Black Beauty*, though published as recently as 1877, was really a throwback to that kind of writing. Jefferies showed that animals could play a different kind of role, and though *Wood Magic* came out very like Aesop or *Reynard the Fox*, it sowed new ideas in the minds of certain writers of the next generation. Indeed, those passages where Bevis talks to the Wind and the Brook, sentimental though they are, could have come straight out of 'The Piper at the Gates of Dawn' in *The Wind in the Willows*.

*

Bevis is a much more robust book than *Wood Magic*, and the opening two chapters are among the best pieces of description of a child's imaginative life ever printed. They mark an enormous step forward from the saccharine 'Beautiful Child' writings, and they even have the edge over Mark Twain's *Tom Sawyer* and *Huckleberry Finn* in that they are not part of a dramatic (and therefore inherently improbable) story. They simply describe Bevis, now aged about ten, occupying himself during a typical late spring day at the farm. They start with no preamble or self-consciousness:

> One morning a large wooden case was brought to the farmhouse, and Bevis, impatient to see what was in it, ran for the hard chisel and the hammer, and would not consent to put off the work of undoing it for a moment. It must be done directly. The case was very broad and nearly square, but only a few inches deep, and was formed of thin boards. They placed it for him upon the floor, and, kneeling down, he tapped the chisel driving the edge in under the lid, and so starting the nails. Twice he hit his fingers in his haste, once so hard that he dropped the hammer, but he picked it up again and went on as before, till he had loosened the lid all round.

The contents of the case are of no interest – merely a picture purchased by his parents – but the case itself has possibilities. First, Bevis considers splitting up the boards and making a hut out of them. He starts to do this, but gets distracted by other things. Suddenly it occurs to him 'what a capital raft the picture packing-case would make', and he is off at the double to try and achieve this. The main problem is to caulk the planks so that the water will not come in, and he borrows or steals all kinds of rags, rope, and other stuffings from around the house and farm to do this. Then he has to transport the raft the hundred-and-twenty yards to the brook. He tries dragging it across the field, but it is far too heavy, even with wooden poles underneath it for rollers. He gives up, and decides to 'go indoors and sit down and play at something else'.

He thinks about making bullets out of an old piece of lead pipe, or hammering a nail into an arrowhead, or mending his broken fishing rod. 'But he did not feel much inclined to do that either; he had half a mind to go up in the bench-room, and take the lock of the old gun to pieces to see how it worked.' Instead, he opens his favourite book and reads the old ballad of King Estmere; this gives him the idea of getting his old cutlass and slashing away at the meadow flowers, pretending they are Saracens and he is St George. And once outside again, he remembers the raft.

> What he wanted to do was to launch his raft before anyone saw or guessed what he was about, so that it might be a surprise to them and a triumph to him. Especially he was anxious to do it before Mark came; he might come across the fields any minute, or along the road, and Bevis wished to be afloat, so that Mark might admire his boat, and ask permission to step on board.

Bevis finds John the farm-hand, and tries to bribe him to help drag the raft, but the Bailiff is keeping an eye on John, so this is no good. At last he persuades the carter's boy to help, with his horse. The raft is brought to the water's edge, and is launched just as Mark arrives, but Bevis's triumph is brief, for only the bottom has been caulked, not the sides, and the water comes in. The caulking is completed with the aid of his friend Mark's handkerchief and handfuls of moss, and now the raft can sail. In an ecstatic moment, Bevis floats off down the brook:

> Then there was a straight course, a broad and open reach, at which he shouted with delight. The wind came behind and pushed his back like a sail, and the little silvery ripples ran before him, and dashed against the shore, destroying themselves and their shadows under them at the same time. The raft floated without piloting here, steadily on. Bevis lifted his pole and waved his hand in triumph.

But again, the exhilaration is brief. Round the bend, the stream is blocked by a fallen willow. The raft can go no further. Bevis and Mark contemplate sawing the tree in half, burning it, even blowing it up with gunpowder, or digging a canal round it. The Bailiff watches them.

> 'I thinks you be stopped,' said the Bailiff, having now looked at the tree more carefully. 'He be main thick' – with a certain sympathy for stolid, inanimate obstruction.

Stopped they are; the raft has to be left where it is, and the journey is over.

If Jefferies had concluded *Bevis* there, he would have produced a masterpiece. Scarcely anywhere else in literature is there quite such a vivid, sympathetic, uncondescending account of a boy's intense absorption in a task he has set himself-and at the same time his fitful attitude to the whole thing, for Bevis (like most children) loses interest as soon as things get too difficult, and goes off to do something else, only resuming the task when it takes his fancy again. The relationship with Mark and the adults is perfectly drawn. Mark is both a companion in adventure and a rival, sometimes to be fought against. Bevis's parents are not named or described, merely vaguely present as an uninteresting part of the scenery: simply 'the people'.

> He had to wash his hands, and by the time Mark and he reached the table the rest had finished. The people looked at them rather blackly, but they did not mind or notice in the least, for their minds were full of projects to remove the willow, about which they whispered to each other.

There is not a word out of place in this, not a touch of adult perspective or detachment from Bevis's world.

But *Bevis* is fifty-two chapters long – it was originally published in three volumes – and Jefferies cannot sustain this extraordinarily high level of writing for long. The raft is left in the brook, and Bevis and Mark set out to explore the Long Pond (Coate Water), which they rename 'The New Sea'. There is boating (in proper craft this time), swimming, 'war' between two gangs of boys, and a disappearance to camp on an island – very much *Tom Sawyer* territory, in fact, and at inordinate length, with neither the humour of Mark Twain nor the perfect poise of Jefferies' own opening chapters.

These later chapters of *Bevis* have often been recognised as the precursor of a whole genre of 'holiday adventure' stories for children. The Canadian author Ernest Thompson Seton followed Jefferies' lead in *Two Little Savages* (1903), about two boys camping out in the wilds, while Arthur Ransome's *Swallows and Amazons*, a generation later, in effect adapted *Bevis* for twentieth-century children. But the opening 'raft' chapters of *Bevis* have a greater claim to importance in the development of writing for children than does all the boating-fighting-camping narrative later in the book. In these opening chapters, Jefferies was refining the manner of writing *about* children far more than other Victorians had dreamt possible. And among those who seem to have taken note of what he had done was Kenneth Grahame.

2

Kenneth Grahame and the search for Arcadia

Bevis fails to hold our attention for its whole length because it lacks a sense of personal urgency. It is, in the end, a rather clinical exercise in entering a child's mind, without any vital private need to do this on the part of the author. Kenneth Grahame, repeating the experiment, avoided Jefferies' mistake, and got inside the experience of childhood while managing to communicate great excitement to the reader. He did this because the revisiting of his childhood was a journey which had an intense private purpose for him. And once he had done it, other writers, less anxiously involved, could follow his lead successfully.

*

Anyone studying Grahame's life and work will quickly find himself indebted to Peter Green's immensely skilful biography of him (1959), arguably the best book ever written about an English children's author. Nevertheless, Green may be wrong in one of his major conclusions. Chiefly on the evidence of Grahame's two books about childhood, *The Golden Age* (1895) and *Dream Days* (1898), he concludes that Grahame had a largely unhappy childhood, marked by emotional deprivation, and suggests that it was this which largely influenced him to write these two books – and so, indirectly, to become the author, a decade later, of *The Wind in the Willows*. Yet *The Golden Age* and *Dream Days* seem to suggest precisely the opposite – that Grahame's childhood (or at least the part of it that these two books deal with) was unusually happy.

Grahame was born in 1859, the son of an Edinburgh lawyer who shortly after the boy's birth became a legal official in Argyllshire, and moved his wife and family there. Kenneth was the third child; when he was five, his mother gave birth to another, and shortly afterwards she died of scarlet fever. The father decided that he could not cope with the children after his wife's death, and sent them south to live with her mother, a Mrs Ingles, who resided in the Thames-side village of Cookham Dene in Berkshire. There Kenneth, his two brothers, and his

sister, spent about three years, after which their grandmother decided
that the house was not suitable for her any longer, and took them with
her to a cottage at Cranbourne in the same county. Next, Mr Grahame
decided that after all he would like to have his children back, and they
were duly sent up to Scotland; but the experiment was not a success,
and back they came. The father, always a *bon viveur*, now devoted
most of his energies to the bottle, and soon vanished to France, where
he seems to have scraped some sort of a living by teaching English.
Kenneth never saw him again alive, but many years later was suddenly
summoned across the Channel to sort things out after the father had
died penniless in a Le Havre boarding house.

Peter Green makes out (as do the biographers of Lewis Carroll) that
it was the death of the mother which profoundly affected his subject,
and caused a trauma which was closely related to his becoming a writer.
The father, he says, meant by comparison nothing at all to Kenneth,
who presumably resented the casting-out of himself and his siblings
after their mother's death. That experience cannot exactly have
endeared his father to Kenneth; and yet one wonders whether Mr
Grahame senior should be dismissed quite so briskly from the son's
life. There are two important facts about him: that he took to drink, and
that he ran away to France. Both were forms of escape from the intolerable pressures of life, and it is exactly this kind of escape – this ducking
responsibility – which forms a major theme in Grahame's writing. His
first published book, *Pagan Papers* (1893), which came out in the year
after his father's death, is brimful of fanciful accounts of men who do
just the sort of thing his father had done:

> This is how Fothergill changed his life and died to Bloomsbury. One
> morning he made his way to the Whitechapel Road, and there he
> bought a barrow . . . He passed out of our lives by way of the
> Bayswater road . . .

> That stockbroker . . . who was missed from his wonted place one
> settling-day! . . . They found him in a wild nook of Hampshire.
> Ragged, sun-burnt, . . . he was tickling trout with godless native
> urchins . . .

> 'Mr —— did not attend at his office today, having been hanged at
> eight o'clock in the morning for horse-stealing.' . . .

> There was once an old cashier in some ancient City establishment,
> whose practice was to spend his yearly holiday in relieving some
> turnpike-man at his post . . .

And so on and so on. Respectable City men run away, become lock-

1. Charles Kingsley in the garden at Eversley Rectory. Artist and date unknown.

2. Charles and Fanny Kingsley at Eversley, from *The Bookman*, 1919.

3. The hallowed lovemaking of Charles and Fanny. A drawing by Charles Kingsley, first published in Susan Chitty's *The Beast and the Monk* (1974).

4. Lewis Carroll as a young man, by an unknown photographer.

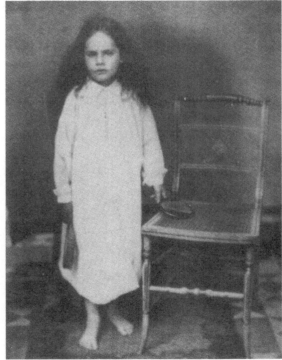

5. 'It Won't Come Smooth.' An 1863 photograph of Irene, one of the children of George MacDonald, taken by Lewis Carroll.

6. An illustration of Alice by the author himself to the manuscript of *Alice's Adventures Under Ground*.

7. Lewis Carroll photographed with Mrs George MacDonald and four of her children in 1862. Taken from Greville MacDonald's life of his father.

8. George MacDonald. A photograph thought to be by Lewis Carroll.

9. An illustration by Arthur Hughes to the first edition of *At the Back of the North Wind*.

10. Louisa May Alcott. The frontispiece to her *Life, Letters and Journals* (1889).

11. Amos Bronson Alcott, father of Louisa May: a seer or a charlatan?

12. Richard Jefferies, whose *Bevis* made a whole new genre of children's books possible. An engraving by William Strang.

13. 'The Willow Was Obstinate.' A drawing by E. H. Shepard from the 1932 edition of *Bevis*.

14. Kenneth Grahame in about 1895.

15. 'The Listener.' Alastair Grahame, to whom Toad's adventures were first told. From Elspeth Grahame's *First Whisper of The Wind in the Willows* (1945).

GREEN BANK HOTEL.
FALMOUTH
10th May 1907.

My darling Mouse

This is a birth-day letter,
to wish you very many happy returns
of the day. I wish we could have
been all together, but we shall
meet again soon, & then we will
have Tea &c. I have sent you two
picture books, one about Bre'r
Rabbit, from Buddy, & one about
some other animals, from Mummy.
And we have sent you a boat,

painted red, with mast =sails, to
sail in the round pond by the
windmill — & Mummy has sent you
a boat-hook to catch it when it
comes to shore. Also Mummy has
sent you some sand-toys, to play
in the sand with, and a card game

Have you heard about the
Toad? He was never taken prisoner
by brigands at all. It was all a
horrid low trick off his. He wrote
that letter himself — the letter saying
that a hundred pounds must be
put in the hollow tree. And he got
out of the window early one morning,
& went off to a town called Buggleton
& went to the Red Lion Hotel & there
he found a party that had just
motored down from London, & "
while they were having breakfast he

16. Part of the letter to Alastair Grahame beginning the story of *The Wind in the Willows*.

17.   E. Nesbit with a 'Magic City' she built for children.

18.   'We Die In Captivity.' An illustration by
H. R. Millar to E. Nesbit's *Wet Magic* (1913).

19.   Beatrix Potter (left, holding toy rabbit) with
one of her cousins (from Margaret Lane's *The Tale
of Beatrix Potter*).

Eastwood Dunkeld
Sep 4th 93

My dear Noel,
                    I don't know what to
write to you, so I shall tell you a story
                about four little rabbits
                        whose names were —

Flopsy, Mopsy Cottontail

and Peter

They lived with their mother in a
sand bank under the root of a
big fir tree.

20. Beatrix Potter's letter to Noël Moore containing the first version of The Tale of Peter Rabbit
(from Margaret Lane's The Tale of Beatrix Potter).

21. Beatrix Potter with her brother and father.

22. Beatrix Potter in old age.

23. J. M. Barrie. The frontispiece to the 1931 edition of his plays.

24. Mark Rylance, a male Peter Pan in the 1983 revival of the Royal Shakespeare Company's production.

25. A. A. Milne, Christopher Robin, and Pooh.

26. Galleon's Lap, drawn by E. H. Shepard.

keepers on the Thames, turn into vagabonds wandering the remote country villages, 'die to Bloomsbury'. And all this is described with the deepest envy and admiration, and not a hint of censure. Is not Grahame, in these musings (which contain a germ of the characters of Toad, Rat, and Mole), looking wistfully over his shoulder at his father's all-too-successful escape? Certainly Grahame's passion for things continental, the constant longing to follow the sun southwards which possessed him from his early adult years, and which he was only able to gratify by occasional and rather sober trips through Europe, seems to have been motivated by a desire to follow in his father's steps. All these feelings united to create one pole of his personality, which we might call the Wanderer.

At the other pole was Kenneth Grahame the Home-lover. All those moves from one house to another in childhood must have played a part in his obsession with creating a snug, neat little home for himself, which runs through *The Wind in the Willows* (Mole End, Rat's bachelor home, Badger's splendid underground quarters) and may also be discerned in his early essays and letters. To a friend, he confessed that he had a recurrent dream of

> a gradual awakening to consciousness in a certain little room, very dear and familiar . . . always the same feeling of a home-coming, of the world shut out, of the ideal encasement. On the shelves were a few books – a very few – but just the editions I had sighed for, the editions which refuse to turn up, or which poverty glowers at on alien shelves. On the walls were a print or two, a woodcut, an etching – not many . . . All was modest – Oh, so very modest! But all was my very own, and, what was more, everything in the room was exactly right.[82]

All Grahame's writing was produced by tension between those two poles, the Wanderer and the Home-lover. *The Wind in the Willows* was the outstanding result of it, but one may also observe it in *The Golden Age* and *Dream Days*, which are explorations of the security and home-lovingness of childhood, and also a search for some more distant goal, which can only be achieved by the child wandering away from home, either in imagination or in actual fact.

Neither book conveys any sense of deep unhappiness, of regret for parents dead and lost, of a lack of love. The two books describe a family of parentless children living in the house of some maiden aunts, under the supervision of these ladies, a governess, and the occasional visiting uncle; and after the narrator's initial observation that he and his brothers and sisters lacked 'a proper equipment of parents' there is not even a hint of regret for what might have been. Certainly Aunt Eliza (who is the nearest we get to a portrait of Grahame's grandmother) is a rather unlikeable, unsympathetic Victorian who lacks even the slightest understanding or tolerance of what children like doing and thinking; and she and the others of her kind are characterised by the narrator as 'the Olympians', both stupid and indifferent to children's needs. But the Olympians play only a small part in the story. Sometimes, quite unpredictably, they intervene in the doings of Edward, Harold, Selina, Charlotte, and the nameless boy-narrator, as when a circus visit is promised by them, and is then suddenly withdrawn to be replaced by a threatened garden party. They may be relied upon, too, to punish apparent wrongdoing without any questioning of its real nature or cause. But for most of the time the Olympians are simply not in evidence; the children are left free to do what they want, to an extent that would astonish their modern successors, and such rules as do exist – for instance, attendance at schoolroom lessons – are broken again and again without dire consequences:

> Harold would slip off directly after dinner, going alone, so as not to arouse suspicion, as we were not allowed to go into the town by ourselves. It was nearly two miles to our small metropolis, but there would be plenty of time for him to go and return . . . Besides, he might meet the butcher, who was his friend and would give him a lift . . .

> . . . I vowed, as I straddled and spat about the stable-yard in feeble imitation of the coachman, that lessons might go to the Inventor of them. It was only geography that morning, any way: and the practical thing was worth any quantity of bookish theory. As for me, I was going on my travels . . .

> Harold tumbled out of the trough in the excess of his emotion. 'But we aren't allowed to go on the water by ourselves,' he cried.
> 'No,' said Edward, with fine scorn: 'we aren't allowed; and Jason wasn't allowed either, I daresay. But he *went*!' . . .
> We made our way down to the stream, and captured the farmer's boat without let or hindrance . . .

And though the circus visit has been called off, the children nevertheless manage to get there, accepting a random offer of a lift from a neighbour, the Funny Man. The Olympians have about as little actual influence on their lives as did the original Olympians on the daily lives of the Greeks; Grahame, who knew his classical literature pretty well, chose their name carefully.

These books, then, are not the product of an unhappy childhood. On the contrary, they are a record of a time so free from worry, so peculiarly happy, that later life could never quite measure up to it. Grahame once remarked to a friend that

I feel I should never be surprised to meet myself as I was when a little chap of five, suddenly coming round a corner . . . I can remember everything I felt then; the part of my brain I used from four till about seven can never have altered.[83]

That his character at that age – the time he was living at Cookham Dene – should seem to him detached from the rest of his life indicates that his experiences in those years must have seemed utterly different from anything that happened before or after; one is reminded of C. S. Lewis's remark that his time in the trenches during the First World War, and the memory of all the horrors there, 'is too cut off from the rest of my experience and often seems to have happened to someone else'. Great unhappiness would presumably produce this effect; but in Grahame's case we can scarcely doubt, from the evidence of *The Golden Age* and *Dream Days*, that it was exactly the reverse which inspired this sense of detachment – his childhood self had experienced a life of freedom, contentment, and excitement which other experiences could never match.

His achievement in these books was, of course, the recovery of this childhood self, the ability to bring it alive again on the page. Not that the books are autobiography: it is impossible to relate much in them with any certainty to Grahame's actual experiences (for example, there are five children in them, as opposed to the four Grahames), and Peter Green points out that at least some details in them were taken from other families and children of his acquaintance. None the less a process of recall has taken place. Grahame does not assume the *persona* of his child-self, and narrate the books in that voice; perhaps he had felt that Jefferies' *Bevis* (which he would have known well, being an admirer of Jefferies' ruralist writings) lacked a certain vitality because its author had chosen to see everything in it through the boy's eyes. Instead, Grahame retains all his adult sophistication, and uses it to describe the child's feelings. The result seems arch at first, and certainly the prose is sometimes irritatingly ornate;[84] but the reader who is prepared to accept this device uncomplainingly soon finds that it creates a 'Chinese box' effect, and the presence of Grahame-the-child becomes oddly more real because Grahame-the-adult seems to be stressing his separateness from him:

Why does a coming bereavement project no thin faint voice, no shadow of its woe, to warn its happy, heedless victims? Why cannot Olympians ever think it worth while to give some hint of the thunder-bolts they are silently forging? And why, oh, why did it never enter any of our thick heads that the day would come when even Charlotte would be considered too matronly for toys?

This comes in a story – the final one in the collections – which tells how the toys are packed up, without the children's consent, to be sent off to a London hospital; but, late at night, the children raid the parcel, extract a few of their favourites, and bury them in the garden – not so that they can play with them again, but because 'The connexion was not entirely broken now – one link remained between us and them.' The meaning of the metaphor is obvious: for Grahame, and so for his readers, childhood itself lies buried at the foot of that tree in the paddock; a few turns of the spade, and it will be out in the light again. *The Golden Age* and *Dream Days* are themselves an act of exhumation.

A lesser writer than Grahame might have performed that act with no deeper purpose than mere nostalgia; the result would then have been trite. But Grahame has no particular interest in childhood for its own sake; he is not setting out, as Jefferies was, to understand the emotions and the imagination of boyhood just for itself; nor is he trying to show his readers how sweet or charming children really are – such as the creators of the Beautiful Child had done, with horrid results. Indeed, Grahame's children are not especially likeable. They have no special depths of character – Edward, the eldest, is rather shallow, and neither of the girls has anything in particular to commend her; only Harold, the younger boy, is at all a memorable figure in himself, possessed of a quirky imagination. They are all far less entertaining to read about, in themselves, than E. Nesbit's Bastable children. The point is that to write about them, and what they thought and felt, was only the halfway house in Grahame's self-imposed mission. He wished to revisit childhood because of the possibilities it offered of Escape.

*

If the notion of Escape was planted in him by his father's behaviour during his early years, the later part of his childhood and his early adult life seem to have encouraged him to contemplate a kind of spiritual running-away because of the constraints they imposed on him. He was sent to St Edward's School, Oxford, where he had to endure the usual kind of public school toughness, and then was denied his very strong desire to become an Oxford undergraduate. His family believed that a University education would be both unnecessary and expensive, and instead they secured him a clerkship in the Bank of England. Not surprisingly, many commentators, following Peter Green, have regarded Grahame's apparent desire to escape, in his writings, from the world of conventional late Victorian society as a natural result of his having been pressed, in this fashion, into an alien mould.

Yet the facts do not quite accord with this interpretation. However shy and reserved Grahame may have been (and, according to many accounts, he was very retiring in manner), he does not seem to have hated public school at all; indeed he was one of the heroes of St Edward's in his days there, gaining his First XV Rugby colours and becoming the head boy of the school – the behaviour of Mr Toad rather than Mole. And as for the Bank of England, far from being a repressive, authoritarian institution likely to frown upon any individuality of spirit in its · employees, it was in Grahame's day notable, even notorious, for its tolerance and even encouragement of eccentricity. It was a quaint repository of tradition whose staff worked short hours, and where pandemonium often reigned while business was supposedly being conducted – the staff ate and drank heavily on the premises, kept pet animals, and amused themselves at all hours oblivious of decorum. Any distaste Grahame may have felt for the Bank in his early years there is more likely to have been on account of its licentious character than any repression it exercised over him. And the evidence is that, far from hating his work there, he found it extremely congenial; for he rose extremely quickly through its ranks, and in 1898 actually became Secretary, one of its highest offices – at thirty-nine he was one of the youngest people to have done so. No doubt the Bank did inspire conflicting feelings in him – there is some evidence that he found the responsibility of his job there a burden – but it would be wrong to paint it as the monster from which he wished to escape. That monster, if it existed, seems to have been of a more subtle nature; one might suspect it to have been London itself.

By Grahame's day, hatred of urban life, and of the harm that the industrial revolution had steadily done to English society during the previous hundred years, had become a major theme in English writing. After Dickens and Mayhew (and the evangelical writers) had had their say at describing the miseries of the urban poor, there had come those Pre-Raphaelites who believed that a return to sanity lay through medievalism and the old craft methods. A wide range of writers from Ruskin to Kingsley had tried to find other answers to the dilemmas of industrialisation, but no magic solution appeared, and the problem merely got worse and worse. In view of this it is scarcely surprising that more and more writers were seeking landscapes that were far from what Ruskin called 'that great foul city – rattling, growling, smoking, stinking – a ghastly heap of fermenting brickwork, pouring out poison at every pore'.[85]

It was in this climate that the nature writings of Richard Jefferies found an enthusiastic audience, and Grahame was among those who lapped them up. He devoured George Borrow too – he often refers in his writings to *Lavengro*, Borrow's prose Scholar Gipsy tale which offers even wider landscapes into which to escape. Meanwhile, in Grahame's actual daily life, more practical possibilities of flight were offered by his friend F. J. Furnivall, a Muscular Christian (he was a disciple of Maurice) who had founded the Early English Text Society –

thereby reviving many pre-industrial English romantic narratives – and who ran a working men's rowing club on the Thames. Furnivall took Grahame sculling on the river, and seems to have contributed to the character of the Water Rat, with his passion for messing about in boats. Even more important, he was the first person steadily to encourage Grahame with his writing, and it was largely thanks to him that in the late 1880s Grahame began to have essays and prose sketches accepted by London magazines.

Grahame's early writings are very much in the manner of Robert Louis Stevenson – the first Grahame book to be pulished, *Pagan Papers*, closely resembles the style and subject matter of Stevenson's essay collection *Virginibus Puerisque*, which had appeared about a dozen years earlier; there is even an essay in the Stevenson book called 'Child's Play' which may have helped to suggest *The Golden Age*, with its discussion of children's imaginations. *Pagan Papers* also owes a little to the Decadents, with whom Grahame was marginally associated (he published several pieces in the *Yellow Book*), in its praise of the rural god Pan, whom Grahame claims to detect lurking in all the most secluded rural spots. But the 'paganism' of the book is not really of a kind that the Beardsley–Wilde circle would have understood: Grahame's pagan desires are not remotely priapic, but simply epicurean in the old classical way, and in essay after essay he extols the pleasures of the hearty country walk, the pints of beer and the tobacco pipe in the rural inn – much as his unconscious disciple C. S. Lewis did half a century later. And even these are only halfway houses in the great game of Escape: the Ridgeway along the Berkshire downs is chiefly loved not for the pleasures it itself can offer, but because it leads to a gleam of the English Channel, and so over to Europe and the Mediterranean climate where living can really begin. And what is Grahame escaping from? From the machine age, not because of the harm it had done to its workers or its city dwellers (Grahame took no interest himself in such social problems), but because it denied the possibility of dreaming dreams and seeing visions. Grahame did not actually dislike machines for themselves – he speaks of having 'a sentimental weakness for the night-piercing whistle', and even of 'the enchanted pages of the railway A.B.C.' The trouble is that they were not enchanted enough: 'The crowning wrong that is wrought us of furnace and piston-rod', he writes, 'lies in their annihilation of the steadfast mystery of the horizon, so that the imagination no longer begins to work at the point where vision ceases.' He pleads for a return to the story-book world, in which 'there was always a chance of touching the Happy Isles'.

The first part of *Pagan Papers* is all in this mode, with its whimsical accounts of vanishing stockbrokers and City men who become tramps. The second part consists of the realisation of the dream of Escape in much richer terms – for in *Pagan Papers* were first printed many of the sketches that later went to make up *The Golden Age*. In this context, more than when they later appeared in a separate book, their function in Grahame's psyche becomes clear. By returning to childhood in these prose sketches, he is able to indulge the Escape dream to its fullest. For the five children who dwell under the shadow of the Olympians are constantly escaping, in fact and in imagination, from their mundane lives into worlds of quite extraordinary fancy.

The dominating notion in these *Golden Age* sketches is that of the Good Place, the Golden City, an Arcadia which can always be reached in imagination, and whose shores one may occasionally touch in fact. In one of the stories (in *Dream Days*) the narrator confides to a girl-neighbour his familiarity with just such a place:

> 'Of course it's just a place I imagine . . . but it's an awfully nice place – the nicest place you ever saw . . . Generally it begins by – well, you're going up a broad, clear river in a sort of boat. You're not rowing or anything – you're just moving along. And there's beautiful grass meadows on both sides, and the river's very full, quite up to the level of the grass. And you glide along by the edge. And the people are haymaking there, and playing games, and walking about; and they shout to you, and you shout back to them and they bring you things to eat out of their baskets, and let you drink out of their bottles; and some of 'em are the nice people you read about in books. And so at last you come to the Palace steps . . .'

In this instance the Palace itself proves something of a disappointment to the adult reader – its contents are chiefly chocolates, sweets, and fizzy drinks. The dream, in fact, is more enticingly suggested when the goal of the Golden City is not quite reached, as in the story 'Its Walls Were as of Jasper', in which the children visit, in their imagination, the Arcadian landscape in one of the pictures which hangs in the Olympians' house, but can never quite see what lies behind the corner. Sometimes they make actual journeys and discover real approximations to the Good Place. In one story the narrator crawls through a fence and finds himself in a garden fit for a fairy tale, with what seems to be a real Princess being courted by a Prince. The grown-ups do not disillusion him, for the very good reason that his child's perception of them actually enriches their own lives. In another, similar story the children go boating up the river (how often water occurs in this context with Grahame) and find a remote house and garden where a girl they meet there seems to them a true fairy tale creature. And indeed she really has been imprisoned by an aunt, after an unhappy love affair. Best of all, in the story 'The Roman Road', the narrator encounters an Artist (clearly the adult Grahame himself) who, to his astonishment, shares his own

dream of Arcadia, and would dearly love to get there – despite the fact
that he has been to, and actually lives in, what the boy imagines to be a
real Arcadia, the city of Rome:

> 'You haven't been to Rome, have you?' I inquired.
> 'Rather,' he replied briefly: 'I live there. . . . I'm a sort of Ulysses –
> seen men and cities, you know. In fact, about the only place I never
> got to was the Fortunate Island . . .'
> 'Wouldn't you like,' I inquired, 'to find a city without any people
> in it at all?'

The boy goes on to describe his Good Place in childish terms: 'You go
into the shops, and take anything you want – chocolates and magic-
lanterns and injirubber balls – and there's nothing to pay . . .' And to his
surprise, the Artist understands him:

> 'Do you know,' he said presently, 'I've met one or two fellows from
> time to time, who have been to a city like yours – perhaps it was the
> same one. They won't talk much about it – only broken hints, now
> and then; but they've been there sure enough. They don't seem to
> care about anything in particular – and everything's the same to
> them, rough or smooth; and sooner or later they slip off and
> disappear; and you never see them again. Gone back, I suppose.'
> 'Of course,' said I. 'Don't see what they ever came away for; *I*
> wouldn't . . .'

And so the adult Grahame and the boy Grahame part company,
vowing to meet again one day in that city, and the boy

> went down-heartedly from the man who understood me, back to the
> house where I never could do anything right. How was it that
> everything seemed natural and sensible to him, which these uncles,
> vicars, and other grown-up men took for the merest tomfoolery?
> Well, he would explain this, and many another thing, when we met
> again . . . Perhaps he would be in armour next time – why not? He
> would look well in armour, I thought. And I would take care to get
> there first, and see the sunlight flash and play on his helmet and
> shield, as he rode up the High Street of the Golden City.
> Meantime, there only remained the finding it. An easy matter.

*

The Golden Age became a bestseller when it was published in 1895, but
its popularity was not on account of its delicate, subtle accounts of the
search for Arcadia. It was loved by the majority of its readers simply

because here at last was an unsentimental, funny, but still true-to-life way of portraying children. A few reviewers – true Olympians – were simply unable to believe that children can be as contemptuous towards adults as those in Grahame's book are to the aunts and uncles; one Professor Sully, author of a book called *Children's Ways*, spoke sternly about 'a dishonour done to the sacred cause of childhood . . . a tone of cynical superiority which runs through the volume'. Those who had worshipped the Beautiful Child for several decades were, not surprisingly, disconcerted to have their idol dethroned in favour of a more realistic image. But most reviewers recognised a masterpiece, and agreed with Swinburne, who spoke of *The Golden Age* as 'well-nigh too praiseworthy for praise'. Grahame's reputation was made at one stroke; he became a literary lion, and when *Dream Days* appeared three years later it was lapped up just as greedily by the public. And in that same year, 1898, E. Nesbit began to write her Bastable stories, which showed very clearly the influence of Grahame in the way she portrayed children.

Grahame himself meanwhile fell virtually silent as a writer for many years after *Dream Days* was published. Did he feel he had betrayed a very personal secret in talking so publicly of his search for Arcadia, for the Golden City? At all events he seemed not to know where to look next in his quest for it.

3

E. Nesbit
a Victorian in disguise

E. Nesbit was a likely sort of person to adapt and popularise Grahame's vision of childhood. She was an energetic hack, keen to try anything in the struggle to support her wayward husband and her odd household. She seized on Grahame's idea, and made it the prototype of a series of highly popular books which have led her to be regarded as a great children's writer. Yet if one inspects those books closely, doubts begin to emerge as to the real nature of her talent.

*

Edith Nesbit was born in London in 1858, the year before Grahame. She was the daughter of a distinguished agricultural chemist who died when she was only three. She may well have felt this loss very deeply; absent or dead fathers form a recognisable motif in her children's books, and there is a tear-jerking moment at the end of *The Railway Children* when Roberta is unexpectedly reunited with her papa: '"Oh! my Daddy, my Daddy!" That scream went like a knife into the heart of everyone in the train . . .' But, rather typically, Nesbit, always keen to squeeze good value out of an idea, used precisely the same words at the end of *The House of Arden*: 'In one flash she was across the room and in her father's arms, sobbing and laughing and saying again and again – "Oh, my daddy! Oh, my daddy, my daddy!"'

After the father's death, Edith Nesbit's mother ran his Agricultural College for a little while on her own, displaying the kind of stamina Mother shows in *The Railway Children* when she supports her family after the father has been put in prison. Then, when Edith was about nine, her mother decided to take the family abroad in the hope of improving the health of one of the elder daughters – Edith (always known as Daisy in her childhood) was the youngest of six. From this time on, Edith never had a settled home. She was sent to a number of boarding schools in Britain and on the Continent, most of them fairly deplorable, and her life in middle childhood seems to have been chiefly marked by a series of nightmare terrors. There was a horrific occasion when she was taken into a crypt full of mummified bodies at Bordeaux; this gave her 'nights and nights of anguish and horror'. Staying with a doctor's family, she mixed some of his medicines together for a prank, then suffered agonies of remorse, believing that his patients would die. At night, when the gas-jet had been turned down, she would see corpses and skeletons among the shadows of her bedroom. Fears like this dominate her memoirs of childhood,[86] and led her to 'pray fervently, tearfully, that when I should be grown up I might never forget what I thought and felt and suffered then'.

Yet her works of fiction about childhood contain nothing of these fears and horrors.[87] There is a notable absence of threat of any kind, and the children in them, even when their outward circumstances are not pleasant, are sustained by a cheerful, even complacent, sense of security very different from the anxieties experienced by the young Edith Nesbit. Perhaps she wanted to rewrite her childhood, and to give the Bastables and her other child heroes a depth of happiness she had never known; perhaps she simply thought the reading public would not care for anything less placid. At all events she did not answer her own prayer for total recall.

Of course, her childhood was not all horrors, and there were a few years during her early teens when the family was living at Halstead Hall in Kent, the kind of rambling country house and garden which she glorified in *The Wouldbegoods* and other books. She also had happy memories of the Bastable-like activities of her brothers and herself – the shooting of the fox and the search for the source of the stream in *The Wouldbegoods* were closely based on episodes involving her brothers Alfred and Harry. She also began to make a little money by getting poetry accepted for publication, like Noël Bastable. Then, at about the age of twenty, she fell in love with Hubert Bland.

This curious person was described as a 'Brush Manufacturer' on the certificate of his marriage to Edith, which took place in her twenty-second year, when she was seven months pregnant. But if Bland ever ran a brush business it was short lived; like the Bastables' father he seems to have been susceptible to fraud by his partners. Early in their marriage he began to go in for journalism, and some of Edith's early published work was written in collaboration with him. He was also a founder member of the Fabian Society.

A reader searching for superficial evidence of Edith Nesbit's socialism will not have far to look in her books. There is an episode in *The Phoenix and the Carpet* when the Queen of Babylon comments on the treatment of London's 'slaves', the working classes: '"How wretched and poor and neglected they seem . . . Why don't their masters see that they're better fed and better clothed.' And in *The Phoenix and the Carpet* a small piece of social justice is done when the

Cook, worn out by her dreary chores below stairs, is allowed to remain
in the South Seas as queen of a tribe of savages. Yet any deep concern
with changing the existing social order is notably lacking from the
Nesbit books.

The children, even if temporarily afflicted with poverty, are securely
middle class.[88] Every family, however poor, has its servants,[89] and the
cooks, parlourmaids, and the rest seem by implication to be inferior beings in every kind of way – in *Five Children and It* it is arranged that the
servants shall not be able to see the results of the Psammead's magic, and
though this is a necessary plot device one also feels it to be a comment on
their place in the social hierarchy. It may be argued that Nesbit was
simply typical of her time in her acceptance of the domination of the
middle classes, and her apparent assumption that only middle-class
children are appropriate heroes for children's books. Yet things might
have gone otherwise. Charles Kingsley and George MacDonald, following the evangelical tradition, had made poor children their heroes,
while in America, Mark Twain had concentrated on the grubby end of
society. Mrs Ewing, the children's writer whom Nesbit admired above
all other, had produced a crop of tales about poor orphans. After
Nesbit, on the other hand, English children's writers almost unremit-
tingly chose middle-class protagonists, until there was a conscious (indeed self-conscious) revolution against this in the 1950s. Nesbit seems
to be at least partially responsible for the extraordinarily narrow social
compass of English juvenile fiction for the first half of the twentieth
century.

In fact there is no real contradiction between her life and her work.
Her support of the socialist cause was only skin deep. She revelled in
the atmosphere created by the Fabians without having much intellectual grasp of their doctrines. It was all very daring and exciting: she cut
her hair short and considered this very wild; she smoked in public,
which seemed equally 'fast'; she thought Sidney Webb rather comic,
and fell in love with George Bernard Shaw. She liked to interrupt
Fabian discussions by asking for a glass of water, or, as Shaw put it,
'staging a faint'. Her socialism was about on a level with that diehard
evangelical children's book *Jessica's First Prayer*, which she loved; she
said that its account of the poor London waif turned out of the chapel
because she is too grimy made 'my eyes smart and my throat grow
lumpy'.

When Women's Suffrage became a public issue she declared herself
opposed to it, and she caricatured the Suffragettes in the figure of the
Pretenderette in *The Magic City* (1910). Her only real intellectual
enthusiasm was the Baconian theory, to which she became addicted in
her later years. She wasted hours of her friends' time trying to convince
them that Bacon wrote Shakespeare, and went in for long mathematical
calculations to 'prove' this, quite unabashed by her incompetence at

even simple arithmetic. According to her biographer Doris Langley Moore, J. C. Squire once 'sat with her till two in the morning while she worked out a Bacon "proof" which rested on the assumption that four thirteens made forty-two'.

She took to wearing 'aesthetic' clothes, and drifted about looking rather like Isadora Duncan. Her billowing dresses began to seem more and more eccentric as she grew older and put on weight. She revelled in the *outré* fashions and tastes of her time without having much idea what they were really about. She was a child in adult clothes. Doris Langley Moore writes of her:

> She was exceedingly lithe and athletic, and even after the birth of four children far more adept than the average Victorian woman in riding, swimming, and running . . . She was proud of being able to do fancy skipping, and in appreciative company would perform a dancer's high kick, or bend backwards across a gate until her head nearly touched the ground . . . Dressed in aesthetic clothes, daringly corsetless, she would lie at full length on the rug before the fire with the dogs beside her – so oblivious to the extreme unconventionality of her attitude that she charmed the young people, and disarmed the elderly . . . Her manner was as gay and careless as a child's. Indeed she had a child's flexibility almost all her life in recovering from every possible distress. Neither anger, nor worry, nor even grief itself, save in its direct extremity, could ever master her for long.[90]

This childlike resilience was a distinct asset, given her domestic situation. Her husband Hubert Bland seemed at first sight an altogether more adult, rational being than Edith, and he quickly made some reputation as an editor and newspaper columnist. He was intellectually active in the Fabian Society, where he was known as 'the Tory Socialist' on account of his distinctively Conservative appearance, with monocle and bristling moustache, and his anti-liberal line on such issues as sexual freedom; he declared himself an earnest opponent of those advocates of free love (such as H. G. Wells) whose voices were beginning to be heard in Fabian circles. On the other hand, his private life was an exact negation of this.

After six years of marriage, and by the time she herself had three children, Edith discovered that her friend Alice Hoatson, who had helped to get some of her earliest work into print and who now acted as 'companion-help' to the Blands, was pregnant. Edith magnanimously decided to adopt the baby and pass it off as her own, and this was duly done. But scarcely had the arrangement been entered into and the baby born than Edith discovered that the father was her own husband Hubert. There was a violent quarrel, and Edith tried to throw Alice Hoatson and the baby out of the house. Hubert answered that if they went, so did he, whereupon Edith consented to continue with the adoption plan, and the child, Rosamund, was brought up as her own.

A decade or so later, Alice Hoatson gave birth to another child by Hubert, and the whole business was repeated. (Edith also discovered early in her marriage that Hubert had fathered a child on a woman in Beckenham whom he had promised to marry.) Neither Rosamund nor the second Hoatson child, John, was aware until adolescence that Edith was not their mother and they were really the offspring of the insipid 'companion'. The discovery, when it happened, was not pleasant. Indeed one might imagine that the atmosphere in the Bland household would have been thoroughly poisonous. George Bernard Shaw remarked of Edith and Hubert: 'No two people were ever married who were better calculated to make the worst of each other.' Yet H. G. Wells observed of Bland's entanglements: 'All this E. Nesbit not only detested and mitigated and tolerated, but presided over and I think found exceedingly interesting.'

She seems to have had a child's detachment from the turmoil. Certainly she remained deeply fond of Hubert. After his death in 1914 she wrote to a friend: 'Without Hubert everything is so unmeaning.' And she behaved in a curiously childlike fashion over another pair of tragedies in her life, the deaths of two of her children. One was in fact a still-birth, in about 1886; it would have been her fourth child. Doris Langley Moore records that she 'grieved as much over it as if it had been her first-born'. It was to be buried in the garden, this being then legally possible, and Alice Hoatson laid it out in a long basket decked with flowers. But Edith would not give it up, and clung to it desperately; Hubert and Alice had to struggle with her before she would let them inter it. Fifteen years later her son Fabian, then in his mid-teens, underwent an operation for the removal of his tonsils, which was performed at home – a common practice at the time. For no apparent reason he died under the anaesthetic, and Edith simply refused to accept that he would not come back to life. For two hours after the doctor had departed she, Hubert, and Alice tried to revive him, and when the others had given up hope she rushed round the house collecting hot-water bottles in the hope of warming him to life again. As a final desperate gesture she set the candles intended for his next birthday around his bed, in the hope that they would somehow provide the warmth. So a child tries to revive a dead pet animal, or mend a broken doll.

It is striking how many of those who knew her compared her to a child. Richard le Gallienne, meeting her when she was about thirty, recalled

> her tall, lithe, boyish-girl figure admirably set off by her plain 'socialist' gown, her short hair, and her large, vivid eyes . . . like a

tom-boyish sister slightly older than myself. She suggested adventure, playing truant, robbing orchards, or even running away to sea. I was hers from that moment.[91]

Nesbit, indeed, spoke of herself as a child, or at least an adolescent. 'When I am happy I feel nineteen,' she remarked, and in *The Treasure Seekers* she drew a portrait of herself (as the writer 'Mrs Leslie') as 'a jolly sort of grown-up boy in a dress and hat'. She had a childish lack of understanding of the needs of other people – including her own children, whom she dressed and disciplined simply according to her current whim, as if they were dolls. Her not infrequent bad temper was like a child's, and she had to be coaxed out of it as if she were still in childhood:

> At mealtimes [writes Doris Langley Moore] there were often stormy outbursts which ended in her rushing from the table and violently slamming the doors as she retired to her study. The children would be left staring uncomfortably at their pudding plates, and Hubert Bland. . . would be heard at the door of her room begging to be let in. Then there would be an affectionate reconciliation . . . and she would penitently kiss everyone all round and tackle the pudding obediently.[92]

One notes how often in these comparisons of Edith with a child she is described as tomboyish, or even as a boy. Her adoption of the *persona* of Oswald Bastable as narrator for *The Treasure Seekers* seems to have answered a deep need. There is scarcely any suggestion in biographical records that she found other women sexually attractive, and one cannot detect that she felt herself to be cast in the wrong gender as did Louisa Alcott. She simply seems to have preferred to think of herself as a boy. This would seem to be one reason for her adoption of the sexually anonymous 'E. Nesbit' as her *nom de plume* from her first publications onwards. Many readers writing to her for the first time assumed her to be male – H. G. Wells decided that she was named 'Ernest', and continued to call her this throughout their friendship – and there is no evidence that this displeased her in the least.

*

She wrote, like Mother in *The Railway Children*, chiefly to keep her family from starvation. She longed to be a great poet, but there is no evidence that what she wrote really gratified any deep emotional or intellectual need. Her early books suggest that she had nothing in particular to write about, but was simply an intelligent craftsman, determined to squeeze a living by one of the few paying occupations readily available at that time to educated women – literary hack-work.

She turned out narrative poems in the style of Tennyson, and had quite
a success with a collection of them, *Lays and Legends* (1886). She and
Hubert wrote nondescript popular fiction together under the pseudonym 'Fabian Bland', and she produced such bits and pieces as *Grim
Tales* (1893), a mixture of Poe and light romantic fiction. She showed
no unusual talent, no special gift at characterisation, verse-style, or
anything else; simply a capacity for hard work. But this was enough to
earn her, by the mid-1890s, a modest reputation as a readable author
and poet.

Children's books featured among her hack-work from quite early
on; they had such titles as *Pussy Tales* and *Doggy Tales*. She was in the
Molesworth tradition, a competent, professional, entirely uninspired
lady children's author. Then the *Girl's Own Paper* commissioned her
to write some reminiscences of her childhood, and this, coupled with
the appearance a few months later of Grahame's *Dream Days*, seems to
have suggested to her the idea of writing something rather new in
English children's fiction. Some of the stories which afterwards made
up *The Treasure Seekers* appeared in magazines during 1898, and the
book itself came out a year later. Suddenly her name was made.

The Story of the Treasure Seekers, to give it its full title, seemed
entirely new in its predominantly comic treatment of children. Nesbit
had taken the formula of *The Golden Age* and *Dream Days* – a family of
children able to conduct their lives with very little adult supervision –
and used it for a series of comic set-pieces. The comedy was achieved
partly through the characters of three of the children: the idealistic poet
Noël, the would-be-heroic Oswald, and the youngest, H.O. (Horace
Octavius); another brother, Dicky, and the girls, Dora and Alice, are
less sharply characterised. But the chief source of humour is the
narration; Oswald himself tells the story, though he tries to disguise his
identity and to praise 'Oswald' dispassionately as though he were not
himself:

> It is one of us that tells this story – but I shall not tell you which: only
> at the very end perhaps I will . . . It was Oswald who first thought
> of looking for treasure. Oswald often thinks of very interesting
> things . . .

The sustained humour of *The Treasure Seekers* may be original; the
device of child as narrator is not. It was used in several children's books
which preceded Nesbit's, most notably Dickens's *A Holiday Romance*
(1868) and Mrs Ewing's *A Great Emergency* (1877), and the Ewing
book has something of the flavour of the Bastables. Yet the fact that
Oswald is telling the story, funny as it may be, disguises the true nature
of *The Treasure Seekers*, which is as condescending towards children as
are any of the Beautiful Child books of the Molesworth era.

Oswald, H.O., Noël *et al.* are a very far cry from the sharply observant, shrewd, adult-criticising children of *The Golden Age* and *Dream Days*. There is no doubt in Grahame's books who has the 'right' view of the world: it is the children, and those rare, exceptional adults who are able to share something of their imagination. To them, rather than to the Olympians, is given the proper perception of how things really are. In consequence the children in Grahame's books do not make mistakes, do not make fools of themselves: sheer folly is left to the Olympians. But Nesbit's Bastables are fools from the beginning, albeit holy fools, foolish through extreme innocence. Their understanding of the world around them is simply naïve, and the comedy derives from the collision between their idealism and the naïvety with which they try to carry out the ideals. They decide to go treasure-seeking, 'to restore the fallen fortunes of the House of Bastable' – in itself a notion that would seem ridiculous or irrelevant to the Grahame children, who have no concern whatever with such adult things as money. They dig for treasure in the garden, and are actually persuaded that they have found some by a neighbour's uncle, who drops a couple of half-crowns into the hole.

> I wish Albert-next-door's uncle would come treasure-seeking with us regularly; he must have very sharp eyes: for Dora says she was looking just the minute before at the very place where the second half-crown was picked up from, and *she* never saw it.

Similarly when Noël and Oswald set off to London to try to make money by selling Noël's poems, they are rewarded not by their own industry, but by the patronising kindness of a lady poet and a Fleet Street editor, both of whom take pity on them.[93] Throughout *The Treasure Seekers* and the other Bastable books, adults play this role of kindly protector. There is not one sharp or satirical portrait of an adult; it is all very far from the children's observation of adult fatuities in *The Golden Age*. Moreover, when Nesbit follows Grahame's lead and describes those adults who are prepared to enter imaginatively into the children's games, she displays a similar condescension towards the Bastables. Grahame had portrayed, for example, a bookish country cleric who is able to share a boy's outlook because of the mixture of naïvety and enthusiasm in his own character. But in the Bastable books such characters as Albert-next-door's uncle are actually patronising the children when they pretend to be taking their games seriously. Occasionally the Bastables realise this, and understandably it comes as a shock to them. After discovering that the 'robber' who has supposedly broken into their house and who delights them with stories of his criminal escapades is really a friend of their father's, come to dinner, Oswald says: 'Then we began to understand, and it was like being knocked down, it was so sudden . . . We were dumb with amazement.' But most of the time their world is not broken into by reality, and they live safely cocooned in their own imaginings.

Nesbit herself seems to have realised what she was up to. There is a very revealing passage in one of her adult books, *The Red House* (1902), a popular romantic novel about married life. She arranged it to overlap with a story in *The New Treasure Seekers* (1904) in which the Bastables impersonate a society of antiquaries and so gain entry to the grounds of a country mansion, the Red House, which is occupied by the young couple of the novel. The children's account of the incident, in the short story, is funny and jolly in the usual Bastable manner, but the adult version is rather different. The male narrator of *The Red House* (one half of the married couple) observes crushingly of the Bastables: 'They were much funnier than they meant to be.' The same point about their naïvety is made in a conversation between him and his wife:

'They are very trusting. The world must have been kind to them . . .
'Why aren't all children nice?'
'They are – if they have nice grown-ups belonging to them.'

This is precisely the Bastables' advantage, and disadvantage. Their life is cushioned by 'nice grown-ups', and in doing this the grown-ups are holding them back from maturity, are protecting them from the world as it really is. Unlike the children in *The Golden Age*, one cannot imagine how they will ever grow up.

In fact *The Treasure Seekers* is a strikingly old-fashioned book. Underneath the comedy, the Bastables are steadily being schooled in the accepted adult virtues. Not only do the adults patronise them; they never hesitate to deliver little moral lectures. Albert-next-door's uncle, the adult most involved with their games, is also the one most ready to be plainly didactic:

Albert's uncle came in next day and talked to each of us separately. To Oswald he said many unpleasant things about it being ungentle-manly to spy on ladies, and about minding your own business . . .

When Albert-next-door had gone his uncle sat in the Guy Fawkes armchair and took Alice on his knee . . . At last he said –
'Look here, young 'uns. I like to see you play and enjoy yourselves . . . But what about Albert's mother? Didn't you think how anxious she would be at his not coming home?' . . . He only talks like that when he is very serious, or even angry.

Very often there is no need for adults to impress the desirability of virtuous behaviour on the Bastables – they are aware of it already.

Stricken with conscience because Alice has knowingly used a 'bad sixpence' to pay for a telegram, they make every effort to raise money and replace it with a good one, even to the extent of Oswald putting on ragged clothes and selling flowers outside a railway station. One might suppose from passages such as this that the book is at its heart an old-fashioned moral tale, with the children eventually reaping the reward of good conduct, were it not for the fact that the dénouement (the showering of a fortune on the family by the children's 'Indian Uncle') is chiefly the result not of their virtues but of their simple-mindedness.

The truth is that Nesbit was essentially a late Victorian writer, who accepted the attitude, prevalent in the 1870s and 1880s, that children are delightfully naïve. She belongs to the era of Carrots and Herr Baby. She frequently expressed an enthusiasm for Mrs Ewing, but most of her stories are of the Molesworth rather than the Ewing school. Her only book which might have been written by Mrs Ewing is *The Railway Children* (1906), created after the Bastable chronicle had run its course. Its melodramatic plot, rural setting, and portraits of such people as the Old Gentleman, benefactor of the children, might have come straight from the pages of Ewing. But the moralising is cruder than Ewing would ever have permitted herself:

> Roberta . . . was quite oddly anxious to make other people happy. And she could keep a secret, a tolerably rare accomplishment. Also she had the power of silent sympathy. That sounds rather dull, I know, but it's not so dull as it sounds. It just means that a person is able to know that you are unhappy, and to love you extra on that account, without bothering you by telling you all the time how sorry she is for you . . . So she just loved Mother more and never said a single word that could let Mother know how earnestly her little girl wondered what Mother was unhappy about.

Roberta's naïvety is almost as marked as that of the Bastables. She and her brother and sister are quite unable to comprehend, despite every kind of hint, that their father is in prison. Nesbit keeps them in ignorance partly to achieve the book's climax, but also, one feels, because she likes to shelter children from the real world. The story, competently structured and entertainingly written as it is, ducks out of what might have been its real issues – the children's discovery of the possibility of gross injustice in the adult world (the imprisonment is the result of a mistake) – and does not allow them to experience any real hardships during their supposed poverty (the boy's theft of coal from the railway station is condoned the moment it is discovered). Instead Nesbit contents herself with a series of soap-opera crises, most notably the children's prevention of a train wreck. The only concession to reality is a rather sentimental account of the family helping a political prisoner.

This cocooning of children from the real world is not an obvious feature of Nesbit's fantasy stories, but in these books the issues of the real world scarcely ever threaten to intrude. The children in *Five Children and It* (1902) seem far more mature than the Bastables; they are resourceful, speculative, and equal to virtually any emergency. But they are also entirely unmemorable. (How many readers of *Five Children* and its sequels can recall their names?) They exist merely as figures in the landscape of the plot, virtually undifferentiated except in sex, and without any character beyond the bare demands of the stories. Those stories are exceptionally well crafted, and will be judged by many to be Nesbit's best achievement, but again it must be observed that she knew how to borrow, and the degree of originality in them is comparatively small. The cross-grained Psammead, giver of each day's wishes in *Five Children*, is a cousin of the bad-tempered Cuckoo and Raven in Mrs Molesworth's *The Cuckoo Clock* and *The Tapestry Room*. The children's perpetual inability to make any worthwhile use of the daily wish is the motif of the traditional *Three Wishes*, while the intrusion of magic into the modern world was used as the stuff of fiction a few years before Nesbit by F. Anstey, in *Vice Versa* (1882) and *The Brass Bottle* (1900), the latter being the story of the embarrass-ments caused to a modern young man when he acquires the services of a genie. At the end of *Five Children and It* the children turn to *The Brass Bottle* to find a way of getting out of their difficulties. It seems likely that the Anstey book was the inspiration of the whole story, and so of *The Phoenix and the Carpet* (1904) and *The Story of the Amulet* (1906). Anstey, moreover, was not really a children's writer but an adult humorist who saw the comic possibilities of fantasy, and the Nesbit fantasies have inherited something of this ambiguity of audience. They have the adult polish of the *Strand Magazine*, in the pages of which *Five Children* first appeared – as did *The Brass Bottle*.

An eloquent claim on behalf of Nesbit's talents has been made by Julia Briggs,[94] who has stated that 'all her best books explore the relationship between imagination, fiction, and life . . . Her children live primarily in an imaginative world, largely absorbed from their own reading, and act out their fantasies and expectations in the real world, in the process discovering important truths about that world and about themselves'. Certainly the Nesbit books are full of pointers which suggest this. There are frequent references to the children's favourite works of literature, the *Jungle Book*, La Motte Fouqué's *Sintram*, the Sherlock Holmes stories, the *Ingoldsby Legends*, and suchlike. Such books provide, in effect, manuals of conduct, used by the children to guide their enterprises.

'I'll be Sintram,' said Alice; 'and H.O. can be the Little Master.'
'What about Dicky?'

Oh, I can be the Pilgrim with the bones.'

'Hist!' whispered Alice. 'See his white fairy fur gleaming amid yonder covert!'

And I saw a bit of white too. It was Noël's collar, and it had come undone at the back.

So, again and again, the literature-derived dreams come down to earth. But are the children any wiser? Does the acting out of the literary fantasies truly lead the Bastables to discover truths about the real world and about themselves? It is hard not to feel that, at the end of *The Treasure Seekers*, the children are as naïve as when they set out.

*

The success of *The Treasure Seekers* was such that, in the early 1900s, Edith and Hubert Bland were able to enjoy a reasonably prosperous lifestyle, moving to Well House at Eltham in Kent, the 'Moat House' of *The Wouldbegoods*; there are lively accounts of the mildly bohemian house parties they gave there. But this comfortable period came to an end shortly before the First World War with Hubert's gradual blindness and then his death, and Edith found it increasingly hard to support herself by writing – ironically, she did not help her literary career by the sheer number of books she continued to write. She could not rid herself of the habit of hack-work, and her children's stories became progressively less inspired, in such books as *The Magic City* (1910) and *Wet Magic* (1913). The war virtually put an end to her output, and when it was over no publisher seemed to be interested in her. She found a second husband, a good-natured ex-seafaring widower known as 'Skipper', who seems to have been like one of the avuncular adults on the fringe of the Bastables' world. For a time she made a little money by taking in lodgers, then, when finances became impossible, she and Skipper moved into what her biographer politely describes as a bungalow, but which was in fact a pair of ex-War Office sheds. There she spent her final days. It was not until after her death (in 1924) that her children's fiction recovered and maintained its huge popularity. She is an author whose methods are comparatively easy to copy, and many have done so, though whether to the ultimate benefit of children's literature seems questionable.

4
Beatrix Potter
the ironist in Arcadia

There is perhaps a stereotype in many people's minds of the typical children's writer of the late Victorian and Edwardian periods. He or she is supposed to have been a lonely, withdrawn, introverted individual, scarcely able to achieve normal human relationships, and only capable of communicating his or her deepest feelings by talking to children or writing books for them. The creation of children's literature by such a person is, in other words, interpreted largely as an act of therapy for a damaged personality.

Beatrix Potter has generally been regarded in this light. The standard picture of her is derived from Margaret Lane's very readable biography *The Tale of Beatrix Potter*, first published in 1946. According to this, Beatrix Potter's childhood was 'abnormally secluded and lonely'; she then led a stiflingly boring adolescence and early womanhood, during which her life went on 'without change'; then, when she was still living with her parents as an unmarried daughter, came the writing of the Peter Rabbit books, which at last gave her 'an occupation, an objective'. The therapy having taken place, she was psychologically ready for marriage, and as Mrs William Heelis she quickly grew into an 'endearing and formidable personality' very different from the shy self-effacing Miss Potter of her early days. So says *The Tale of Beatrix Potter*.

Margaret Lane's book is well named, for it is something of a tale about its subject rather than a strictly accurate portrait. If it had appeared a decade or so later it might have been very different, for during the 1950s there came to light a journal kept by Beatrix Potter between the ages of fifteen and thirty, during that period of her life when nothing is supposed to have happened to her. The journal, written in cipher, shows that the young Miss Potter and the old Mrs Heelis were really one and the same person: that from her earliest years she was a determined, self-confident person who gradually and patiently matured as a writer and painter, who knew what she wanted, and was determined to get it. The creation of the children's books did not change her character; they were a natural and inevitable emanation of it at a period when her powers were at their peak.

This new picture of Beatrix Potter[95] is not only of interest in itself. Inevitably it also alters our attitude to her work. Indeed, when her books are looked at in the light of the journal they emerge as a linked, coherent body of writing, in which specific themes are developed and examined. Moreover, though she was writing for the very youngest children, those themes are close to the preoccupations of several of her predecessors and contemporaries in children's literature.

*

She was born eight years later than E. Nesbit and seven later than Kenneth Grahame, in 1866, and so flourished at the end of Victoria's reign. Yet in many ways she seems to have been a Regency figure. She was fascinated to the point of obsession with her paternal grand-mother's reminiscences of her own youth, and would write them down verbatim in her journal: details of clothes, habits of travel, any scrap of information she could cull about the way of life in those days. *The Tailor of Gloucester* is her particular homage to the most elegant era of English society, 'the time of swords and periwigs and full-skirted coats with flowered lappets'. But in fact all her books, with their ironically elegant diction and their emphasis upon the comedy of manners, have something about them of that period.

She devoured her grandmother's reminiscences with such an appetite largely because they provided a lively diversion from the stultified conversational round of her own home life. She was the daughter of Rupert and Helen Potter, as solidly respectable a couple as ever lived in the Kensington district of Victorian London. Both had inherited decent portions of their families' North Country cotton fortunes, and Beatrix's father never needed to practise his chosen profession of barrister. His life was on the whole unexciting, and Margaret Lane has a splendid passage in her biography in which she describes the tedium she imagines to have dominated 2 Bolton Gardens, the house in which the Potters lived:

> The ticking of the grandfather clock could be heard all over the house, like a slow heart-beat, and there were other reliable indica-tions of the time of day. At the same hour every morning Mr and Mrs Rupert Potter came down to the dining-room for breakfast, a meal consumed in silence. Between ten and eleven Mr Potter left for his club. At one o'clock a tray furnished with a small cutlet and a helping of rice pudding went up to the nursery by the back stairs, and as the clock struck two the carriage was at the door and Mrs Potter, small and inflexibly upright and dressed in black, came down the whitened

steps and got into it, and was driven away. At six o'clock Mr Cox, the butler, could be observed through the dining-room windows preparing a solemn ritual with napkins and spoons and forks on the mahogany table. Soon the curtains would be drawn and the nursery lamp be extinguished, and to the street the house would give no further evidence of life.

Certainly life in Bolton Gardens must have had its oppressive moments. Long afterwards, Beatrix spoke of the house as 'my unloved birthplace'. Yet her journal does not suggest that tedium was the dominant characteristic of her childhood; quite the opposite.

It is true that she was an only child until the age of five, but thereafter she had the companionship of her younger brother Bertram, and though he was away at school for much of the time, the two shared many hobbies and amusements. More to the point, much of her childhood was not spent in Bolton Gardens at all, but in two places visited regularly by her parents: Camfield Place, her paternal grand-mother's country house in Hertfordshire, and Dalguise House on the River Tay in Perthshire, which her father rented for summer visits for twelve consecutive years during her childhood. In both these places she was deeply happy, so much so that all life thereafter seemed an anticlimax, and she looked back to those times with feelings very close to those Kenneth Grahame had felt for the golden age of his own youth.

She wrote at length about both places in her journal, looking back at them when they were already chiefly things of the past. Life at her grandmother's house seemed to her in recollection a 'perfect whole, where all things are a part, the notes of the stable clock and the all pervading smell of new-mown hay, the distant sounds of the farmyard, the feeling of plenty, well-assured, indolent wealth, honourably earned and wisely spent, charity without ostentation, opulence without pride . . .'[96] Visits to Dalguise gave her an even greater sense of perfection; returning to it in her late teens, she realised how much its landscape had meant to her, and wrote simply in her journal: 'It is home.'

This sense of childhood security lost, but somehow recoverable by an act of the imagination, seems to have motivated her writings for children. But the recovery of the lost Arcadia is for her only the first stage in the process. Peter Rabbit and his fellows certainly move through a landscape as perfect in terms of physical beauty as that of Camfield or Dalguise. But the evocation of that landscape in words and pictures is not enough for Beatrix Potter; perhaps partly because, by the time she came to create her books, she had discovered and begun to inhabit another real Arcadia, the village of Sawrey in the Lake District, which she came to love deeply and where she gradually made her home, as escape from the parental fold became possible.[97] There was no need to be yearningly nostalgic about a childhood paradise in her stories; she had her feet planted on the soil of an adult one. Instead, she used the Arcadian setting as an ironic contrast and background to the blackly comic themes of her stories.

And yet she, above all Victorian and Edwardian children's writers, seems to have consciously understood the importance to the adult imagination of the childhood Arcadia. At the age of only eighteen she wrote in her journal:

> As we struggle on, the thoughts of that peaceful past time of childhood comes to us like soft music and a blissful vision through the snow. We do not wish we were back in it, unless we are daily broken-down, for the very good reason that it is impossible to be so, but it keeps one up, and there is a vague feeling that one day there will again be rest.

*

'As we struggle on . . .' What was it that already made her, at eighteen, regard life as a struggle? Simply, it seems, the constant tension at home between her own very strong will and her parents' cautious, fussy natures. By the time she was in her teens she had determined to be a painter, and she felt she was not receiving sufficient parental encouragement. Certainly she was allowed to have lessons, first in drawing (from a governess) and then in oils (from a professional lady painter), but she thought little of her instructors, and fretted that her mother did not give her more support – on a typical occasion she was stopped from painting, one winter's day, 'because mamma says the dressing-room [in which she was working] is too cold'. This was the kind of thing which seems to have caused family rows. She does not describe these directly in the journal, but often hints at them, writing of 'my self-will which brings me into so many scrapes', and declaring: 'My temper has been boiling like a kettle.'

And yet, if the thing is looked at a little more objectively, she seems to have been treated pretty well by her parents. Her father, far from being a dull old stick who simply pottered to and fro between his club and Bolton Gardens, was passionately interested in art and artists. He bought whatever pictures he could afford, including some of the originals of Randolph Caldecott's marvellous nursery rhyme illustrations, thereby influencing Beatrix's own style as an illustrator. He and the family (Beatrix included) were close friends of the painter Millais, in whose studio Mr Potter spent many hours, often taking photographs of sitters to help his friend's portrait work. He was an excellent amateur photographer, and Millais' celebrated picture 'Bubbles' was done partly with the aid of a plate Mr Potter had taken of the subject, the artist's grandson. Beatrix herself was encouraged by her father to become adept with the camera, though she never seems to have achieved much, perhaps because she mostly chose to photograph animals, who would not sit still long enough.

Her father also took her to the Royal Academy year after year, and her journal is full of strongly worded pieces of art criticism. She had innate good judgement, and though she saw very little great art until she was in her mid-teens she instinctively preferred it to the average Academy canvases. Turner she judged to be 'the greatest landscape painter that has ever lived'; Doré she considered merely vulgar, but she enjoyed the cartoons of Richard Doyle and of Phiz. She also knew exactly why she herself had to paint: it was 'the irresistible desire to copy any beautiful object which strikes the eye . . . and when I have a bad time come over me it is a stronger desire than ever, and settles on the queerest things, worse than queer sometimes. Last time, in the middle of September, I caught myself in the back yard making a careful and admiring copy of the swill bucket, and the laugh it gave me brought me round.'

The real enemy to her becoming a full-time painter seems to have been not parental discouragement but her own shyness, which she regarded as a family failing. It made her deeply reluctant to confess her ambitions (she never seems to have mentioned them to Millais) or to do anything to display her talent until she was in her thirties, although long before that she had developed a fine technique with line and water-colour. (Oil she never found congenial.) Yet she observed of her shyness: 'It is one of the peculiarities of my nature that when there is anything to be shy about, I don't care in the least.'

Though very reserved on the surface, she was privately full of firmly held opinions, by no means all of them conventional. She thought it ridiculous, for example, to fuss about nudity in art: 'The ostentatious covering of certain parts only, merely showing that the painter considers there is something which should be concealed, is far worse than pure unabashed nudity,' she wrote in her journal. Her family were Unitarians, but she privately rejected even this rather bare form of conventional religion: 'All outward forms of religion are almost useless, and are the cause of endless strife,' she wrote. 'What do Creeds matter, what possible difference does it make to anyone today whether the doctrine of the resurrection is correct or incorrect, or the miracles . . . Believe there is a great power silently working all things for good, behave yourself and never mind the rest.'

This was written when she was eighteen, by which time she had also developed a lively interest in politics. Gladstone was one of her family's pet hates (her father took a portrait picture of him in Millais' studio, but would not doff his hat when he met him in the street), and again and again Beatrix records gossip about the 'Old Gentleman' and his government. She was also horrified and fascinated by the unrest of the

times, particularly the frequent dynamitings in London by the Irish
home rule fanatics, and the public meetings of working men which
seemed to threaten riot or revolution. 'Times are awful,' she recorded in
1885. 'Father says we shall have the taxes ½ crown in a pound and
conscription . . . There is scarcely a night without the news-criers come
round the silent streets, sometimes after ten o'clock . . . Things of evil
omen, who ever heard of them proclaiming good tidings?'

There is much in her journal to suggest that she might easily have
become a novelist. She writes long descriptions of visits to relations or
family acquaintances, dwelling on nuances of behaviour and little
details of setting with a novelist's relish. 'The old butler hurried up the
steep staircase like a beetle. He turned out his feet at right angles; they
were very large, or rather his shiny shoes were, I could not make out his
feet, they were all knobs. I was much impressed by them as he went up
before, two steps at a time.' She has a particular eye for the niceties of
middle-class decorum, such as the prejudice against 'trade'. 'The house
was built in '59 by old Mr Ross,' she writes of a villa in which her family
is staying. 'I do not know if I ought to mention it, but I *believe* he was a
baker. He afterwards went to Australia and found a nugget which was
more genteel.' And she is tickled to see Millais trying to impress the
Duchess of Edinburgh, whose daughter is coming for a sitting, by
hiring an extra butler, simply because the Duchess has treated him as a
tradesman.

But it was paint, not words, that drew her attention most demand-
ingly during the years in which her character was developing. Nor can
one imagine her as an Edwardian novelist. Her literary imagination was
rooted firmly in the era of Jane Austen,[98] and her conscious stylistic
model was no less than the Authorised Version of the Bible. 'The sweet
rhythm of the authorised translation,' she called it, and one may
observe how often she uses biblical cadences for comic effect, and
employs a psalm-like caesura in the middle of her sentences:

> As the fish would not come off the plate, they put it into the red-hot
> crinkly paper fire in the kitchen; but it would not burn either. (*The
> Tale of Two Bad Mice*)

> But the trout was so displeased with the taste of the macintosh, that
> in less than half a minute it spat him out again; and the only thing it
> swallowed was Mr Jeremy's galoshes. (*The Tale of Jeremy Fisher*)

> He opened his mouth most unnecessarily wide; he certainly had not
> a tooth in his head. (*The Tale of Mrs Tittlemouse*)

She required a setting and a subject matter in which this formal irony
could flourish, and one cannot imagine it much at home in the themes
of the adult Edwardian novel.

In any case her imagination was particularly attracted by animals. No doubt this had begun in early childhood simply as a compensation for a certain emotional deprivation, but by the time she reached her teens it was a marked peculiarity. Again, her parents' attitude seems to have been one of tolerance, even encouragement; for she was allowed to keep all kinds of creatures, both alive and dead. She and her brother Bertram would bring corpses home from country rambles and dissect them to study their anatomy. Live specimens soon outnumbered dead ones; she kept as pets, at various times, a snake, a dormouse (who lived to be so old that its eyebrows turned white), a frog, a bat, and an entire family of snails, not to mention rats, hedgehogs, and various rabbits, whom she would take around on leather leads as if they were dogs. It was partly a kind of playing-with-dolls, partly a way of developing her talents at drawing and painting (for she became expert at getting them to sit still long enough for her pencil and brush), and partly an irrepressible urge to see them in human terms.

Quite where this urge came from is hard to say. She may have acquired something of it from childhood reading. Books in which animals took the main part, generally acting as commentators on human society, had been written specially for children since the mid-eighteenth century, in a tradition derived from Aesop and such medieval beast-epics as *Reynard the Fox*. More immediately, Beatrix Potter probably drew inspiration from Joel Chandler Harris's *Uncle Remus* (1880), which she certainly read when she was young. Yet one feels that she could have written her own tales had Harris's books never existed. The cunning of Brer Rabbit and Brer Fox, typical trickster-figures of folk-tale, is a far cry from the sedately civilised nastiness of Mr Tod, or Jemima Puddle-Duck's 'elegantly dressed gentleman' with 'black prick ears and sandy coloured whiskers' (the fox who lures her to his shed), or the snuff-taking Samuel Whiskers.

She completely avoided the trap of sentimentality in writing about animals. Though her pets were obviously close favourites, she recorded their deaths or misadventures coolly in her journal. And she seems to have had a special affection for the memory of her great-grandfather Abraham Crompton, who used to pick snails off an ivy-covered wall in his garden and eat them alive.

*

It was in the early 1890s, when she was in her mid-thirties, that she began to write picture-letters to children of her acquaintance about the supposed adventures of her pets. She also determined at about the same time to get some of her drawings of animals dressed in human clothes accepted for publication, and she duly placed several with a London greetings card firm. But several more years went by before *The Tale of Peter Rabbit*, her first fully fledged story, was complete in every detail.

Even then, like Lewis Carroll, she published the first edition at her own expense, and only when it proved an undisputed success did the London publishing house of Warne make her an offer for her work. So it was not until 1902 that she could sit down with confidence to produce the body of writing and drawing for which she had been preparing so long.

Reading through the Beatrix Potter books in order of publication, one discerns not only their very adult view of the world – surely recalled by anyone who knew them in childhood – but also the fact that they are a connected body of writing, dealing stage by stage with a set of themes.

In the first stage, admittedly, the stones are very simple and the themes not ambitious. *The Tale of Peter Rabbit* itself, though her most famous book, is actually almost her least remarkable, certainly one of her least ambitious. Yet its single theme is a dark one, familiar in folk-tales: the pursuit of a hapless individual (Peter) by a vengeful giant (Mr McGregor the gardener). Peter is the youngest of his family and should therefore, according to fairy-tale principles, be the luckiest; but he is a fourth child, not a third, and the luck has passed him by. The nature of the threat is made clear to him at the beginning: 'Your Father was put in a pie by Mrs McGregor.' But he ignores this old legend, and ventures, Jack-and-the-beanstalk fashion, into the ogre's very castle:

> Flopsy, Mopsy, and Cottontail, who were good little bunnies, went down the lane to gather blackberries: but Peter, who was very naughty, ran straight away to Mr McGregor's garden, and squeezed under the gate!

He begins to help himself to the giant's treasure ('First he ate some lettuces and some French beans; and then he ate some radishes'), but comes face to face with the giant and takes to his heels. Strikingly, his eventual escape is utterly unheroic; no folk-tale hero would arrive home in a pathetic condition and be put to bed by his mother as a punishment; moreover she

> made some camomile tea; and she gave a dose of it to Peter! 'One table-spoonful to be taken at bed-time.' But Flopsy, Mopsy, and Cottontail had bread and milk and blackberries for supper.

The expectations of the folk-tale or fairy story have been upset. Instead of being presented with the ordered, Utopian universe of folklóre, where heroes can be heroes and giants are properly defeated, we have a much more true-to-life account of an individual's unpleasant encounter with a force greater than himself. *Peter Rabbit*, though slight, is an ironic comment on the giant-killer stories.[99]

The other three books which concern Peter Rabbit himself continue to develop this theme. *The Tale of Benjamin Bunny* (1904) and *The Tale of the Flopsy Bunnies* (1909) are progressive stages in the defeat of Mr McGregor, who by the end of *Flopsy Bunnies* has been made into a proper fool, just as giants should be. But there are enemies even more unpleasant than giants, traitors among one's own race. *The Tale of Mr Tod* (1912) has for its villain somebody who should by rights be the rabbits' ally: the badger Tommy Brock, who turns ogre when they are off their guard. And in *Mr Tod*, as in *Peter Rabbit*, there is no heroic victory; the 'heroes', Peter and Benjamin, merely grab the rabbit-babies and run for their lives while Brock's attention is distracted by his enemy Mr Tod. The *Peter Rabbit* sequence ends as it began, with the ignominy of flight.

Two other Beatrix Potter stories, both early, deal with the motif of ogre and little man. *The Tale of Squirrel Nutkin* (1903) is an exercise in taking the 'hero' as close as possible to the ogre without getting eaten up. Nutkin, indeed, goes too far; while the other squirrels soberly present their tributes to Old Brown, the owl on whose island they are nutting, Nutkin behaves like a Brer Rabbit or Till Eulenspiegel, dancing up and down under Old Brown's very beak and chanting riddles at him. Instead of being content to observe time-honoured religious rituals and make sacrifice to the tribal god, he laughs in that god's very face – and Beatrix Potter is fully aware of the threatening nature of the riddle-game in which Nutkin tries to engage Old Brown:[100]

> Nutkin was excessively impertinent in his manner. He bobbed up and down like a little red *cherry*, singing –
>
> > 'Riddle me, riddle me, rot-tot-tote!
> > A little wee man, in a red red coat!
> > A staff in his hand, and a stone in his throat;
> > If you tell me this riddle, I'll give you a groat.'
>
> Now this riddle is as old as the hills; Mr Brown paid no attention whatever to Nutkin.

The riddle, like others chanted by Nutkin, is indeed 'as old as the hills', and one of the strengths of Beatrix Potter's work is that it is rooted again and again in traditional nursery rhymes and folk-tales, from which it gains resonances beyond the immediate story.

Squirrel Nutkin fares worse than Peter Rabbit, who merely lost his clothes in the encounter with Mr McGregor; Nutkin has his tail pulled off, a castration-like calamity which ends the story with striking abruptness:

Old Brown carried Nutkin into his house, and held him up by the tail, intending to skin him; but Nutkin pulled so very hard that his tail broke in two, and he dashed up the staircase and escaped out of the attic window. And to this day, if you meet Nutkin up a tree and ask him a riddle, he will throw sticks at you, and stamp his feet and scold, and shout – 'Cuck-cuck-cuck-cur-r-r-cuck-k-k!'

The Tale of Jeremy Fisher (1906), the other story in this early group which deals with the aggressor-and-victim theme, resembles *Peter Rabbit* in that the hero escapes with no worse injury than the loss of his clothes and his possessions. On the other hand, Mr Jeremy Fisher, a frog, is actually seized in the jaws of his antagonist the trout:

> . . . a really *frightful* thing it would have been, if Mr Jeremy had not been wearing a macintosh! A great big enormous trout came up – ker-pflop-p-p-p! with a splash – and it seized Mr Jeremy with a snap, 'Ow! Ow! Ow!' – and then it turned and dived down to the bottom of the pond!

The whole of *Jeremy Fisher*, in which the story develops with sinister slowness and is pervaded by the oppressive dampness of the river atmosphere, is an accumulation of threats. More subtle in this respect than *Peter Rabbit* and *Squirrel Nutkin*, the book suggests that there are worse things than ogres. Dangers lurk around every corner, and perpetual vigilance is necessary. Long before the appearance of the trout, Jeremy Fisher has been frightened by a water-rat and injured by a stickleback which he inadvertently lands with his fishing line. Nor is it a simple matter of hero and enemies: Jeremy Fisher himself is a predator to smaller creatures, for he eats a butterfly sandwich for his lunch, and at the end of the book he dines off 'roasted grasshopper with lady-bird sauce'.

*

The theme of predator and victim is present in the Potter books to the end, but comparatively few of them (and those mostly early ones) make it their principal motif. In a second stage of her writing, Beatrix Potter dwells largely on a very different notion, the imagination of an Arcadian landscape and society. Her search for Arcadia, like Kenneth Grahame's, was no doubt partly motivated by the desire to return to what she called 'that peaceful past time of childhood'. *The Tale of Mrs Tiggy-Winkle* (1905) surely derives from this, for it is the little girl Lucie who is able to climb the hillside (again, a kind of fairy-tale journey) and discover the old hedgehog who is washerwoman to the animals and birds, and whose kitchen, like Badger's house in *The Wind in the Willows* and Bilbo's hobbit-hole in *The Hobbit*, is a visible manifestation of Arcadian peace and security. Yet while no external threat enters this most utopian of Potter's books, there is none the less something faintly sinister about Mrs Tiggy-Winkle herself:

> Her little black nose went sniffle, sniffle, snuffle, and her eyes went twinkle, twinkle; and underneath her cap – where Lucie had yellow curls – that little person had PRICKLES!

And at the end, the dream is shattered: Lucie turns round at the stile and sees not the cheerful dumpy washerwoman making her way back up the hillside, but a little brown hedgehog running away as if in fear. Beatrix Potter will never allow the Arcadian vision to remain untainted by threat or fear. Her world is, on almost every page of her books, as alarming as Alice's.

The other book in which she deliberately creates a utopia is *The Tailor of Gloucester* (1903). This was her own favourite of all her stories, and one can see why, for in it she indulges her own fascination with the era of her grandparents and great-grandparents. Here again is that central Arcadian scene, the snug kitchen (in this case the tailor's home) in which every kind of really valuable comfort is to be found. Nemesis is not absent: the tailor is threatened by poverty and illness, and is cheated by his own cat. But all is finally turned to good. The mice, preserved by the tailor from becoming the cat's dinner, show their gratitude by taking over the sick tailor's work for him, just as the elves help the poor shoemaker in Grimm. While this takes place, there is a carolling of nursery rhymes, sung by the animals and birds at midnight on Christmas Eve in the attics and on the rooftops of snowbound Gloucester. It is a strikingly beautiful scene, rendered all the more effective by the grumbles of the mouse-deprived cat Simpkin as he trudges through the snow. Fairy tale, nursery rhyme, and Arcadian fantasy all come together for a moment in perfect balance. No wonder Beatrix Potter was proud of the book.

But she was not content to repeat herself, and her work soon moved on to a third stage, in which Arcadian settings were used as a backdrop for a dissection of social pretension. *The Tale of Two Bad Mice* (1904), *The Pie and the Patty-Pan* (1905), *The Tale of Tom Kitten* (1907), and *The Tale of Mrs Tittlemouse* (1910) are all comedies of manners. In *Two Bad Mice* the target is the pretentious, over-furnished, middle-class life of the dolls' house, surely a reflection of that led by the Potters in Bolton Gardens. The house, into which come the destructive mice Tom Thumb and Hunca Munca (whose names refer to Fielding's burlesque), is a typical late Victorian mansion in which everything is for show rather than use. The food appears to be superb, but 'underneath the shiny paint it was made of nothing but plaster'.[101] The mice expose the pretensions and pull everything to pieces. Similarly *The Pie and the*

Patty-Pan is an elaborate farce which satirises social politeness. The dog Ribby, who has perfect party manners and knows all the conventions, thinks it impolite to tell her hostess what she really wants or does not want to eat, and in consequence has to indulge in an elaborate deception, which is a dismal failure and has ludicrous consequences. *The Tale of Tom Kitten* deals with the folly of forcing children into tidy clothes and of trying to make a good impression on visitors. *The Tale of Mrs Tittlemouse*, perhaps the most subtle of this sequence of stories, portrays that all too familiar social figure, the unwanted guest. Mr Jackson the toad makes himself tiresomely at home in the parlour of the house-proud, socially conscious Mrs Tittle-mouse. In all these stories the setting suggests a Utopia – the dolls' house in *Two Bad Mice*, the village of Sawrey in *The Pie and the Patty-Pan* and *Tom Kitten*, and the snug kitchen in *Mrs Tittlemouse* – but the events are a reminder of the impossibility of dwelling in the Arcadian dream.

In the third and penultimate stage of her writing, Beatrix Potter returns to the motif of pursuit and pursuer; but now the canvas is much larger, the irony sharper, the comedy more black. *The Tale of Jemima Puddle-Duck* (1908) is, as Beatrix Potter herself pointed out, a reworking of *Little Red Riding-Hood*; the sexual implications are even clearer than in Perrault's story, with Jemima strongly suggesting an empty-headed maiden and the fox behaving exactly like an elegant, caddish Victorian seducer.

The Roly-Poly Pudding (1908), afterwards retitled *The Tale of Samuel Whiskers*, is perhaps Beatrix Potter's masterpiece, in which comedy and irony are perfectly held in balance. It is certainly in this book that her language is at its most ironic. She has often been censured for using long words which children do not understand, but the deliberately over-elaborate vocabulary is a principal instrument of the comedy. In *Peter Rabbit* the hero, trapped in Mr McGregor's garden, gives himself up for lost, but 'some friendly sparrows . . . implored him to exert himself'. In *The Pie and the Patty-Pan* the ridiculous Dr Maggoty, summoned by Ribby because Duchess believes she has swallowed a patty-pan, 'accompanied her with alacrity', so that their progress through Sawrey 'was most conspicuous' – a perfect descrip-tion of social embarrassment. Now, in *The Roly-Poly Pudding*, the most elegant diction is put into the mouths of the two old rats who have been debating how best to cook and eat Tom Kitten:

> 'I fear that we shall be obliged to leave this pudding.'
> 'But I am persuaded that the knots would have proved indigest-ible, whatever you may urge to the contrary.'

It is very funny and very nasty, and it is much to her credit that Beatrix Potter dared to serve up such strong meat to small children.

*

In the last stage of her writing she turned to an autobiographical theme. All through her twenties and thirties she had continued to live with her parents, but as her fortieth birthday approached she became engaged to Norman Warne, a member of the family who published her books. However, he died before they could marry, and this particular escape route to independence was shut off for the time being. It was not until 1913 that she at last acquired a husband, a meek country solicitor named William Heelis, who was quite happy to play second fiddle to her. Not surprisingly, Escape is the dominant theme of what she wrote in this period and after: *The Tale of Pigling Bland* (1913), *The Tale of Johnny Town-Mouse* (1918), *The Fairy Caravan* (1929), and *The Tale of Little Pig Robinson* (1930). Of these only *Pigling Bland* matches up to her fine work of the middle period, being written in the heat of her own actual escape. The others are rather low-key meditations on freedom and running away. But *Pigling Bland* is tightly constructed and intricate, based on three nursery rhymes ('Tom, Tom, the Piper's Son', 'Over the Hills and Far Away', and 'This Little Pig Went to Market').

Pigling does not want to go to market, but at first he obeys the rules:

> He glanced wistfully along the road towards the hills and then set off walking obediently the other way, buttoning up his coat against the rain. He had never wanted to go, and the idea of standing all by himself in a crowded market, to be stared at, pushed, and hired by some big strange farmer was very disagreeable –
>
> 'I wish I could have a little garden and grow potatoes,' said Pigling Bland.

Beatrix Potter had for many years glanced wistfully at the hills, but had walked obediently the other way, remaining in the family fold and working off some of her feelings about the society which imprisoned her by creating her bitter little stories. Now escape had come, when she was almost in her fiftieth year – it is notable that Pigling and his lady-love Pigwig escape across the county border by pretending to be *old*. And when the moment of actual escape is reached, the story becomes too exhilarating for prose:

> They ran, and they ran, and they ran down the hill, and across a short cut on level green turf at the bottom, between pebble beds and rushes.
>
> They came to the river, they came to the bridge – they crossed it hand in hand –
>
> then over the hills and far away she danced with Pigling Bland!

5

The Wind in the Willows

Though the notion of Escape dominates *The Golden Age* and *Dream Days* as strongly as it does the stories of Beatrix Potter, Kenneth Grahame was incapable of finding any real-life escape route from the pressures of his existence. In the years that followed the publication of *Dream Days* (in 1898) he became even more deeply trapped in a life which was far from what he desired. The consequence was that, for a whole decade after *Dream Days* had appeared, he maintained a virtual literary silence.

One can deduce from *The Golden Age* and its sequel that Grahame was not short on the romantic instinct; if those stories are to be trusted, he had, at least in childhood, a habit of falling in love with unattainable idealised females (a baker's wife, a girl in spangled tights at the circus, and other dream-princesses). It appears that their very unattainability was part of the attraction; certainly Grahame reached his late thirties without coming anywhere within hailing distance of marriage, and the only relationship which might have led that way seems[102] to have ended because the lady (apparently a cousin) was too 'forward', and actually made advances to him. But then, quite suddenly, he was hooked and landed by one Elspeth Thomson.

She was the daughter of a Scottish inventor whose mother had remarried after the father's death, and had brought Elspeth to London. The girl – if she could still be called that, for she was only two years younger than Grahame – was a kind of ferociously flirtatious blue-stocking. As a child she had specialised in whimsically precocious friendships with Tennyson and other great literary men, and she had kept up the habit of pursuing successful writers. Grahame was at first merely one such prey. Unfortunately the fact that he wrote stories about children made her all the more fascinated by him. By the late 1890s the fashion for sentimentality towards children and childhood was at its height. Grahame's own writings had helped to nurture it, though of course they were not intended to be taken sentimentally. Elspeth Thomson was among those who adored *The Golden Age* simply because it was about children, without realising that it was implicitly opposed to soft-hearted attitudes towards the young. In fact

she was a worshipper at that by now much-visited temple, the shrine of
the Beautiful Child. And she even enrolled Grahame himself temporarily into her religion.

> Wensdy arnoon
> My Dearie
> Fanx fr mornin letter wich I redd *insted* o gettin up & ketchin a
> bote wot wos goin to Exmouf it wasn't tickler erly but Id ad a rarver
> wakefle nite so ventchly I sor the bote steem orf . . . My room as a
> balkiny & a stript ornin & looks over the arber so I sees the botes I
> orter ketch goin orf wich is next bes ter ketchin of em . . .
> Goodbye darlin pet & I wish you were here . . .
>
> > Your lovin
> > Dino[103]

This – though one finds it hard to believe it at first – is Kenneth
Grahame writing to Elspeth Thomson in the early months of their
courtship. Mock baby-talk was the *lingua franca* between the two of
them, though one can hardly imagine it was a language Grahame would
ever have wished to speak, left to his own devices. But Elspeth
conducted things very cunningly, taking advantage of an illness of his
to pay unchaperoned visits, thereby compromising him (it seems) to a
point where marriage was almost obligatory. They were married in the
summer of 1899. There is a tradition that Grahame's sister Helen,
astonished by the newspaper announcement of the impending wedding
and herself detesting Elspeth, asked Kenneth if the marriage was really
going ahead, and he answered in a tone of the deepest gloom, 'I suppose
so; I suppose so.'

It was a disaster from the beginning. Elspeth immediately conceived
a child, but it would appear that Kenneth thereafter shied away from
sex. Elspeth poured out, in the bad poems she wrote in large quantities,
her resentment at his coldness and neglect of her, and when the child,
Alastair, was born she made him the focus of all her hopes and
affections. Unfortunately Alastair was blind in one eye from birth and
generally sickly, but Elspeth treated him as an incipient genius, so that
he developed a precocious, cheeky manner which nauseated Grahame's
friends.

Grahame himself made a few feeble efforts to extricate himself from
the situation. He spent as much time as possible in the company of male
friends who understood and shared his nature and his tastes, notably
Arthur Quiller-Couch, at whose home at Fowey in Cornwall he was a
frequent visitor. The Fowey river and estuary contributed more than is
generally realised to the setting of *The Wind in the Willows*, while
another Fowey resident, a mildly eccentric boating bachelor called
Edward Atkinson, seems to have been among those whose personality

went to make up the Water Rat. Another form of Escape tried by
Grahame in the early days of his marriage was moving his family back
to the setting of the happiest part of his childhood; for in 1907 he took
a house at Cookham Dene by the Thames. But nothing could really
ease things. During 1904 both parties made more serious moves to
extricate themselves: Elspeth spent much of the year away from home,
taking the cure at a Lincolnshire spa, and while she was still away
Kenneth set off alone for Spain on one of his southward migrations that
were as near as he dared go to real escaping. But then Alastair
contracted peritonitis, and both parents had to return home. No
further attempts at a separation were made, possibly because by this
time Kenneth had begun to rediscover his old escape route, writing.

> Presently the tactful Mole slipped away and returned with a pencil
> and a few half-sheets of paper, which he placed on the table at his
> friend's elbow . . . When he peeped in again some time later, the Rat
> was absorbed and deaf to the world; alternately scribbling and
> sucking the top of his pencil. It is true that he sucked a good deal
> more than he scribbled; but it was joy to the Mole to know that the
> cure had at least begun.

*

The Wind in the Willows began as bedtime stories for Alastair in May
1904, just as the child had reached his fourth birthday. Or rather, that
part of the book which concerns the adventures of Toad originated in
this fashion. But those adventures form only one of several layers in the
book; the others are very different in character, and one cannot imagine
that their creation had much to do with Grahame's son.

Alastair was nevertheless the catalyst for the simplest elements in the
story. The original night-time tales told to him sound much as if they
were in imitation of Beatrix Potter, whose books were just then
beginning to appear, with great success; they were certainly known to
Grahame, for the rabbits in his short story 'Bertie's Escapade', written
at the same time as *The Wind in the Willows*, are called Peter and Benjie.
The first stories told to Alastair are reported to have been about 'moles,
giraffes & water-rats', a fairly random selection of the sort of creatures
Beatrix Potter might have written about, though the giraffe seems
incongruous and soon dropped out. The Toad appears to have arrived
fairly early on. Probably the saga continued in a random way over the
next three years; certainly in May 1907 when Alastair was on holiday
with his governess, his father was writing him story-letters in which
Toad's adventures were well under way. The first of these letters refers
to Toad supposedly being 'taken prisoner by brigands' and a ransom
being demanded, but this proves to have been one of Toad's tricks; the

truth (the letter says) is that he climbed out of the window early one morning, went to a hotel, stole a motor car, and has vanished. 'I fear he is a low bad animal,' says Alastair's father. In subsequent letters, written over the next four months, Toad's exploits are described much as in the published book, at first in terse synopsis form, but gradually in full-length narrative.[104]

The book could have been published in this form, simply as a farcical account of the career of the irrepressible Toad. Grahame, however, seems to have shown no desire to do this, and quite rightly. Toad's encounters with the English judicial system – police, magistrate, prison warders – and his flight from prison via engine cab, canal boat, and stolen horse have a certain energy, resembling eighteenth-century picaresque, and Toad is an amiable trickster of the standard folk-tale type. But this idiom was not Graham's *forte*, and he does not seem very comfortable in it. There is a certain amount of parody – of Harrison Ainsworth's historical novels in the scene where Toad arrives at the prison ('"Oddsbodikins!" said the sergeant of police . . . "Rouse thee, old loon, and take over from us this vile Toad, a criminal of deepest guilt"'), and of George Borrow's *Lavengro*, in the scene where Toad sells the horse to the gypsy ('"He's a blood horse, he is, partly; not the part you see, of course – another part"'). But this all suggests uneasiness of authorial control; the parodies would mean nothing to children, so who is Grahame writing for? As W. W. Robson has observed, in the prison sequence 'the authorial or editorial voice itself seems to have gone slightly crazy'.[105] Perhaps Grahame felt he should be writing a different kind of book. At all events he was soon doing so.

He continued to work at Toad's adventures after the story-telling to Alastair had ceased, at the encouragement of Constance Smedley, an American lady who represented the magazine *Everybody's* in England. She lived near Grahame in Berkshire and was sent by her editor to persuade him to write another book. It seems that she discovered that he was telling the story of Toad to Alastair, and encouraged him to put it on paper; under protest he responded, and this later stage of work on *The Wind in the Willows* brought it gradually to the form we know. It was published in 1908.

*

There is nothing remarkable about the fact that the original bedtime stories for Grahame's son concerned animals. Largely thanks to Beatrix Potter, many Edwardian children (or at least those with inventive parents or nursemaids) must have been listening to the same sort of thing. Alastair himself was nicknamed Mouse. But at some point Grahame must have realised, if only subconsciously, that an animal story also provided the perfect vehicle for the kind of thing he most wanted to write.

His disastrous marriage had made him turn with deeper passion than ever to the things that had concerned him in *Pagan Papers* and the *Golden Age* stories: complete emotional freedom from the control of 'grown ups'; a boyish delight in outdoor pursuits sought not for muscular exercise but spiritual refreshment; and always a longing glance towards the far horizon which offers the possibility of complete and utter Escape – flight to an Arcadia even more perfect than that offered by these daydreams. Suddenly, in the chapters of *The Wind in the Willows* that he wrote after the Toad adventures were complete, all these things burst out.

And bursting out is just what happens at the beginning of the book. As anyone who studies it alongside Grahame's biography must realise, Mole's burrowing up to the surface at the start of Chapter One is the author himself letting his deepest preoccupations break out from their prison in his mind and come into the daylight. Pretence does not have to be kept up any more. 'This is fine!' Mole says to himself. 'This is better than whitewashing!'

The greatness of *The Wind in the Willows* lies largely in what comes next. Of all the Victorians and Edwardians who tried to create Arcadia in print, only Grahame really managed it. His opening chapter gives a full, rich portrait of the earthly paradise,[106] expressed in a symbol that is likely to strike a chord with all readers and was particularly meaningful to his own generation: the River.

The immediate source of the landscape and characters of *The Wind in the Willows* – apart from the slight influence of Beatrix Potter on the Toad chapters – is Richard Jefferies. In *Bevis* you may find the same languorous description of water's edge and woodland, while *Wood Magic* supplies the notion of tribal and social upheavals among the animals, and even has passages where words are whispered by the reeds, the river, and the wind. But there is little suggestion of Grahame's River – with a capital R – in Jefferies' book. Rivers are, of course, timeless symbols in literature, but the late Victorians found a special meaning in them. By the middle of the nineteenth century, Britain's rivers in general and the Thames in particular had been tamed by a system of locks and weirs, and the decline of the old commercial barge traffic (taken away first by canals and then by railways) left them open, as they had never been before, as a pleasure ground for anyone who cared to pick up a pair of oars. In consequence, thousands of those who lived in the sprawling towns and whose lives were dominated by urban industrial society – Londoners very much among them – were taking to the water. Grahame had observed this during his early days at the Bank of England, when he helped with F. J. Furnivall's working-men's rowing club. Indeed, he seems to have known about the River as an escape route since his schooldays at St Edward's in Oxford, where there was not only the Thames but its tributary the Cherwell to explore in

skiff or punt.[107] Many times in *The Golden Age* the experience of
Escape is bound up with a journey by water, usually along a willow-
fringed river; and so it must have been for many young men in
Grahame's time. One literary result of this was Jerome K. Jerome's
Three Men in a Boat (1889), to which *The Wind in the Willows* has
more than a slight resemblance. Jerome's book, though outwardly far
more comic than Grahame's, slips again and again into ponderous
musings which, poor stuff though they are, show their author's
awareness of the River as a numinous subject.

Grahame, then, was choosing a very popular symbol when he
expressed the Arcadian life in terms of the River Bank. In many ways he
was writing specifically about the *bachelor* Arcadia, unencumbered by
women. Mole's first meeting with the Water Rat, their picnic together
with its catalogue of good food, and their homeward row during which
Mole makes a fool of himself by grabbing the oars and upsetting the
boat, is a perfect expression of the delights of the all-male life as enjoyed
by Grahame in the company of such friends as Furnivall, Quiller-
Couch, and his Fowey boating acquaintance Edward Atkinson – a life
without many responsibilities, but certainly not without etiquette. The
shy, slightly effeminate, and privately rebellious Mole, bursting out
from his private confines, is both coming to terms with his own nature
as he 'entered into the joy of running water' (a phrase strikingly
reminiscent of *The Water-Babies*) and is being initiated into the
outdoor, gently muscular world that Kingsley, Furnivall, and the other
Christian Socialists knew so well, a world which offered them a form of
Escape which was quite adequate for high days and holidays.

It is in one sense a very restrained world. No questions must be asked
about people's private activities, and Badger and Otter appear and
vanish without apology ('Animal etiquette forbade any sort of comment on the sudden disappearance of one's friends at any moment, for
any reason or no reason whatever'). But there is deeply warm
friendship for anyone who wants it and is acceptable to this all-male
group:

> 'Look here! I really think you had better come and stop with me for a
> little time . . . And I'll teach you to row, and to swim, and you'll soon
> be as handy on the water as any of us.' The Mole was so touched by
> his kind manner of speaking that he could find no voice to answer
> him; and he had to brush away a tear or two with the back of his paw.

Only three things mar the perfection of the landscape. One is the
Wild Wood. In recent years it has become customary to regard *The
Wind in the Willows* largely as a social allegory, with the Wild Wood
and its inhabitants standing for the rebellious proletariat. This layer of
meaning undoubtedly exists within the book, as we shall see; but in the

opening chapter it is not touched upon. Here, with the River Bank standing so clearly for all that is good, comradely, and humane in (male) human nature, the Wild Wood intrudes itself darkly into a corner of the picture as a symbol of the unpleasant possibilities of one's personal psychology, the unhealthy imaginings (presumably chiefly sexual) which are apt to cause disturbances when vigilance is relaxed:

> 'Well, of course – there – are others,' explained the Rat in a hesitating sort of way. 'Weasels – and stoats – and foxes – and so on. They're all right in a way – I'm very good friends with them – pass the time of day when we meet, and all that – but they break out sometimes, there's no denying it, and then – well, you can't really trust them, and that's the fact.'

The second threat is one we have met already in Grahame's writings. The River is not in itself the extent of the visible landscape; it forms a boundary or frontier, and there are other possibilities beyond it, chief among them the allure of the far horizon, the Wide World, 'Where it's all blue and dim, and one sees what may be hills or perhaps they mayn't, and something like the smoke of towns, or is it only cloud-drift?' This is Escape taken to its furthest possibilities, real flight from all responsibility, just as Grahame's father had flown from his family and vanished across the Channel. In *The Golden Age*, full-blown Escape of this sort was treated as a positive, morally acceptable goal – the Roman Road to the perfect city. In *The Wind in the Willows*, a more mature work which shows the imprint of Grahame's increased knowledge of the world, it is recognised for what it really is, a dangerous siren-call that the person of sense cannot dare to listen to:

> 'Beyond the Wild Wood comes the Wide World,' said the Rat. 'And that's something that doesn't matter, either to you or me. I've never been there, and I'm never going, nor you either, if you've got any sense at all. Don't ever refer to it again, please.'

But Grahame also knows that the call cannot be silenced, and later in the book it is the disciplined Rat, rather than the inquisitive, jejune Mole, who responds to it and nearly succumbs.

The third and final threat to the River Bank, and to the stability of the dream, is that which in the event nearly triumphs: Toad Hall. It was a work of some ingenuity for Grahame to link his comic narrative about Toad to his Arcadian vision of the River Bank.[108] Later in the book, Toad's uncertain social position, his *nouveau riche* ambitions, are the principal source of the comedy. But at the beginning, before *The Wind in the Willows* has become a social parable, Toad is not a *parvenu* so much as a psychological misfit. In the structure of the book's first chapter he represents the threat to the individual from the excesses of his own nature. He constantly 'goes over the top'. While Rat and Mole indulge soberly in the gentle pleasure of 'messing about in boats', Toad goes 'a-pleasuring' to excess, and gorges himself on what should be simple delights:

> 'Once, it was nothing but sailing,' said the Rat. 'Then he tired of that and took to punting. Nothing would please him but to punt all day and every day, and a nice mess he made of it. Last year it was house-boating . . . He was going to spend the rest of his life in a house-boat. It's all the same, whatever he takes up; he gets tired of it, and starts on something fresh.'
> 'Such a good fellow, too,' remarked the Otter reflectively. 'But no stability – especially in a boat!'

'Stability' is precisely the quality that Toad lacks. He is certainly 'a good fellow': even at the height of his misdemeanours he retains the fundamental sympathy of his fellow-creatures. But he cannot refrain from over indulgence, and he entirely lacks that *gravitas* or sobriety which is abundantly possessed by Mole, Rat, and Badger, and which is essential to the proper enjoyment of the Arcadian life of the River Bank. Many real-life models for Toad have been suggested: Grahame may have had in mind the tantrums and outrageous behaviour which his own son Alastair is reported to have often indulged in; he may very likely have been thinking of Oscar Wilde, whose scandalous excesses had recently (he was imprisoned in 1895) implicated much of English male society, particularly the Yellow Book circle in which Grahame himself had briefly moved. What seems certain is that, within the structure of the early chapters of *The Wind in the Willows*, Toad is meant to represent Everyman as much as are Mole and Rat, but in his case Everyman run riot. He is not, in this early part of the book, a Till Eulenspiegel or a jester so much as a warning.

The second chapter, 'The Open Road', expounds this further. Toad's *hubris* has now led him to dismiss the River as a 'silly boyish amusement', and he sets off for 'the Life Adventurous'. But his attempt to reach the Wide World – the ultimate Escape – by such crude means is doomed to failure. Toad is restlessly dissatisfied with the new horizons; the journey ends in the ditch (with the ruin of the horse-drawn caravan), and Toad's sights become set on yet another form of excess (the fast motor car). His companions Rat and Mole pine for the River Bank.

By now, we may suspect that the River is not just a symbol for the perfect bachelor life, but for something greater, perhaps Imagination itself. Is not Mole the apprentice artist discovering the possibilities of the imaginative life, and being initiated into it by Rat, already practised in it? We are constantly being told that Rat is a poet; Mole is at first contemptuous of his poetry-writing:

'I don't know that I think so *very* much of that little song, Rat,' observed the Mole, cautiously. He was no poet himself and didn't care who knew it; and he had a candid nature.

But his increasing experience of the River Bank changes his attitude. When he and Rat encounter the great god Pan on the enchanted island, Mole cannot at first hear the music of the Pan-pipes which bewitches Rat, but then he does:

Breathless and transfixed the Mole stopped rowing as the liquid run of that glad piping broke on him like a wave, caught him up, and possessed him utterly.

And finally, when Rat is undergoing a spiritual-psychological crisis, and is fighting the siren-call of the south in 'Wayfarers All', it is Mole who perceives that the cure for his friend's condition is poetry – and who himself turns poet in his attempt to win his friend back to the River Bank:

Casually, then, and with seeming indifference, the Mole turned his talk to the harvest that was being gathered in, the towering wagons and their straining teams, the growing ricks, and the large moon rising over bare acres dotted with sheaves. He talked of the reddening apples around, of the browning nuts, of jams and preserves and the distilling of cordials; till by easy stages such as these he reached midwinter, its hearty joys and its snug home life, and then he became simply lyrical.

By the conclusion of the book, then, Mole is fully initiated into the life of the Imagination, the life of the artist. He who at the start 'was no poet' is now 'simply lyrical'.

Toad is a poet too, but his odes are hymns of self-love; not without merit, perhaps, and a little resembling the boasts of great heroes in ancient literature, but ultimately the poetry of excess and self-indulgence:

He got so puffed up with conceit that he made up a song as he walked in praise of himself . . . It was perhaps the most conceited song that any animal ever composed.

'The world has held great Heroes,
As history-books have showed;
But never a name to go down to fame
Compared with that of Toad!'

Yet Toad, too, grows in wisdom, and by the end of the book has learnt to keep his boastful poems to himself. He recites 'Toad's Last Little Song' in the privacy of his bedroom, and then, descending to the banquet celebrating his return to Toad Hall, maintains a discreet silence. Poetry has been restored to its rightful place in the order of things.

If the Wild Wood – the subject of the book's third chapter – symbolises the darker side of human psychology, it also has a place in that layer of *The Wind in the Willows* which examines the proper and improper role of Imagination in the individual's life. Here, it seems to stand for the tangle of rich and dangerous symbolism which threatens the mental life of even the most sober of artists. The image is not unusual; for example, Charles Williams, friend of C. S. Lewis, used the wood Broceliande to carry just this meaning in his Arthurian cycle of poems, *Taliessin through Logres*. Williams described this wood as 'a place of making', from which either good or evil imaginings may come, and so it is with Grahame's Wild Wood.

The most striking fact about the Wild Wood is that, despite its threatening nature, Badger dwells at the heart of it; and Badger is the most wise and perfectly balanced character in the book, with his gruff common sense, his dislike of triviality (he chooses to come into Society only when it suits him), and his strength of character which can – at least temporarily – master even the excesses of Toad. Badger is, of course, a portrait of a certain kind of English landed gentleman, but he is far more. He is the still centre around which the book's various storms may rage, but who is scarcely touched by them. He is, one may surmise, the deepest level of the imaginative mind, not easily accessible; perhaps he stands for inspiration, only visiting the artist when it chooses, and then behaving just as it wishes. 'You must not only take him *as* you find him, but *when* you find him,' Rat says of Badger. Above all he is not to be sought out deliberately: 'It's quite out of the question, because he lives in the very middle of the Wild Wood.' The deepest level of the imagination dwells (as surely it must) right in the middle of spiritual or psychological danger.

Mole, the artist who has not yet learnt the wisdom of his craft, ignores all warnings and determines to plunge into this danger zone in the hope of getting some sort of imaginative reward. He 'formed the resolution to go out by himself and explore the Wild Wood, and perhaps strike up an acquaintance with Mr Badger'. The result is predictable: at close quarters the wood terrifies him, with its nightmare visions of sinister faces, its whistlings, and its patterings. Again, the wood's threat may be sexual – the artist's mental equilibrium is perhaps being threatened particularly by sensual imaginings. Rat's remedy for it is male companionship: 'If we have to come, we come in couples, at least; then we're generally all right.' Yet when Mole collapses in terror at the very centre of the wood, it offers, surprisingly, a womb-like security:

> At last he took refuge in the deep dark hollow of an old beech tree, which offered shelter, concealment – perhaps even safety, but who could tell?

So Anodos takes refuge in the arms of the maternal beech tree in George MacDonald's *Phantastes*: '"Why, you baby!" said she, and kissed me with the sweetest kiss of wind and odours.'

But the Wild Wood offers, at the heart of its sexual tangle, an even more womb-like refuge than the hollow of the beech: Badger's own home, entered by 'A long, gloomy, and, to tell the truth, decidedly shabby passage'. The words 'womb-like' are, indeed, quite inadequate to describe the sense of security and return to childhood conveyed by Grahame's description of Badger's home. And with this description, we come to the heart of Grahame's Arcadian dream.

*

The description is worth quoting at length. Badger flings open a stout oak door, and Rat and Mole find themselves in his kitchen:

> The floor was well-worn red brick, and on the wide hearth burnt a fire of logs, between two attractive chimney-corners tucked away in the wall, well out of any suspicion of draught. A couple of high-backed settles, facing each other on either side of the fire, gave further sitting accommodation for the sociably disposed. In the middle of the room stood a long table of plain boards placed on trestles, with benches down each side. At one end of it, where an arm-chair stood pushed back, were spread the remains of the Badger's plain but ample supper. Rows of spotless plates winked from the shelves of the dresser at the far end of the room, and from the rafters overhead hung hams, bundles of dried herbs, nets of onions and baskets of eggs. It seemed a place where heroes could fitly feast after victory, where weary harvesters could line up in scores along the table and keep their Harvest Home with mirth and song, or where two or three friends of simple tastes could sit about as they pleased and eat and smoke and talk in comfort and contentment. The ruddy brick floor smiled up at the smoky ceiling; the oaken settles, shiny with long wear, exchanged cheerful glances with each other; plates on the dresser grinned at pots on the shelf, and the merry firelight flickered and played over everything without distinction.

The Kitchen, described in these terms, is as universal a symbol as the River. Whereas the River is the expression of the adult Arcadia, with its challenges and its rules and its excitements, the Kitchen suggests another kind of Golden Age.

Its appeal is multiple. It hints at the mead-halls of such poems as *Beowulf*; Grahame says that 'heroes could fitly feast' in it, a phrase whose alliteration faintly recalls Anglo-Saxon verse. To Grahame's generation it must also have had William Morris-like hints of an earlier, pre-industrial, and therefore ideal society where distinctions of class seemed unimportant when food was being dealt out, and men of all ranks sat together in the lord's hall or by the yeoman farmer's hearthside. And, more sharply for Edwardian readers than for those of the present day, there is a suggestion too of a return to childhood. Many of Grahame's generation spent much of their early life being cared for by domestic servants, and so as small children lingered often in the kitchen, watching the pots and the joints of meat cooking on the great ranges or spits. Walter de la Mare, born fourteen years after Grahame, was still in time to have this experience, shared with his brothers and sisters. As his biographer Theresa Whistler writes:

> They had their breakfast in the kitchen with Pattie [the servant], while [their mother] was served her toast alone . . . in the drawing room . . . The children's lives revolved in great part around Pattie's spry, neat figure in the kitchen . . . Pattie's big old range had a roasting jack with a winding clock, and dripping-pan underneath. When the children came home ravenous from school, if a joint was roasting, Pattie would open the little door below and supply them with hot bread and dripping . . . In [de la Mare's] fairy tales for children, magic and remoteness are often given for backcloth an old-fashioned kitchen, minutely described and as warmly relished.[109]

There is a suggestion of the Kitchen in many of the outstanding children's books which preceded *The Wind in the Willows*. In *The Water-Babies*, Tom comes, at the end of his exhausting climb down Lewthwaite Crag, to the cottage of the old school-dame, where he peeps through the door:

> And there sat by the empty fireplace, which was filled with a pot of sweet herbs, the nicest old woman that ever was seen . . . At her feet sat the grandfather of all the cats . . . Such a pleasant cottage it was, with a shiny clean stone floor, and curious old prints on the walls, and an old black oak sideboard full of bright pewter and brass dishes . . .

George MacDonald's preferred symbol of deep security is the Library in the Castle, yet even he touches upon the Kitchen at moments. It is from a cottage kitchen that Tangle and Mossy set out on their quest in

'The Golden Key', while in *The Princess and Curdie* the moral decay of the king's household is largely expressed in terms of the disgusting state of the castle kitchen:

> Everywhere was filth and disorder. Mangy turnspit dogs were lying about, and grey rats were gnawing at refuse in the sinks. . . . [Curdie] longed for one glimpse of his mother's poor little kitchen, so clean and bright and airy.

Lewis Carroll, of course, was not concerned with the establishment of a positive Arcadia, but his anti-Arcadia has, as one of its most memorable features, a kitchen where everything has gone deliberately wrong:

> The door led right into a large kitchen, which was full of smoke from one end to the other . . . The cook took the cauldron of soup off the fire, and at once set to work throwing everything within her reach at the Duchess and the baby – the fire-irons came first: then followed a shower of saucepans, plates, and dishes.

Beatrix Potter's Mrs Tiggy-Winkle and Tailor of Gloucester, both true Arcadians, live in kitchens, but it was left to Grahame to give full expression to this symbol of deep, childlike security. As Rat and Mole sit down to supper by Badger's great hearth, they find themselves truly 'in safe anchorage', and know 'that the cold and trackless Wild Wood just left outside was miles and miles away, and all that they had suffered in it a half-forgotten dream'.

*

It is now – and only now – that *The Wind in the Willows* begins to become a social drama, a narrative about the English middle class and the threat to its stability. The meditations on the subject of the artistic imagination, on Escape, and on the deep need the individual has for the womb-like security of home, do not disappear from the book. They return in force in the chapters 'Dulce Domum' and 'Wayfarers All', while the Pan chapter 'The Piper at the Gates of Dawn' is an attempt to go beyond the plain, homely Arcadia of Badger's kitchen and describe a more spiritualised utopia. But, in general, after Badger's home has been reached the book turns into something more like a socio-political allegory.

Something of class distinction has been suggested from the beginning. The Mole, scrabbling up to the surface and running across the meadows in his delight at freedom, brushes officious toll-gate-keeping rabbits aside in a manner resembling that of a member of the upper middle class dealing with tiresome government clerks. On the other hand, when he first meets the Rat there is a suggestion that here is someone subtly his social superior, who leads a leisured gentlemanly existence while Mole is a creature of routine, who inhabits a more lowly home. Badger, of course, is a member of the old aristocracy, living unmolested in the very heart of the Wild Wood by virtue of the authority that birth and breeding have conferred upon him, not to mention his vast tunnelled dwelling which gives him access to any part of the landscape – the great country house and its estate dominating the villagers. The young hedgehogs sheltering from the snow and break-fasting in his kitchen refer to him as 'the Master', and address Rat and Mole as 'sir' and 'you gentlemen'. When Badger shows Mole the extent of his underground domain, and explains that it owes its grandeur to the fact that it is the ruins of an ancient city, Grahame is surely suggesting that society at its best and most stable is built on the foundations of past cultures.

Toad represents the opposite of this stability. His exact social position is never made clear; he is described as behaving like 'a blend of the Squire and the College Don', and it is clear that Toad Hall has been in his family for more than one generation; yet the narrative constantly gives the impression that he is a *parvenu* whose family has bought its way into the squirearchy rather than inherited its position. Badger censures Toad for 'squandering the money your father left you', and there seems to be a hint that Mr Toad senior made that money in the cotton trade or something less decorous.[110] What is absolutely certain is that Toad's behaviour is letting the side down, is threatening the position of the entire *bourgeoisie* and upper class. Badger says to him severely:

'You knew it must come to this, sooner or later . . . You're getting us animals a bad name in the district by your furious driving and your smashes and your rows with the police. Independence is all very well, but we animals never allow our friends to make fools of themselves beyond a certain limit; and that limit you've reached.'

This passage is to some extent misleading, in that it suggests that Toad's sin is to damage the reputation of the animal inhabitants of the River Bank with 'the police', that is, the humans. Grahame is not, however, talking about this. (He is never certain about the animals' relation to the human world around them – this is perhaps the one major flaw in the concept of the book[111] – and at times, as here, the uncertainty obtrudes.) What he is really saying is that Toad is letting down his class and exposing it to danger, as subsequent events make clear. Toad's absence in prison leaves Toad Hall vacant for the Wild Wooders to occupy and claim as their own. Irresponsible behaviour among the *bourgeoisie*, the *rentier* class, has weakened the defences of that part of society, and made it vulnerable to riot and revolution.

One can have little doubt that this layer of meaning exists within the book. It appeared in print, in 1908, at a time when England, like much of western society, had experienced many decades of social unrest, and when anarchy or revolution was an all too familiar terror. Peter Green, in his biography of Grahame, speaks of the Wild Wooders as 'like the urban mob-anarchists of every Edwardian upper-middle-class nightmare'. He argues persuasively that the story has 'an unmistakable social symbolism'. Yet it is hard to persuade oneself that Grahame was so very much aware of this symbolism, or took much conscious interest in contemporary social unrest. Certainly, shortly before he began to invent the Toad element in the book's plot, in November 1903, he himself was threatened at gunpoint in the Bank of England by a lunatic of socialist tendencies, and this episode is perhaps echoed at the moment when a ferret sentry fires at Toad. But apart from this, there is little evidence that Grahame took the kind of interest in current social events that may be found, for example, in Beatrix Potter's journal. One is inclined to judge that the 'social symbolism' of *The Wind in the Willows* is in the nature of almost accidental colouring, acquired because of the time in which it was written, rather than present strongly in its author's mind.

The parallels between the Wild Wooders and the socialist–anarchist mob threat are not in any case very many. Mole, walking through the Wild Wood and seeing 'evil wedge-shaped faces', may be experiencing something of the emotions of an Edwardian gentleman inadvertently finding himself in the London slums, but the episode has more about it of nightmare than rational social fear. Moreover, the Wild Wooders, inasmuch as they are described at all (and remarkably little is actually said about them), do not behave like a working-class mob. When they get possession of Toad Hall they act just like dissipated gentry – like Toad himself, in fact, 'lying in bed half the day, and breakfast at all hours . . . Eating your grub, and drinking your drink, and making bad jokes about you'. The speech given by the Chief Weasel is not rabble-rousing by a mob leader but a typical piece of after-dinner oratory at a banquet:

> 'Well, I do not propose to detain you much longer' – (great applause) – 'but before I resume my seat' (renewed cheering) – 'I should like to say one word about our kind host, Mr Toad. We all know Toad!' – (great laughter) . . .

This is the atmosphere of an undergraduate dining club, or a cheerful gathering of City clerks, not a piece of revolutionary fervour. *The Wind in the Willows* does not anticipate *Animal Farm*.

If, despite this, the Wild Wooders are *en masse* the social inferiors of the River Bankers – and there is no clear evidence to support this – then possibly they represent the rural rather than the urban working classes, for there is a passage near the end of the book where a mother weasel speaks to her child much as a cottager might have addressed her offspring when the local gentry of Grahame's era came in sight:

> 'Look, baby! There goes the great Mr Toad! And that's the gallant Water Rat, a terrible fighter, walking along o' him! And yonder comes the famous Mr Mole, of whom you so often have heard your father tell!'

In fact, one suspects that Grahame himself saw the behaviour of the Wild Wooders not in terms of contemporary English society, but as something like the suitors of Penelope in the *Odyssey*, who have to be cast out by Ulysses before he can regain his home. The final chapter of *The Wind in the Willows* is entitled 'The Return of Ulysses', and Peter Green has pointed out that there are other Homeric references within the book, most notably the description of the arming of Badger, Rat, Mole, and Toad before their attack on Toad Hall.

*

If one accepts that *The Wind in the Willows* is not primarily a social parable, one is likely to judge that the dominating element of the book is that which celebrates the pleasures of existence among the River Bankers. Within this part of the story, on the simpler level, Grahame is talking about the cheerful bachelor-like existence of himself and his friends, as they lead the kind of life sought by men of their class since the days of Kingsley and Tom Hughes.[112] More subtly, he is concerned with the artistic imagination and its delights and dangers. And this higher level is the only one which easily assimilates everything in the book, and makes a coherent whole of it.

On this level, Rat and Mole are not simply the apprentice and the experienced artists, but different facets of the same artistic mind. Mole is by turns timorous and rash, while Rat alternates between dreamer and practical man-of-the-world. One begins gradually to feel that Mole is the artist's personality as a human being (he closely resembles many aspects of Kenneth Grahame himself), while Rat is an expression of the two sides of an artist's actual work: inspiration (Rat's dreaminess) and craftsmanship (his practical knowledge of boats). The meeting ground of the two is the River, Imagination itself, with its 'babbling procession of the best stories in the world, sent from the heart of the earth to be told at last to the insatiable sea'.

Both Rat and Mole are vulnerable to certain urges which threaten to upset the stability of the relationship. Mole is markedly home-loving, and would half like to desert the River Bank (imagination and artistic creation) for the very mundane pleasures of his own home. In 'Dulce Domum', the brilliant chapter describing his rediscovery of that home one winter's evening, Grahame subtly suggests that Mole has no real artistic taste: the courtyard of his house is decorated with 'brackets carrying plaster statuary – Garibaldi, and the infant Samuel, and Queen Victoria, and other heroes of modern Italy'; and in the centre of a goldfish pond is 'a fanciful erection clothed in . . . cockle-shells and topped by a large silvered glass ball that reflected everything all wrong and had a very pleasing effect'. The hint of vulgarity, of mass-produced works of art purchased from chain stores, contributes to a picture of the reluctant artist fleeing for his real pleasures to very off-duty surroundings. Rat wisely allows Mole a night in this setting before luring him back to the River Bank and his true vocation. Rat himself has an equally strong temptation in the opposite direction, to abandon the life of the imagination for a life of purely sensual pleasure. The Sea Rat – an exact mirror-image of himself in all but experience – tries to lure him away from his own habitat and occupations into a world that is not merely Grahame's adored Mediterranean landscape but also a life of lotus-eating, a lazy tasting of pleasure that spells death to artistic creation. (The Sea Rat, it should be noted, is not himself a sailor; he takes no part in the work of the crew, but lazes in the captain's cabin while they are labouring.) Was Grahame thinking particularly of the excesses of some of his fellow-writers of the 'nineties?

Within this scheme of the book, with Badger (as we have said) personifying pure inspiration, and Toad's adventures symbolising the threat to the artist from the unstable nature of his own personality,[113] one turns to the chapter 'The Piper at the Gates of Dawn', which stands at the centre of the book, in the expectation that here Grahame will make some positive statement about the artistic imagination which will bind the rest of the book together. But any such expectation is disappointed. Grahame has chosen, at this crucial place, to introduce yet another major character or symbol, the great god Pan himself, whose pipes are heard and who is then glimpsed himself by Rat and Mole. The episode makes plenty of sense within the book's examination of the theme of the artistic mind: it is Rat (as we have noted) who hears the Pan-pipes first, and Mole only comes to be aware of the presence of the god thanks to the persuasion and influence of Rat ('Now you must surely hear it! Ah – at last – I see you do!') But Pan does not seem to be the right figure to stand for the pure artistic inspiration, the experience of real poetry, which is what the chapter is intended to convey.

Grahame, it should be noted at this point, rejected conventional religion. *The Golden Age* mocks the Olympians for going to church on Sundays 'though they betrayed no greater delight in the experience than ourselves'. Peter Green records that the Calvinism of his parental upbringing followed by the 'social Anglicanism' of his grandmother's home 'had damned Grahame's natural spring of faith at the source'. He was drawn aesthetically to the ritual of the Roman Catholic church, which lured him as did all things Mediterranean, but his rational mind could not apparently accept Christian doctrine. In this, of course, he resembled other outstanding practitioners of children's literature, and like them he wrote for children partly because it seemed to offer a way to the discovery of an alternative religion. But though his River Bank and Wild Wood stir, at the moment when he is writing most subtly, something like religious awe in the reader, he is quite unable to evoke specifically religious feelings just at the moment when he wants to. 'The Piper at the Gates of Dawn' is embarrassing because it summons up the very 'nineties figure of Pan, who reappears again and again in mediocre 'pagan' writings of the period by Grahame and his contemporaries. Grahame's description of him is a ghastly error in taste:

> . . . the rippling muscles on the arm that lay across the broad chest, the long supple hand still holding the pan-pipes only just fallen away from the parted lips; . . . the splendid curves of the shaggy limbs disposed in majestic ease on the sward . . .

Just when we should be encountering pure poetry we have a piece of bad late Victorian art, with the sexual potency of the Pan of classical literature replaced by something resembling 'The Light of the World'. W. W. Robson has suggested that people who dislike 'The Piper at the Gates of Dawn' do so because they are hostile to religion. But this is to suppose that the chapter conveys any real sense of the religious or numinous.

However, it not only misses true religious art but is redundant within the scheme of the book. Badger and the Wild Wood are surely more than adequate symbols for the deepest level of the artistic imagination, and Mole's encounter with them both is the book's central crisis. The River Bank stands perfectly for the day-to-day life of the artist. The exploration of these themes in the supposedly more heightened terms of 'The Piper at the Gates of Dawn' is just not necessary; the thing has already been done as well as it possibly could be.

*

The Wind in the Willows has nothing to do with childhood or children, except in that it can be enjoyed by the young, who thereby experience (though they do not rationally understand) what its author has to say, and are able to sense some of its resonances. C. S. Lewis observed that it is a perfect example of the kind of story which can express things without explaining them. Taking as an example the character of Badger, whom he described as an 'amalgam of high rank, coarse manners, gruffness, shyness and goodness', Lewis argued that 'The child who has once met Mr Badger has got ever afterwards, in its bones, a knowledge of humanity and English social history which it certainly couldn't get from any abstraction.' In this sense *The Wind in the Willows* has a claim to be regarded as the finest achievement of children's literature up to the date at which it was written, and perhaps afterwards. It is crammed full of experience of human character, almost unfailingly wise and mature in its judgements, and yet largely accessible to children.[114] It does not frighten in the way that *Alice* often does; it is never condescending, nor does it present an oversimplified view of the world. It has nearly as much irony and comedy as Beatrix Potter's stories while being far more ambitious. Yet it is also faulty. 'The Piper at the Gates of Dawn' is an error of judgement on a grand scale, and there are smaller lapses again and again in the book – the awkward question of the human-animal relationship, the self-conscious self-parodying authorial manner during the account of Toad's brush with the law, and overindulgent scenic descriptions, reminiscent of Richard Jefferies or Edward Thomas at their most run-of-the-mill. Though it is fine enough in structure, one feels that it is often shakily executed, and that the exercise could scarcely be repeated successfully, so near does it come at times to collapse.

Certainly Grahame himself never repeated it. *The Wind in the Willows* was his last book, and after it he gave up the struggle to rescue himself from his marriage and the general impossibility of his life. He resigned early from the Bank of England and led an empty retirement. His son Alastair, to whom the book had first been told, was found dead on a railway line while an undergraduate at Oxford in 1920, and though the inquest verdict was accidental death the evidence points to suicide. This event provides an ironic link with another Edwardian who wrote a great work of literature for children; for the child who, more than any other, was the 'real' Peter Pan met his death a year later, in not dissimilar circumstances and only a few miles away from that of the boy who had provided the impetus for *The Wind in the Willows*.

6

J. M. Barrie and *Peter Pan*
'That terrible masterpiece'

The Wind in the Willows took many years to make a public impact. At first many readers thought it inferior to Grahame's *The Golden Age*, and it was not until after the First World War that it came to be recognised as his greatest work, and its charm and depth of character-isation came to be properly appreciated. On the other hand, J. M. Barrie's play *Peter Pan* was a success from its very first performance, at the Duke of York's Theatre, London, on 27 December 1904. The audience's response – both adults and children – was wildly enthusias-tic; the play thereafter became an annual fixture in London each Christmas and also toured Britain for much of the year, as well as being performed from coast to coast in America. Moreover, it initiated – or played a larger part than any other work in initiating – a fashion for 'fairy' literature and illustration in the Edwardian nursery, a fashion that scarcely abated until the 1930s. The effect of *Peter Pan* was, in other words, more immediate than that of any earlier work of children's literature, *Alice in Wonderland* included. Any discussion of the play and its author needs to be conducted with this in mind. We are dealing here not just with a piece of imaginative creation by one man, but with a public phenomenon.

The play has generally been recognised since its first appearance as, in its strange way, a work of genius. Yet it also inspires, even from its warmest admirers, expressions of distaste: at its whimsicality, its sentimentality, and perhaps other qualities not so immediately apparent. Nowhere has the reaction to it been better expressed than by someone who was very close to its author and the writing of it: Peter Llewelyn Davies, whose own first name supplied that of its hero. Looking back at it many years later and contemplating the effect it had had on him and his brothers, and perhaps on a whole generation, he called it 'that terrible masterpiece'.[115]

*

James Matthew Barrie spent much of his life writing about himself. The greater part of his prose fiction and a large proportion of his many plays are taken up with an attempt to express his own very peculiar character. In a sense, therefore, the biographer or critic has much to draw on when trying to understand Barrie and his work. But Barrie, by this very act of writing so much about himself, made himself into a character in his own literature, and we should be very wary in accepting his account of himself as the literal truth. Barrie created, fleshed out, observed, and manipulated a character called 'J. M. Barrie', with as much whimsy, sentimentality, and cold detachment as he put into the character of Peter Pan. We must be on our guard, therefore, when examining his writings for clues towards the personality behind them. It is all something of a circle.

Certainly the first part of his life could be Act One of a typical Barrie drama – but that is exactly how Barrie, writing about it in adult years, wanted it to seem. The scene is Kirriemuir, a small town north of Dundee; James is the ninth child of a weaver, and he passes the first six years of his life in unclouded happiness. Then his thirteen-year-old brother dies after a skating accident; his mother takes to her bed, inconsolable; and James discovers that only he has the power to bring a smile back to her lips.

> . . . there came to me my sister, the daughter my mother loved the best . . . and she told me to go ben[116] to my mother and say to her that she still had another boy. I went ben excitedly, but the room was dark, and when I heard the door shut and no sound come from the bed I was afraid, and I stood still. I suppose I was breathing hard, or perhaps I was crying, for after a time I heard a listless voice that had never been listless before say, 'Is that you?' I think the tone hurt me, for I made no answer, and then the voice said more anxiously 'Is that you?' again. I thought it was the dead boy she was speaking to, and I said in a little lonely voice, 'No, it's no him, it's just me.' Then I heard a cry, and my mother turned in bed, and though it was dark I knew that she was holding out her arms.
>
> After that I sat a great deal in her bed trying to make her forget him, which was my crafty way of playing physician . . . At first, they say, I was often jealous, stopping her fond memories with the cry, 'Do you mind nothing about me' but that did not last; its place was taken by an intense desire (again, I think, my sister must have breathed it into life) to become so like him that even my mother should not see the difference . . . He had such a cheery way of whistling, she had told me, it had always brightened her at her work to hear him whistling, and when he whistled he stood with his legs apart, and his hands in the pockets of his knickerbockers. I decided to trust to this, so one day after I had learned his whistle . . . from boys

who had been his comrades, I secretly put on a suit of his clothes . . .
and thus disguised I slipped, unknown to the others, into my
mother's room. Quaking, I doubt not, yet so pleased, I stood still
until she saw me, and then – how it must have hurt her! 'Listen!' I
cried in a glow of triumph, and I stretched my legs wide apart and
plunged my hands into the pockets of my knickerbockers, and began
to whistle.[117]

One might add: 'Curtain. End of Act One, Scene One.' We now pass
on to Scene Two, in which mother and son become especially close to
each other, and she shares in the flowering of his childish imagination.
Then comes the less pleasant Act Two, in which a youthful Jimmy
Barrie sets off for Edinburgh University and, arriving there, finds
himself to be not quite like other young men.

Yes, Barrie the dramatist is firmly in command of the reader's
reactions. But beneath the undoubted artifice of his account of himself
in childhood lies one undoubtedly true thing. At some point – and the
impersonating-the-dead-brother incident is as plausible as any – he
seems to have discovered that he had the power of stepping into other
people's shoes, of adopting their personalities; and this in turn gave him
a way of influencing those closest to him. As an adult he would enthrall
children by becoming a child himself, and outdoing them in the childish
energy of his imagination. It was this that filled up *Peter Pan* with its
splendid jumble of pirates, redskins, fairies, and mermaids, all done
without the faintest condescension. A moment later he could slip into
the part of a 'gentle, whimsical, lonely old bachelor' (his description of
himself in *The Little White Bird*), who would have loved to have had
children of his own, and so would seek them out and solace himself
with their company. He could think himself just as easily into the
character of a mother or an unhappy wife or a girl on the brink of
marriage. This ability at shape-changing accounts for the fact that his
plays, wildly whimsical as their plots usually are, are full of entirely
three-dimensional characters. Like Dickens, he would think himself
into every personality he created. But the corollary of this was that he
found it extraordinarily difficult to engage in real relationships. No one
ever seems to have got close to 'the real J.M.B.', if there was such a
person.

Barrie had nearly reached this state of affairs by the time he became a
student at Edinburgh. He kept a notebook recording his impressions of
human character, chiefly his own. At first he usually referred to himself
in the first person singular:

Men can't get together without talking filth.
Far finer and nobler things in the world than loving a girl & getting
her.
Greatest horror – dream I am married – wake up shrieking.

But gradually, stepping back from his own predicament, he slipped into the third person:

> He is very young looking – trial of his life that he is always thought a boy.

He was indeed 'very young looking'. He only grew to be five feet three inches high, and despite a moustache he retained a markedly boyish look until old age. He was in this respect quite literally a boy who couldn't grow up. His life's work consisted in transforming this unavoidable state of affairs into something willed – 'the boy who *wouldn't* grow up', which is the subtitle of *Peter Pan*.

The third person habit soon became a fixed one in Barrie's notebooks as he painfully chronicled personal difficulties during his first years of literary success:

> This sentimentalist wants to make girl love him, bullies and orders her (this does it) yet doesn't want to marry.
>   Such a man if an author, wd be studying his love affair for book. Even while proposing, the thought of how it wd *read* wd go thro' him.
>   Literary man can't dislike any one he gets copy out of.

This was written during 1892, when, at the age of thirty-two, he had made quite a name in London as a writer of prose sketches about his Scottish home town, and also was beginning to achieve fame as a playwright. Despite his private expression of horror at the prospect of marriage, he used his involvement with the theatre to get introductions to pretty actresses, and he was soon paying particular attention to one of them, Mary Ansell, who appeared in his second play, *Walker, London*. The notebook entries quoted above apparently refer to her, and they say a good deal about him.

First, he described himself as a 'sentimentalist', which can be taken at face value (Barrie could certainly switch on sentimentality when he wished to), but was also a term he used to describe his ability at stepping psychologically into other people's shoes.[118] The hero of his novel *Sentimental Tommy* (1896) is given that nickname by the village schoolmaster because of his ability to take on other people's feelings as if they were his own. The schoolmaster says of him:

> 'He is constantly playing some new part-playing is hardly the word though, for into each part he puts an earnestness that cheats even himself, until he takes to another. I suppose you want me to give you some idea of his character, and I could tell you what it is at any particular moment; but it changes, sir, I do assure you, almost as

quickly as the circus-rider flings off his layers of waistcoats. A single
puff of wind blows him from one character to another, and he may be
noble and vicious, and a tyrant and a slave, and hard as granite and
melting as butter in the sun, all in one forenoon. All you can be sure
of is that whatever he is he will be it in excess.'

Barrie knew perfectly well that this was a description of himself. One
might consequently say that the very description, the distancing from
his own character, was yet another kind of role-playing.

In his notebook entries he talks about 'bullying' and 'ordering' Mary
Ansell without really wanting to marry her. This was to be characteristic of all his relationships. He loved to play the manipulator, to be God
to other people; to shape their lives, arrange their friendships, make
them as dependent on him as he possibly could – yet he shrank back
from any real commitment to them himself. The unhappiness of his
marriage, and the strange nature of his later relationship with the boys
who became his wards and who inspired *Peter Pan*, has naturally
always aroused speculations about his sexuality. The easiest solution is
to suppose that he was impotent with women and had paederastic
inclinations. But there is no evidence to support the charge of
impotence, while those of the boys who survived into adult life
strenuously denied that there was any conscious sexual element in the
relationship. The truth may be that actual sexuality of any kind played
no part at all in Barrie's personality: all his sexual energies seem to have
been diverted from their usual course into this passionate desire to
manipulate other people. He wished to stand above them and pull the
strings rather than be on stage alongside them. He was ultimately cold,
remote, distant, god-like; and in day to day life he was, as he knew very
well, a writer constantly on the look-out for copy: 'Literary man can't
dislike anyone he gets copy out of.'

So he went through with an engagement and marriage to Mary Ansell
simply to get copy, though it was against his nature to play the part of
husband, a role which aroused expectations of real participation (and
not just sexual) in a relationship. He got his copy quickly enough: even
before the marriage had begun he was at work on *Sentimental Tommy*,
a book which both moaned over and revelled in the predicament of
being such a one as himself; while its sequel, *Tommy and Grizel* (1900),
exulted in the agonies he had experienced in the first six years of
marriage:

> They had a honeymoon by the sea . . . Tommy trying to become a
> lover by taking thought, and Grizel not letting on that it could not be
> done in that way . . . He was a boy only. She knew that, despite all he
> had gone through, he was still a boy. And boys cannot love. Oh, is it
> not cruel to ask a boy to love? . . . He was a boy who could not grow
> up.

Sentimental Tommy was a great success with the public; *Tommy and Grizel*, with its alarming account of a failing marriage, did not go down so well. That mattered little to Barrie (who was making a good living from plays); he had got a good deal of himself sorted out by writing it, and had discovered the role he could most comfortably play ('a boy who could not grow up'). At the end of the second novel he cheerfully and implausibly killed off his hero Tommy, and then turned to the matter of finding a stage on which the boy-who-could-not-grow-up could perform to the greatest effect. Meanwhile his wife remained childless, and took to keeping a series of Newfoundland dogs as a consolation.[119] Barrie even managed to get copy out of the dogs. 'The only occupant of the room at present is Nana the nurse,' reads the opening stage direction in *Peter Pan*, 'reclining, not as you might expect on the one soft chair, but on the floor. She is a Newfoundland dog . . .'

*

Barrie seems to have found some indication of where he should next exercise his peculiar powers when he made friends with Margaret, the small daughter of W. E. Henley, friend of Stevenson and mentor of Grahame. She called Barrie 'my friendy', but this came out as 'fwendy' or 'wendy', and Barrie devised the name 'Wendy'. (He liked women who could not pronounce their r's. 'It appeals to all that is chivalrous in man,' he said of this trait when bestowing it on Lady Caroline Laney in his play *Dear Brutus*.) Margaret Henley died in 1895 at the age of six; Barrie put her into *Sentimental Tommy* as Reddy, a little girl who dies young. Besides resurrecting her as Wendy in *Peter Pan*, he used her again as the dream-child Margaret in *Dear Brutus* (1917). As usual, the maximum of copy was extracted.

The friendship with Margaret Henley was a prologue to the main drama of his life, which far exceeded his marriage in its importance to him, and provided him not merely with copy on a small scale but with a whole world of characters and narrative – a mythology. This, in turn, led both to the creation of his outstanding literary work, and allowed him to inhabit a play of his own making for the rest of his life.

Andrew Birkin's enthralling book *J. M. Barrie and the Lost Boys* (1979) records, so to speak, the text of that drama as it was performed, describing how Barrie took over and manipulated an entire family. First he befriended the two eldest boys, George and Jack Llewelyn Davies, when they were aged five and three, and were walking with their nurse in Kensington Gardens. Their younger brothers Peter, Michael, and Nicholas were drawn on to the stage in turn. The father, a not very successful London barrister, remained largely in the wings, and when he came on stage he was no more sympathetic to the goings-on than is Mr Darling in *Peter Pan*. The mother, Sylvia Llewelyn

Davies, shared the centre of the stage with the boys, not only playing the role of Mrs Darling but also acting Wendy to Barrie's Peter.

In Act One, which lasted from 1897 to 1903, Barrie got to know the boys, paid particular attention to George, the eldest and most good-looking, and wrote *The Little White Bird* (1902), which both described (in whimsical and heightened terms) his complicated feelings about the family and took the first steps towards creating the myth of Peter Pan. In Act Two (1904 to 1906) the family, somewhat astonished, found itself enshrined in the play *Peter Pan*, and basked not altogether comfortably in the glory reflected from it; meanwhile Barrie carefully moulded Michael, the fourth boy and the one who took George's place in his affections after George grew up, into the shape of Peter Pan himself. Act Three brought the drama to a climax: first the boys' father and then their mother died of cancer, and Barrie himself (whose marriage was dissolved after his wife's adultery in 1909) took over the role of parent, just as Wendy does for the Lost Boys in *Peter Pan*. Only in the fourth and final act (1910–21) does one feel that Barrie slightly lost authorial control of the play; and even so the dramatic tension was retained to the end, with George Llewelyn Davies dying on the Western Front in 1915 and Michael, fretting at the role of boy-who-wouldn't-grow-up, drowning mysteriously while an Oxford under-graduate, in what has often been thought to be a suicide pact with a friend.[120] An Epilogue shows Barrie as a lonely figure pacing the floor of his London flat, high above the Thames, in a room filled with photographs of his boys.

This drama was really his greatest achievement, and in a sense *Peter Pan* was only an offshoot of it, an attempt to express it in other than realistic terms. Certainly the play becomes doubly charged with meaning and nuance when one re-reads it after studying Andrew Birkin's account of the Barrie–Llewelyn Davies saga. Sensibly, Birkin does not try to explain Barrie's motives in involving himself so deeply with the family, but simply implies that the boys and their parents were a canvas on which this extraordinary artist, this manipulator of personalities, chose to work. Yet if little more need be said about the personal origins of *Peter Pan*, this still leaves us asking what there was in the play which touched such a crucial public nerve. Why did the private, half-mad dream of such a strange individual have such huge appeal to playgoers and readers? Why is Peter Pan one of the immortals of literature?

*

Peter Pan is the only piece of Barrie's writing that gets the whole Barrie into it. As Tommy says to his wife in *Tommy and Grizel* when he is writing 'The Wandering Child' (a story that contains one of the first germs of *Peter Pan*), 'It is myself who is writing at last, Grizel.'

Peter is in a sense made up out of many people, as was Barrie himself. His origin partly lies in Barrie's dead brother David, who had remained alive as a child in his mother's mind – 'When I first became a man . . . he was still a boy of thirteen,' Barrie wrote. His first name came from Peter Llewelyn Davies, who when still a baby became the subject of stories told by Barrie to the older boys, George and Jack. According to these stories Peter, like all babies, had once been a bird and could still fly out of his nursery window and back to Kensington Gardens, because his mother had forgotten to weigh him at birth. From these stories came the 'Peter Pan' chapters in *The Little White Bird* (afterwards re-issued with Arthur Rackham illustrations as *Peter Pan in Kensington Gardens*), which describe not the Peter Pan of the play but a baby, half mortal, who lives in the Gardens, understands the speech of the play, and is met by children who hide there at night after the gates have been locked. The character of Peter in the play owes something too to the personality of George, whose friendship with himself Barrie describes in *The Little White Bird*, where he calls him 'David' (the name of his own dead brother). The chapter of this book which recounts how 'David' comes to stay with the narrator, is undressed by him, and finally demands to sleep in the narrator's own bed, comes as near to the explicitly sexual as anything in Barrie's writings, and if taken alone would lead one to suppose Barrie to have been plainly paedophiliac by inclination:

'Why David,' said I, sitting up, 'do you want to come into my bed?'

'Mother said I wasn't to want it unless you wanted it first,' he squeaked.

'It is what I have been wanting all the time,' said I, and then without more ado the little white figure rose and flung itself at me. For the rest of the night he lay on me and across me, and sometimes his feet were at the bottom of the bed and sometimes on the pillow, but he always retained possession of my finger, and occasionally he woke me to say that he was sleeping with me. I had not a good night. I lay thinking.

But even if his feelings for George Llewelyn Davies came near to real sexual passion, one suspects that even here Barrie was still really collecting copy, was gathering his strength for the major literary act of his life, the creation of the Boy Who Wouldn't Grow Up.

The principal model for Peter Pan is, of course, Barrie himself. Peter is everything that Barrie had been and had become. He is neither child nor adult, and he is entirely sexless. This sexlessness became all the more apparent when the play was first staged, in 1904, for then and in all subsequent English productions for nearly eighty years the part of Peter was played by an actress. But Barrie had not particularly intended

this, and when Miles Anderson took the title role in the 1982 Royal
Shakespeare Company production in London it became apparent that
the sexlessness, the inability to engage in real relationships, the ultimate
loneliness, are all there in Barrie's text, and dominate the character
whatever the actual sex of the performer.

Peter is also an adventure-story addict, just as Barrie had been in
childhood (when he soaked himself in Penny Dreadfuls and in *Treasure
Island*) and had remained. In student days Barrie wrote in his
notebook: 'Want to stop everybody in street & ask if they've read "The
Coral Island". Feel sorry if not.' Peter's adventures in the Never Never
Land,[121] and those of the Lost Boys, are largely inspired by Ballantyne's
The Coral Island,[122] together with touches of Robert Louis Stevenson;
and on this level the play is a joyful celebration of children's literature
itself, and of the rich imagination which is childhood's greatest asset.
Yet, typically, Barrie does not let Peter simply indulge in this; Peter is
always standing back from the action, and regarding it and himself in a
quizzical light. He loves to hear *stories*; indeed it is this which brings
him to the Darling nursery in the first place:

> WENDY: Peter, why did you come to our nursery window?
> PETER: To try to hear stories. None of us knows any stories.

And, as Wendy observes at the end of the play, the stories he likes to
hear best are 'the ones about yourself'. But he cannot really distinguish
between the stories which are true and those which are simply stories.
By the end of the play he has forgotten anything that has happened in it:

> WENDY: Fancy your forgetting the lost boys, and even Captain
> Hook!
> PETER: Well, then?
> WENDY: I haven't seen Tink this time.
> PETER: Who?
> WENDY: Oh dear! I suppose it is because you have so many
> adventures.
> PETER (*relieved*): 'Course it is.

Nor are all the adventures themselves 'real' ones. We are told that the
Lost Boys wear coats of 'the skins of animals they think they have shot',
and in the Home Under the Ground non-existent meals are sometimes
served:

> It is a pretend meal this evening [says the opening stage-direction to
> Act IV], with nothing whatever on the table, not a mug, nor a crust,
> nor a spoon . . . The pretend meals are not Wendy's idea; indeed she
> was rather startled to find, on arriving, that Peter knew of no other

kind, and she is not absolutely certain even now that he does eat the other kind, though no one appears to do it more heartily. He insists that the pretend meals should be partaken of with gusto, and we see his band doing their best to obey orders.

Barrie seems to be saying that the childish imagination, splendid as it is, has the most terrible limitations, and can never (without growing up) come to terms with the real world. *Peter Pan* thus manages – and it is a triumph of ingenuity – both to celebrate imagination and to give a rather chilling warning of its limitations. And is Barrie also suggesting that even the most brilliant and effective writer – such as himself – does not know whether to believe in his own creations? The theme of belief, so important (as we shall see) to *Peter Pan* at its deepest level, is touched on here.

Peter 'is' Barrie in so many other respects. He is the manipulator of other people's emotions, who carries them off from the real world that they inhabit to a country of his own invention, where they can act parts that he chooses for them in dramas of his own devising. He is also the outsider, the observer, who flirts with both mother and child (just as Barrie did), but who in the end is cut off from real relationships. 'There could not have been a lovelier sight,' Barrie writes in *Peter and Wendy*, his 1911 novelisation of the play, describing Mrs Darling's joyful reunion with her children,

> but there was none to see it except a strange boy who was staring in at the window. He had ecstasies innumerable that other children can never know; but he was looking through the window at the one joy from which he must be for ever barred.

From this isolation, this knowledge that he is not a 'real' person, comes Peter's otherwise inexplicable sadness, which pervades the play and provides a superbly judged counterpoint to what would otherwise be an overabundance of 'adventures'. Again Barrie is reminding his audience of the limitations as well as the marvels of childhood, and of the price that has to be paid by those who choose to remain as children. Though the play is in a sense a celebration of immaturity, it is an awful warning to those who choose to remain immature.

In this sense it advances beyond *The Wind in the Willows* in its exploration of personality. Rat, Mole, Toad, and perhaps even Badger are on one level children: their world is an Arcadia from which the principal responsibilities of adult life (sexual relationships, the need to earn money and support dependants) are totally absent. The 'real' world outside is represented by Grahame in such ludicrous terms (the magistrates' court, the gaol, and the other scenes of Toad's escapades) that the reader is encouraged to believe that they do not in truth exist.

The dream is self-sufficient; there is no need to 'grow up' or awaken. Barrie, though he appears to be extolling the joys of not growing up, of remaining within the dream, is in fact saying just the opposite, for the events of *Peter Pan* are framed by a 'real' world in which money has to be earned and family relationships can be extremely difficult. Mr Darling, with his bad temper and his money worries, has been put into the play to make just this point. Moreover, the Never Never Land is a deliberately unreal Arcadia: it is visibly stuck together out of bits of well-known stories, and to visit it requires an act of belief which the children cannot sustain as they grow up. *Peter Pan* is arguably more 'true to life' in this respect than is any other major work of children's literature which preceded it. To use J. R. R. Tolkien's terms for the two layers of narrative found in many works of fantasy, it not only presents us with a 'secondary' (make-believe) world, but reminds us that the 'primary' (real) world is there all the time, and must be returned to if maturity is to be achieved.

But Peter rejects the possibility of returning to it:

PETER (*passionately*): I don't want to go to school and learn solemn things. No one is going to catch me, lady, and make me a man. I want always to be a little boy and to have fun.

For him, in consequence, there can be no maturity, no increase in wisdom, no procreation, not even death. There is only forgetting and starting out all over again. Peter is condemned to live out the same events every time a new generation of children follows him to the Never Never Land; this much is made clear by the continuation of the story in *Peter and Wendy*, and is indicated by Barrie's difficulty in finding a satisfactory ending for the play.[123] There can be no ending, only a return to the beginning.

On the negative side then, Peter is a victim of his own worship of immaturity. On the positive side, he expresses almost everything that children's literature up to 1904 had been trying to say and do. He is at the same time a child himself and a child's dream-figure, the archetypal hero both of magical fairy tale and adventure story. Indeed he is so archetypal that one almost begins to believe Barrie's assertion about the play that, 'I have no recollection of having written it.' He seems not just the invention of one writer, but a character from mythology. He is god-like. Indeed in a sense he is God-like.

Gillian Avery has observed that the fairy-fashion which over-whelmed English nurseries and their books after the success of *Peter Pan* invoked something akin to religious feeling.

There was during these years a yearning in those who wrote for children to present them with some sort of faith to replace the

Christian teaching which had been implicit in Victorian books (even with writers who had no particularly fervent religious feelings) and which had become unfashionable. Children's writers generally deprecated the 'progressive' attitude . . . which sought to remove all mystery and to base everything on scientific fact. They also recognized that it is difficult to preach an ethic convincingly in the absence of a faith, and so fairies became the new guardian angels.[124]

This in a way was what Barrie himself was doing in *Peter Pan*. But he was attempting more than his imitators tried to do. He was following in the steps of Charles Kingsley, George MacDonald, and Kenneth Grahame: working from a largely religious impulse, he was attempting to replace conventional religion with something of his own devising which would summon up religious feelings in his child and adult readers. And unlike them he made a complete success of it. *Peter Pan* is an alternative religion.

*

Kenneth Grahame's vision of Pan in 'The Piper at the Gates of Dawn' fails to invoke real religious awe because it takes over a stock symbol and uses it without any depth of feeling. But Barrie, unlike Grahame, was able to write with deep feeling about a character whom he named Pan.

Barrie's choice of 'Pan' as Peter's second name was, to say the least, ingenious. It implies that Peter is a figure of classical mythology, and Barrie deliberately enhances that impression in *The Little White Bird* in the passage where Peter is first introduced to the reader:

> If you ask your mother whether she knew about Peter Pan when she was a little girl, she will say, 'Why, of course I did, child'; and if you ask her whether he rode on a goat in those days, she will say, 'What a foolish question to ask; certainly he did.' Then if you ask your grandmother whether she knew about Peter Pan when she was a girl, she also says, 'Why, of course I did, child,' but if you ask her whether he rode on a goat in those days, she says she never heard of his having a goat . . . Therefore there was no goat when your grandmother was a little girl . . . Of course, it also shows that Peter is ever so old, but he is really always the same age, so that does not matter in the least.

Barrie cleverly presents his brand new creation as being something of indescribable antiquity, and children first reading or hearing about Peter Pan take on board the notion that he is a mythological figure – which, of course, he nowadays almost is, since today's grandparents really did first encounter him in their own childhood.

Peter Pan has almost nothing about him of the classical Pan except his
pipes and (in *The Little White Bird*) the brief appearance of the goat.
But Barrie was influenced less by ancient tradition than by recent
fashion, for Pan was a recurrent figure in the work of those 'nineties
writers who turned their backs on Christian doctrine but wished to
evoke religious awe. As Theresa Whistler has pointed out in her life of
Walter de la Mare, Pan was ubiquitous in the writings of the generation
that immediately preceded Barrie's:

> The Romantics had used Pan with genuine symbolic truth, but in
> their descendants he came to be a general convenience for represent-
> ing almost any anarchic impulse from the Id – the life-force, sexual
> corruption, even the downright Satanic (as in Arthur Machen). At
> the other end of the spectrum comes the wistful, mystical sentimen-
> tality of Kenneth Grahame's 'Piper at the Gates of Dawn'. It was at
> once a cloying and a muddy cult.

Barrie rescued Pan from the hands of that cult. Or rather he used the
name of Pan in order to arouse in his audience the sort of quasi-
religious awareness that the cult had created.

Peter Pan is in many respects remarkably like the central figure of the
Christian religion. At one moment he goes willingly towards death so
as to save another, proclaiming: 'To die will be an awfully big
adventure.' He can bring the dead back to life: when Wendy is shot to
the ground by Tootles' arrow he revives her by building the Wendy-
house around her.[125] He can perform other miracles too. 'Where is
Peter?' asks a stage direction in Act V, Scene 1.

> The incredible boy has apparently forgotten his recent doings, and
> is sitting on a barrel playing upon his pipes. This may surprise
> others but does not surprise Hook. Lifting a blunderbuss he strikes
> forlornly not at the boy but at the barrel, which is hurled across the
> deck. Peter remains sitting in the air still playing upon his pipes. At
> this sight the great heart of Hook breaks.

Peter is surely Christ-like when he takes the children on a journey
through the skies to his own heavenly land. The Lost Boys who dwell
there seem to be the souls of the dead; Peter says of them: 'They are the
children who fall out of their prams when the nurse is looking the other
way.' Like Christ on earth, he is half human, half immortal. Like
Christ, his only close relationship is that of son to mother.

Hook is the Satan to Peter's Christ, a Satan in the manner of *Paradise
Lost*.[126] Despite his supposedly nightmare qualities he is not really a
figure of terror (as is, say, Blind Pew in *Treasure Island*) but a morally
ambiguous and, as Peter says, 'not unheroic' character. He has the

injured and more than slightly comic pride of a fallen angel nursing his dignity. There is surely a Miltonic air about his speech on the deck of the *Jolly Roger*:

> How still the night is; nothing sounds alive. Now is the hour when children in their homes are a-bed; their lips bright-browned with the good-night chocolate, and their tongues drowsily searching for belated crumbs housed insecurely on their shining cheeks. Compare with them the children on this boat about to walk the plank. Split my infinitives, but 'tis my hour of triumph . . . And yet some disky spirit compels me to make my dying speech, lest when dying there be no time for it. All mortals envy me, yet better perhaps for Hook to have had less ambition! . . . No little children love me. I am told they play at Peter Pan, and the strongest always chooses to be Peter. They would rather be a Twin than Hook; they force the baby to be Hook. The baby! that is where the canker gnaws.

An odd little detail suggests that Barrie could have been thinking specifically of Milton's Satan when he created Hook. In *The Little White Bird* he writes of the stories about shipwreck that he tells to David and his friend Oliver: 'We wrecked everybody of note, including all Homer's most taking characters and the hero of *Paradise Lost*.' Since Dryden's time it had been a critical commonplace to regard Satan as the real hero of the poem.

To encounter Peter Pan and Hook – the Christ and Satan of Barrie's religion – is something that can only be achieved by belief. The play is largely about faith. The Darling children can only fly if they 'think lovely wonderful thoughts and they lift you up in the air'; the fairy dust sprinkled on them by Peter is not in itself enough (faith is necessary as well as the sacraments). At the end of the story, as it is told in *Peter and Wendy*, the children gradually lose their belief in Peter, and so cannot see him any longer:

> Michael believed longer than the other boys, though they jeered at him; so he was with Wendy when Peter came for her at the end of the first year . . .
> Next year he did not come to her . . . Michael came and whispered, with a shiver, 'Perhaps there is no such person, Wendy!'

And, at the greatest crisis in the play, not only the characters in it but the audience itself is called on to make a demonstration of faith:

> PETER: . . . Tink, dear Tink, are you dying? . . . She says – she says she thinks she could get well again if children believed in fairies! (*He rises and throws out his arms he knows not to whom, perhaps to the boys*

and girls of whom he is not one.) Do you believe in fairies? Say quick
that you believe! If you believe, clap your hands!

Those who first staged the play, in 1904, were naturally uncertain that
they would get a favourable response to this at the first performance,
especially as the audience that evening was mostly adult. Accordingly it
was arranged that the musicians in the orchestra should put down their
instruments and lead the clapping. This proved unnecessary, both then
and on all subsequent occasions. There may well have been, as Barrie
suggests in the stage direction and in *Peter and Wendy*, 'a few little
beasts' who 'hissed', but the clapping overwhelmed them. The public
affirmed its faith in Barrie's newly minted religion.

Of course, it was not really new. Barrie was dealing with symbols
which children's writers had been using for almost a half century before
him. Most of all he had taken up that familiar figure the Beautiful Child
and had turned it to brilliant use. In fact he had split it into two. One
half he made into a child-god, Peter Pan himself, who is an expression
of all that the child-worshippers of Mrs Molesworth's generation had
tried to say. Peter is a kind of heavenly equivalent of Little Lord
Fauntleroy. The other half, the mortal child (in the characters of
Wendy and her brothers), is like Wordsworth's infant who comes into
this world at birth with a memory of the heavenly life he used to lead.
But Barrie's children have not come from the Christian heaven, but
from fairyland. David in *The Little White Bird* is told by the narrator
that like all children he was once a bird, who lived among the fairies and
could understand their language. Babies can still speak fairy talk, which
sounds meaningless to grown-ups, and older children can recall
something of it, and of their previous existence. David comes to believe
this. 'He never tires of this story, but I notice that it is now he who tells
it to me rather than I to him,' observes the narrator complacently.

If one still doubts that Barrie was invoking religious feelings, one
need only turn to the Llewelyn Davies boys themselves. Theirs was just
that sort of 'progressive' family which rejected conventional religion:
André Birkin reports that the three youngest boys were not christened
– this was to be 'a choice [they] should be allowed to make for
[themselves] later on'. Yet 'Michael had been brought up to believe in
Peter Pan as other children believe in Father Christmas. He knew that
"Uncle Jim" (as he had now begun to call Barrie) had written a play
about Peter, and that the Peter in the play was an actress pretending to
be a boy, but he also knew that there was a real Peter Pan.'

*

Yet Barrie was a man of boxes-within-boxes, and he could not create
anything without mocking and standing back from it. *Peter Pan*

established a quasi-religion, the early twentieth-century fairy cult;[127] but the play itself is, on its deepest level, a satire of religion and a mockery of belief.

'To die will be an awfully big adventure,' says Peter at his grandest moment; but it is a piece of empty self-observing rhetoric. The stage directions to this scene remark that his self-sacrifice in the Mermaids' Lagoon is quite unnecessary – he could perfectly well swim or fly to safety, but he wants to be a hero – and anyway a moment later he is saved when he floats off in the nest of the Never Bird. Moreover, Peter's words derive not from any faith in the Christian after-life, or in any other external religion, but from stories about Peter himself. In *The Little White Bird* it is stated that when children died Peter would 'sing gaily to them when the bell tolls', and 'went part of the way with them, so that they should not be frightened', and it was stories like this which one day prompted George Llewelyn Davies to say to Barrie: 'To die will be an awfully big adventure.' By putting these words into the play Barrie is making Peter in effect a worshipper at his own altar. The apparent religious awe invoked by the speech is therefore utterly deceptive. Peter knows nothing at all about real death, which he could not experience anyway, given the utterly cyclical and sterile nature of his existence. Yet Barrie throws the words in simply for the effect they produce at that moment, and also one suspects for mockery too. It is disturbing to find the seriousness with which they were nevertheless taken. George Llewelyn Davies set off for the battlefields of Flanders with *The Little White Bird* in his pocket, and Charles Frohman, the impresario who had backed the first production of *Peter Pan*, refused a place in one of the lifeboats during the sinking of the Lusitania in 1915 with the reported words: 'Why fear death? It is the greatest adventure in life.' Barrie was convinced that Frohman, who went down with the ship, was quoting from the play.

If Peter is Christ-like, then he is a Christ of an extraordinarily self-regarding kind. As Wendy remarks to him, 'It is so queer that the stories you like best should be the ones about yourself.' Is Barrie here remarking on, say, the overwhelming preoccupation of the Christ of St John's Gospel with his own nature? Is he saying that in the end all religions are utterly introverted, are concerned only with themselves?

Barrie's audience is meant to realise that the Never Never Land is entirely untrue. The 'secondary world' in *Peter Pan* does not exist except in the children's imaginations. The play is constantly hinting at this. The introductory remarks to Act II state that the Land can only be seen in dreams ('In the daytime you think the Never Land is only make-believe . . .') and in *Peter and Wendy* Barrie describes it as simply 'a map of a child's mind', the ideal adventure-land, 'not large and sprawly, you know, with tedious distances between one adventure and another, but nicely crammed'. There is no question about it being real. Unlike his predecessors who created Arcadias, Barrie is constantly stating that his dream-land *is* a dream. The play is a detailed map of the earthly paradise, the secret garden, more detailed than that made by any other writer. But at the same time it is a statement that such a territory is only to be found in the imagination. Barrie invokes religious belief in his creation only to dismiss it as childish nonsense.

And it is this, surely, which accounts for the terrible whimsy which overlays *Peter Pan* and almost everything else that Barrie wrote. He does not believe in his own creations. How could he do so, given his extraordinary detachment of mind from himself, from other people, and from everything they say and do? His whole self is not engaged in the creation of his stories: there is always a part which stands back and mocks them. And so comes the whimsy: it is partly satirical, a deliberate exaggeration and mockery of such things as parental affection and a delight in fairy stories; and it seems also to be a kind of mockery of his audience, a deliberate giving-them-what-they-want, a tongue-in-cheek pandering to the popular taste which demanded pretty stories for the nursery, and liked to hear about loving mothers and beautiful children. It is in this spirit, surely, rather than with any sincerity, that we are told that 'when the first baby laughed for the first time, the laugh broke into a thousand pieces and they all went skipping about, and that was the beginning of fairies'. Barrie wants to show us the appalling depths to which our sentimentality towards children can lead us. One part of him is being horribly sentimental; the other part is standing back and mocking it. Anthony Hope, author of *The Prisoner of Zenda*, was one of the few dissenting voices at the premiere of *Peter* Pan, and is said to have remarked amid the rapturous reception of the play, 'Oh for an hour of Herod.' But Barrie himself is playing Herod to his own creation. At the heart of the sentimental dream is a cynical, mocking voice.

It is clear that Barrie himself never subscribed to his own religion. He faced disease and premature death in those close to him not with the belief that to die would be 'an awfully big adventure' but with the despair of someone who at bottom had nothing to turn to. When Arthur Llewelyn Davies, the boys' father, was found to be dying of cancer of the jaw, Barrie wrote in his notebook: 'There's an ironical little God smiling at us.' It was the nearest he ever came to a positive statement of faith. And after Sylvia Llewelyn Davies had died of cancer he told her son Peter the news 'brokenly, despairingly, without any pretence of philosophy' (Peter's own words).

Admittedly when Michael Llewelyn Davies died by drowning in 1921 Barrie did in a way turn to his own myth for consolation. He had a dream of Michael coming back from death without knowing that he had been drowned, but being obliged to go through the drowning again every year as the anniversary came round, and never growing any older in consequence. Yet this dream led Barrie to reflect on his play, and to admit in his notebook the ultimately horrific nature of its theme: 'It is as if long after writing "P. Pan" its true meaning came to me – Desperate attempt to grow up but can't.'

7

A. A. Milne and *Winnie-the-Pooh*

farewell to the enchanted places

One would hardly expect it to have been Frances Hodgson Burnett who, seven years after the first performance of *Peter Pan* and three after the appearance of *The Wind in the Willows*, should create a work of fiction which, more clearly than any other single book, describes and celebrates the central symbol of the Arcadian movement in English writing for children. Mrs Burnett seems a figure belonging entirely to the heyday of the Beautiful Child, to the late Victorian saccharine portrayal of children at its worst. Was she not the creator of the most notorious work of that period and type? Yet in 1911 came from her pen *The Secret Garden*.

She had become obsessed with a walled garden at Maytham Hall near Rolvenden in Kent, which was for many years her home when she was not in America. In 1907 the lease ran out and she had to leave, and this and the experience of planting a new garden at her Long Island home seems to have started her on the book.

The story of Mary Lennox's experiences at Misselthwaite Manor in Yorkshire, where she discovers a hidden walled garden and brings it back to life, is remembered by many people as one of the most satisfying books of their childhood, and at first it is hard to believe that it came from the same author as *Fauntleroy*. Mrs Burnett herself seems to have realised that she was doing something very different here, for she begins the story by destroying all the stereotypes of her earlier work. Mary is Cedric Errol reversed, the precise opposite of the Beautiful Child: 'the most disagreeable-looking child ever seen'. Her guardian, to whom she is sent after the death of her parents in India, has much the same function as the old Earl in *Fauntleroy*, but he is presented as physically repulsive, a hunchback who shuns other people because of his deformity. Other details seem to have been picked up casually from handy sources. There is a good deal of allusion to the wind 'wuthering' round the manor; the country lad Dickon, who becomes Mary's friend and helper, is a kind of Heathcliff-gone-right; and Colin, the hunchback's bedridden son, is first discovered hidden away in a remote bedroom after Mary hears a cry like that of Mrs Rochester in *Jane Eyre*. George MacDonald's influence seems to be present too: Misselthwaite Manor with its immense numbers of unexplored and uninhabited rooms, and its endless corridors and statues, is surely the castle from *The Princess and the Goblin*, while Mary's discovery of the key and her search for the lock that will fit it recalls MacDonald's 'The Golden Key'. (Mrs Burnett met MacDonald when he was on a lecture tour in the 1870s, and there is every likelihood that she knew his books.) Mary and Dickon's cure of Colin, whom they persuade to walk again, seems to have been suggested by the passage in Johanna Spyri's *Heidi* (1881) where Heidi and Peter teach Clara Sesemann to use her legs. And *The Secret Garden*, besides being made up largely of borrowings, is written in Mrs Burnett's usual careless manner. Characters are crudely drawn and predictable, and the prose style is sloppy. Yet the book is lifted above all this by its choice of central image, the walled rose garden.

Such an image has preoccupied poets and writers from *The Romance of the Rose* to *Four Quartets*, but only on this occasion does it specifically enter children's literature. Something powerful and apparently not fully understood by Mrs Burnett herself comes into the book when Mary finds the door and turns the key:

> She took a long breath and looked behind her up the long walk to see if anyone was coming . . . She held back the swinging curtain of ivy and pushed back the door which opened slowly – slowly.
>
> Then she slipped through it, and shut it behind her, and stood with her back against it, looking about her and breathing quite fast with excitement, and wonder, and delight . . .
>
> 'How still it is!' she whispered. 'How still.'

Mrs Burnett of all people has brought us to the centre of Arcadia, to the 'place of making' that lies at the heart of the Wild Wood. And is not the garden, dead and overgrown when Mary first finds it, reminiscent of another ancient symbol, the Waste Land? Its dead state seems profoundly related to the sickness of Colin, who is a kind of wounded Fisher King. No wonder that the revival of the garden, as Mary tends and weeds and clears away the undergrowth, brings him back to health. Mrs Burnett seems scarcely to understand why this should be so, and tries to suggest that some sort of supernatural 'life-force' is at work:

> Colin's face was not even crossed by a shadow. He was thinking only of the Magic . . . 'The sun is shining – the sun is shining. That is the Magic. The flowers are growing – the roots are stirring. That is the Magic. Being alive is the Magic – being spring is the Magic.

The Magic is in me – the Magic is in me. It is in me – it is in me. It's in every one of us.'

Mrs Burnett cannot comprehend that no Magic is needed to explain the potency of the Secret Garden. But then the Garden, the Enchanted Place itself, is a symbol which greater children's writers than her only dared treat with the utmost delicacy, hinting at it and reaching out towards it rather than grasping it. No wonder that she, having picked it up in her hand, is scarcely sure what she is holding.

The Secret Garden is the last book which uses the Arcadian image quite so confidently. It is the last occasion on which we meet with a Utopia pure and simple. With the next, and really the final appearance of the Enchanted Place in this tradition of writing, the Arcadian vision is used to express a very different set of views about humanity in general and children in particular.

*

Alan Alexander Milne rather regretted that he was his parents' third son. According to fairy-tale tradition, it seemed to mark him out all too predictably for the happy ending. How much more fun to be number one or number two, miss the fortune and the king's daughter, and come to an excitingly nasty end. It was indeed to work out just like that. His eldest brother, Barry, disappeared from the story early on, and, though number two, Ken was the person Alan most loved and admired in childhood, but he too eventually dropped out of the running, leaving Alan to press on alone to success. And when that success came it seemed rather an empty prize.

Born in 1882 at the height of the fashion for the Beautiful Child, A. A. Milne was brought up to look much like Little Lord Fauntleroy. His mother encouraged him to lisp, and he was made to wear his fair hair curling on his shoulders. (His own son Christopher was later to be subjected to the same treatment.) This might seem at odds with the Milne family's severe Scottish Presbyterian background on the paternal side; but Milne's father, who was proprietor and headmaster of a small private school in north London, had rejected the extreme religious views of his own father (a minister) for the kind of liberalism that was being preached by Charles Kingsley and George MacDonald. In the years before his marriage and owning his own school, he had worked in an establishment where the head master preached a sermon to the boys,

> in which he told them that they were all going straight to Hell, or anyhow the boys who hadn't attended in class last week, and he described Hell in words which would terrify anybody who knew that he was going there. And that nice little Mr Milne got permission

to preach to the boys on the next Sunday, and he told them that there was no such place as Hell, and no such thing as Everlasting Fire, but that they would all be very silly if they didn't work now, when work was made easy for them . . . And then he had offered the Headmaster his resignation, but the Headmaster wouldn't hear of it, and said that he was sorry, and that perhaps there wasn't Everlasting Fire after all.

So A. A. Milne tells the story in his autobiography *It's Too Late Now* (1939), and it is clear that he himself was brought up in an atmosphere of religious liberalism. But he too was a child of his age, and he rejected even this liberal view of Christianity, eventually arriving at a position similar to that of Kenneth Grahame, Beatrix Potter, and J. M. Barrie.

He dismissed all organised religion as being merely man-made. 'The long, unlovely hours we laboured through in church' rankled with him as he wrote his autobiography. 'What were we doing there? Even if men believe that the Incomprehensible Being which created this incomprehensible universe is morbidly anxious that little atoms on one of his million worlds should praise him for it in set phrases on every seventh day, is it likely that he should wish them to do so in words which reach no higher than a child's mind?' But for a long time he kept these views to himself. They only became explicit in his autobiography, and though after that he became positively militant and wrote a satirically agnostic poem called *The Norman Church* (1948), one might have supposed until 1939 that he was a thoroughly conventional believer:

> Little Boy kneels at the foot of the bed,
> Droops on the little hands little gold head.
> Hush! Hush! Whisper who dares!
> Christopher Robin is saying his prayers.

Yet Christopher Robin, like the younger Llewelyn Davies boys, was never christened; his father carefully abstained from influencing him in the matter of religious belief, but was delighted when at the age of twenty-four Christopher, too, became agnostic.

Though A. A. Milne rejected conventional belief in God, he was very much prepared to cast human beings in God-like roles. During his own childhood his father, like Mr Fairchild in *The Fairchild Family*, stood in place of God to his son. 'He was the best man I have ever known,' Milne wrote in his autobiography, 'by which I mean the most truly good, the most completely to be trusted, the most incapable of wrong. He differed from our conception of God only because he was shy, which one imagined God not to be, and was funny, which one knew God was not.' In the later part of his own son's childhood, A. A. Milne managed to play the same role to the boy. 'So there I was,' Christopher Milne wrote in his turn in his own autobiography, *The Enchanted Places*

(1974), 'very close indeed to my father, adoring him, admiring him, accepting his ideas . . . An accidental word of reproof or criticism from him and tears would stream from my eyes . . .' This is precisely the relationship in which Pooh, Piglet, and the other toys stand to Christopher Robin: adoring, admiring, fearing only his reproof.

> Christopher Robin came slowly down his tree.
> 'Silly old Bear,' he said, 'what *were* you doing?' . . .
> 'I see now,' said Winnie-the-Pooh. 'I have been Foolish and
> Deluded,' said he, 'and I am a Bear of No Brain at All.'
> 'You're the Best Bear in All the World,' said Christopher Robin
> soothingly.
> 'Am I?' said Pooh hopefully. And then he brightened up suddenly.

If A. A. Milne drew his notions of the relation between God and man from his feelings for his father, it would seem that his ideal for a relationship on the purely human level was his affectionate friendship with his brother Ken. Though Ken was sixteen months the elder, Alan was clearly superior intellectually, and Ken put up with this good-naturedly, never complaining when Alan managed to better his achievements at school. Alan later observed of this:

> Ken had one advantage of me which he was to keep throughout his
> life. He was definitely – nicer . . . kinder, larger-hearted, more
> lovable, more tolerant, sweeter tempered . . . I might be better at
> work and games . . . but 'poor old Ken' or 'dear old Ken' had his
> private right of entry into everybody's heart.

This is the model from which the friendship between Pooh and Piglet was drawn. Pooh, as Piglet himself observes, 'hasn't much Brain', but always manages to survive, chiefly because he is so lovable. Piglet could scarcely be called intelligent – Milne's satirical view of society will not admit such positive qualities as intelligence – and is chiefly character-ised by his fearfulness; yet he has something of Alan's mental perkiness when compared to the solid, dependable, steady 'old Ken'.

Alan was soon soaring above Ken at Westminster, where they were both sent to school; he got a scholarship there when he was only eleven, and showed exceptional ability at mathematics, shooting to the top of the school in that subject at the age of twelve. He might well have become a professional mathematician, like Lewis Carroll. Instead, deprived of the challenge of any further competition (for he had beaten everyone else at Westminster), he stopped working, and when he finally went to Cambridge he achieved only a Third Class in the Mathematical Tripos. Yet, as with Carroll, Milne's humour is that of a mathematician. Each humorous situation in the Pooh books is reached by the logical pursuit of an idea to the point of absurdity. Pooh and Piglet, tracking a Woozle, are in fact following their own footprints round and round the same tree. They dig a trap for Heffalumps and therefore assume that a Heffalump must have been trapped in it. The North Pole is sought, and a pole is duly found, so it must be the right one. There is a mathematical simplicity in such stories very different from, say, the predominantly social comedy of Beatrix Potter's stories, or the humour deriving from the absurd psychology of Toad. Pooh's world is like Alice's in another respect too: people change their shape or their function somewhat unpredictably, and this is treated with an alarming coolness. In the very first story Pooh decides to turn himself into a cloud in order to obtain a honeycomb; later he becomes stuck in Rabbit's hole, and so Rabbit uses his legs as a convenient towel-horse; later still Eyore's tail is discovered doing duty as Owl's bell-rope. Objects change their nature too, and just as disconcertingly. Eyore's birthday presents – a pot of honey and a balloon – turn into an empty jar and a burst fragment, and are perfectly acceptable to Eyore in this form. And there are Alice-like crises of identity: Piglet pretends to be Roo, and when the deception is discovered cannot get his own name back.

> 'There you are!' said Piglet. 'I told you so. I'm Piglet.'
> Christopher Robin shook his head again.
> 'Oh, you're not Piglet,' he said. 'I know Piglet well, and he's *quite* a different colour.'

Any plan embarked upon is likely to produce precisely the opposite consequences from those intended. Rabbit, Piglet, and Pooh set out to 'lose' Tigger in the forest, and as a result become lost themselves. The benevolent plan to build a house for Eyore results in the destruction of the shelter he has just made for himself. This is not quite the world of Nonsense, but it is something very close.

Milne's talent for mathematics was soon diverted into the occupation that came to dominate his life while he was a Cambridge undergraduate: the composition of light verse. He undertook this not as a recreation or amusement, but as an entirely serious task, for his intellect. He taught himself to handle words in the kind of detached manner in which a mathematician deals with figures; they were not to be used to conjure up emotions or even to represent ideas; they were, instead, a challenge in themselves. This process resembles the solving of crossword puzzles; Christopher Milne notes that his father obtained the same kind of quasi-mathematical pleasure from both occupations.

Milne's skill at light verse[128] got him the editorship of the Cambridge undergraduate magazine *Granta*, and this in turn got him contacts in the London offices of *Punch*, the journal that was the mecca of all

British humorists at this period. On leaving Cambridge in 1903, Milne duly set himself up as a freelance writer in London, with his sights aimed at joining the *Punch* staff. He managed this in three years, all at once finding himself Assistant Editor, putting the magazine together under the ponderous eye of the then Editor, Owen Seaman, whose melancholic manner seems to have provided one of the models for Eeyore. But this speedy success presented Milne with a real problem: what was he to write about?

*

A. A. Milne was a very difficult person to get to know on more than a superficial level. His son Christopher wrote: 'My father's heart remained buttoned up all through his life.' He seems to have had no close friends other than his brother Ken in childhood, and eventually for a few years Christopher himself – though he seems to have given almost nothing of himself away, even to Christopher. One has a suspicion that perhaps there simply was no inner man, no secret self: the surface cleverness was perhaps in the end the whole person and not a disguise for a more private level of existence. At all events the greater part of Milne's career shows us the spectacle of a highly alert intellect, with a particular facility at handling words, yet curiously short of subject matter. Humorists, of course, are not required to be 'deep' in the way that a serious novelist is; but they should be able to develop comic 'types' which give flesh and blood to their wit, whether it be Wodehouse's Bertie Wooster and Jeeves or Thurber's eccentric relatives. In his pieces written for *Punch* before the First World War, Milne can be seen setting out on a path much the same as Wodehouse's: there are comic descriptions of country-house parties, the romantic mishaps of young men-about-town, and the like. But Wodehouse's gift for creating exaggerated but believable people is quite lacking, and instead there is a rather weary straining after comic effect.

If one insists on looking for a 'real' A. A. Milne at this stage of his life, an oddly familiar figure begins to show through the facade of the blue-eyed, pipe-smoking, very English-looking young man. He had, he records in his autobiography, 'a notorious distaste for lavatory jokes'; he speaks also of 'wishing that I liked beer and whisky more than I liked rice pudding', and when describing his appearance says, 'I had no beard; I was twenty and very young for that.' The echoes of J. M. Barrie are very striking, and Milne makes no secret of the fact that at this stage of his life Barrie was his principal literary idol. As soon as the task of producing weekly humorous pieces for *Punch* began to pall, he turned to the theatre, and started to write plays very much in the style of Barrie. He also made friends with Barrie himself, who gave him a great deal of help and encouragement in getting the plays put on. He eventually became successful enough as a playwright to go freelance, and did not go back to his *Punch* job after the First World War. Yet his plays are simply Barrie-and-water. Milne the dramatist is adept at creating Barrie-like situations on the stage, but having created them he has no idea what to do with them. To take two plays from his middle years, *The Truth About Blayds* (1921) and *The Dover Road* (1922), for example: the first has an aged and distinguished poet confessing that all his work has been plagiarism, and the second concerns a mysterious gentleman who traps eloping lovers in his country house and tries to persuade them to change their minds. Each would have been a likely topic for Barrie, and one knows that in each of them he would have made far more of the material than Milne does. In Milne's hands the plays really have nothing more to say after the dénouement has been reached and the true facts of the situation made plain.

Milne, then, was not Barrie, however much he may have wished to be. Nor was he Kenneth Grahame. Smitten by *The Wind in the Willows* when it was first published (during his years on the *Punch* staff), he championed it long before its qualities were widely recognised. In one of his early panegyrics of it he said: 'I feel sometimes that it was I who wrote it and recommended it to Kenneth Grahame.' Eventually he turned it into the highly successful children's play, *Toad of Toad Hall* (1929). But Christopher Milne has observed that it was only the part of the book dealing with Toad's adventures that was entirely to his father's taste; the element of it which deals with Mole and Rat and the River (the book's deepest level) meant little to him, and he virtually eliminated it from the play, substituting instead a passage or two of facile sentimentality (such as the opening song, 'Wind in the willows is whispering low'). Milne could in fact no more have written *The Wind in the Willows* than *Peter Pan*.

The First World War came and went without his having found a true *métier* as a writer, though he had become successful enough – largely, as he admitted in his autobiography, due to his being again and again 'not wholly the wrong person in the right place at the right time'. During the war itself he served as a signalling officer on the Somme, was invalided out with trench fever, and was given a job writing patriotic propaganda; these experiences contributed nothing to his imagination as a writer. Nor was his marriage, in 1913, apparently an event of central importance to him. His wife, Dorothy ('Daphne') de Sélincourt, god-daughter of Owen Seaman of *Punch*, seems to have been a brittle, buttoned-up person not dissimilar to Milne himself. Though he frequently declared that she was his 'collaborator' in literary matters, the marriage seems to have been rather a formal, chilling affair, undertaken for the supposed social convenience of both parties rather than because of any great affection. The hints that Christopher Milne drops about this may lead one to imagine A. A. Milne as a would-be bachelor, longing like Kenneth Grahame to escape from the confines of an impossible situation. Yet while in the long run Milne probably would have privately preferred to be unmarried, one has no real sense that there was anything for him to escape to, certainly no River or Open Road. He liked long walks, but chiefly (as Christopher observed) so that he could eat ham-and-eggs at wayside inns at every possible opportunity; there was something here of Pooh's addiction to the honey-pot. Certainly Christopher Milne suggests that his father was sometimes treated a little ungenerously by his mother – he was given the darkest, dampest rooms in the family house for his study and his bedroom. But the figure that emerges from this is not the quietly tragic one of a Kenneth Grahame, but (as Christopher suggests) Eeyore, the gloomy old grey donkey whose self-pity only excites our ridicule.

Christopher, born in 1920, was the only child of the marriage,[129] and at first his presence in the house seems to have made little difference to Milne's life. The child was cared for full-time by a nanny, Daphne Milne having no wish to become involved in the practicalities of baby-care; he only saw his parents at the beginning and end of each day. But when Christopher was three, Milne 'wasted a morning' writing the poem 'Vespers', and thereby opened the first of a series of doors to his major work as a writer.

*

'Vespers', with its refrain 'Christopher Robin is saying his prayers', is the last major appearance in English writing of the Beautiful Child, who by the 1920s had been dominating attitudes to children for nearly half a century. The poem appears at first to subscribe entirely to the Beautiful Child myth, with its description of the 'little gold head' drooping 'on the little hands'. But the Little Boy who 'kneels at the foot of the bed' is not quite so simple or late-Victorian a figure as that. The reader cannot be expected to know that Milne himself does not believe in the God to whom the child is praying – though of course that knowledge affects one's view of the poem. But the point of the poem is that Christopher Robin is *not* praying. He occasionally repeats one of the formulas he has been taught: '*God bless Mummy*. I know that's right.' But immediately he is distracted by something of real interest: 'Wasn't it fun in the bath to-night?' The poem is in fact veiled ridicule of the whole business of formal prayers, the 'set phrases . . . words which reach no higher than a child's mind', against which Milne rails in his autobiography.

The prayers (suggests the poem) are meaningless to the child, compared to the real things in his life – hot baths, dressing-gowns, and the like. And the poem is also a negation of the very image around which it seems to be centred, the Beautiful Child. Christopher Robin may have a 'little gold head', but he is no angel. Milne does not believe that 'Heaven lies about us in our infancy'; the child in 'Vespers', far from having an unsullied perception of the divine, cannot turn his attention from the mundane to the spiritual.

Milne felt very strongly that the Wordsworthian view of childhood was completely wrong. He said so, eloquently and at length, in a 'Preface to Parents' appended to an edition of his children's verses. In this essay he accepts that 'very young children have an artless beauty' which leads adults to suppose that 'Heaven . . . does really . . . lie about the child'. But he argues that this 'outstanding physical quality' is accompanied by 'a natural lack of moral quality, which expresses itself, as Nature always insists on expressing herself, in an egotism entirely ruthless'.[130] The penultimate verse of 'Vespers' is intended to portray exactly this child-egotism:

> Oh! *Thank you, God, for a lovely day.*
> And what was the other I had to say?
> I said 'Bless Daddy,' so what can it be?
> Oh! Now I remember it. *God bless Me.*

There was in a sense no need for 'Beachcomber' (J. B. Morton) to parody the poem, not long after it had first appeared ('Hush, hush, nobody cares, / Christopher Robin has fallen downstairs'). 'Vespers' itself is intended to be an entirely ironic picture of childhood, a rather sarcastic nudge at adults who insist on viewing children as heavenly beings. In fact the irony was not generally perceived, and the poem was taken at face value as a sentimental portrayal of childhood. Milne's perceptions about childish egotism were not a little ahead of their time.[131]

'Vespers' is the nearest Milne came to making a positive statement of belief or philosophy in his writings for children. Placed at the very beginning of them,[132] it is a manifesto of what is to come. We will be shown children, and a childhood world, of considerable physical beauty, but this beauty will be a camouflage for ruthless egotism. To put it another way, children may be Arcadians in their physical appearance, but the Arcadia they inhabit is not an ideal world of fine feelings, not a dream-come-true land at all. It is distinguished by the naked selfishness of its inhabitants.

This is the theme that Milne worked out, first in his children's poems and then in the *Winnie-the-Pooh* stories.

*

The first collection of poems, *When We Were Very Young* (1924),[133] explores the theme tentatively. Its portrayal of childhood owes a lot to

Robert Louis Stevenson's *Child's Garden of Verses*, and many of
Milne's poems in the book are simply Stevensonian explorations of the
childish imagination without any distinguishing mark of Milne other
than his extraordinary facility with rhyme and metre, acquired from
years of writing *Punch* verses. Several pieces even indulge the contemporary taste for fairy poetry, for example 'Twinkletoes', which
describes a fairy flitting from flower to flower. Nevertheless, the book
also contains Milne's first sustained explorations of the 'ruthless
egotism' of childhood.

The best known poem in it after 'Vespers' is 'Buckingham Palace', in
which the two first lines of each verse are

> They're changing guard at Buckingham Palace –
> Christopher Robin went down with Alice.

The poem is an account of the child's perception of the adult world.
This is filtered through Alice-the-nanny's own view of it, which is as
remote from reality as is the boy's. Each of them, child and nanny, is
concerned to find a place for himself or herself in the scheme of what
they see. We are told at the outset that 'Alice is marrying one of the
guard', and at the end Christopher Robin asks 'Do you think the King
knows all about *me*?' The poem is framed by these two pieces of
egotism; Alice and Christopher Robin are only interested in Buckingham Palace for what it can give *them*. In between, the poem is made up
of the child's statements of what he has seen, with the nanny
responding antiphonally. Ostensibly she is bringing him down to earth
and is giving a more sophisticated view of things. In reality she is only
replacing his childish view with hers:

> We saw a guard in a sentry-box.
> 'One of the sergeants looks after their socks,'
>   Says Alice.

> We looked for the King, but he never came.
> 'Well, God take care of him, all the same,'
>   Says Alice.

> They've great big parties inside the grounds.
> 'I wouldn't be King for a hundred pounds,'
>   Says Alice.

> A face looked out, but it wasn't the King's.
> 'He's much too busy a-signing things,'
>   Says Alice.

'Says Alice': the phrase carries echoes of the contemptuous 'Says you'.
And, of course, the narrator's voice – Milne's own – is in the end rather

contemptuous of Alice's spiritual short-sight. She has reduced the King and his court conveniently to her own level, and is even claiming a kind of responsibility for him ('"Well, God take care of him"'). To put it another way, the poem is taking a gently mocking look at the child's and nanny's universe, which appears to be a cosy hierarchy of (from the bottom upwards) Christopher Robin – Alice – the guards – the King – God. Christopher Robin and Alice have remade the King in their own image, just as Milne believed that all religion is man-made. The poem appears to be a celebration of security, just as 'Vespers' appears to be a celebration of a child praying; both poems are in fact deeply mocking, and in 'Buckingham Palace' the mockery is more obvious, for the poem ends with a ruthless assertion of egotism by both protagonists:

> 'Do you think the King knows all about *me*?'
> 'Sure to, dear, but it's time for tea,'
> Says Alice.

Alice panders to Christopher Robin's own egotism, then obstinately reasserts her own world-view – 'It's time for tea'.

Egotism is the predominant theme in all the best poems in the book. In 'Lines and Squares' the child views the London pavements as existing solely for the possibility of offering him adventure: if he treads on the lines between the paving stones the bears will eat him. In 'Market Square' he determines to buy a rabbit, and dismisses the entire market as valueless because it cannot provide one; finally, seeing rabbits all around him on the common, he expresses sheer pity for the market people, ''Cos they haven't got a rabbit, not anywhere there!' The Zoo is seen in similarly self-centred terms; the poem 'At the Zoo' has the refrain 'But *I* gave buns to the elephant when *I* went down to the Zoo!' The marvellous comic narrative 'The King's Breakfast' presents a chidlike monarch who, just like a four-year-old, has his day ruined when he is denied the particular thing he wants to eat:

> The King said,
> 'Bother!'
> And then he said,
> 'Oh, deary me!'
> The King sobbed, 'Oh, deary me!'
> And went back to bed.
> 'Nobody,'
> He whimpered,
> 'Could call me a fussy man;
> I *only* want
> A little bit
> Of butter for
> My bread!'

And the most accomplished piece in *When We Were Very Young*, 'Disobedience', is both the sharpest and the funniest expression of Milne's belief in the 'ruthless egotism' of children.

A small boy – 'James James / Morrison Morrison / Weatherby George Dupree'134 – has frequently warned his mother: 'You must never go down to the end of the town, if you don't go down with me.' She disobeys, and is never seen again. So far, the poem's comedy lies in the simple reversal of parent-child roles. But now we learn of the child's reaction – he 'Told his / Other relations / Not to go blaming *him*', and it is implied that he agrees with the King's view on the matter: '"If people go down to the end of the town, well, what can anyone do?"' In the 'Preface to Parents' in which he discusses the ruthlessness of children, Milne himself picks on this poem in particular as expressing what he is talking about, and says of it: 'It is the truth about a child: children are, indeed, as heartless as that.' Whether he was right must remain a matter for conjecture; Christopher Milne thought not, and wrote in his autobiography that, in circumstances such as James James Morrison Morrison's, at the age of three, he 'might not have missed my mother' and 'would certainly not have missed my father' (a nice back-hander at the poem's author), but 'would have missed Nanny – most desolately'.

Right or wrong in its portrayal of childhood, *When We Were Very Young* caught the imagination of a public beginning to be sated with Peter Pan and the fairy-fashion, and the book was bought in quantities. It went through twelve printings in just over a year and brought Milne a fame which, despite all his apparent successes, had really deserted him up to that time.

He followed it with *Now We Are Six* (1927), which explores the same theme with increased confidence but slightly less subtlety. The tone of the book is summed up by the last poem in it, which concludes:

> But now I am Six, I'm as clever as clever.
> So I think I'll be six now for ever and ever.

There are good things in *Now We Are Six* – among them the blackly comic 'King John's Christmas', in which (as in 'The King's Breakfast') an adult is portrayed as a selfish child, and 'The Knight Whose Armour Didn't Squeak', in which, again, an adult gets away with utterly selfish behaviour that would be condemned in the young. But the book has about it the air of a sequel, of writing to please an audience that knew what to expect. In fact, by the time it appeared Milne had already moved on from these comparatively simple examinations of 'ruthless egotism' to constructing a world peopled exclusively by egotists.

*

Christopher Milne observes that the 'We' in the titles *When We Were Very Young* and *Now We Are Six* is no mere piece of whimsy. In *The Enchanted Places* he suggests that his father's most deeply felt emotion was nostalgia for his own childhood – which had certainly been the happiest period of his life, just as it was with so many of the outstanding children's authors. Christopher feels that his father would have liked to have begun to relive childhood alongside him. But his own reserve and the constant presence of Nanny got in the way, so that he was impelled to do that reliving on paper rather than in the actual company of the boy. As Christopher puts it:

> Some people are good with children. Other are not. It is a gift. You either have it or you don't. My father didn't . . . It was precisely because he was *not* able to play with his small son that his longings sought and found satisfaction in another direction. He wrote about him instead.

Hence the 'We' in the titles of the books of verse. As Christopher Milne observes,

> We grew up side by side and as we grew the books were written . . .
> When I was three he was three. When I was six he was six.

This process of reliving childhood may have encouraged Milne to acquire, in 1925, a Sussex farmhouse for use as a weekend and holiday alternative to the family's London home, for at about the age of eleven he himself had begun a very happy period living in that part of England, where his father established a preparatory school. At all events Cotchford Farm, between Tunbridge Wells and East Grinstead, was to provide the setting for the stories he now started to write about Christopher's toys – a true Arcadian setting, with its sandy wooded landscape on the edge of Ashdown Forest, its small streams and paths. To anyone of imagination, certainly to Christopher and his father, it was a true Enchanted Place.

And, being so idyllic, it provided the perfect ironic backdrop to the foolish, short-sighted goings on among the toys described in *Winnie-the-Pooh* (1926) and *The House at Pooh Corner* (1928). As a setting it is as Arcadian as Grahame's River Bank and Barrie's Never Never Land, but the happenings it witnesses are much closer to those of Beatrix Potter's Sawrey. Milne, indeed, does not even allow his animal characters the breadth of personality that is to be found in the pages of Potter. Peter Rabbit, Tom Kitten, Tommy Brock, and Samuel Whiskers are each a composite of many (human) characteristics. Milne, writing about his son's toys, reverted to an older type of animal story, the fable as practised by Aesop and his many imitators. Milne claimed to be an admirer of *The Wind in the Willows*, but his use of animals (or toy animals) as representatives of human character could scarcely be more different from Grahame's. Pooh, Piglet, and Eeyore exist on a completely different plane from Rat, Mole, and Badger. Grahame's animals are subtle, many layered expressions of their author's ideals. The Pooh toys are as simple and predictable as Milne could make them. The narrative derives not as in Grahame from the characters' gradual discovery of each other's true nature, but from the conjunction and opposition of known quantities. No one, not even the comparatively imaginative Pooh, changes or develops as the story progresses. Christopher Robin gradually grows up, and will eventually leave them (thereby, one imagines, making their continued existence impossible), but this is something of which they remain blithely unaware. In a sense there is no 'story' as such, only a set of incidents which could be put in almost any order. One notes that Milne was brought up on *Uncle Remus*; he claimed not to have been influenced by it, but in construction his work has strong resemblances to Joel Chandler Harris's fable collection.

In 1964 there appeared Frederick C. Crews's book *The Pooh Perplex*, a collection of brilliant parodies of different schools of literary criticism, all taking *Winnie-the-Pooh* for their text. Crews's choice of Milne's work for this exercise was shrewd: trying to analyse the Pooh stones is really futile from the start, because they are almost entirely without layers of secondary meaning. They are exercises in the humorist's art, and almost nothing else. Yet (though to say it puts one in danger of seeming like one of the Crews parodies) there is a little more to them than this. They are, in fact, a continuing exposition of Milne's favourite themes: the selfishness or 'ruthless egotism' of childhood, and humanity's dependence on a God made in its own image.

Pooh, Piglet, and the other toys are really a family of children living their lives under the benevolently watchful eye of a parent-figure, Christopher Robin. This, of course, is exactly how real children treat their toys, exercising over them the domination that they themselves have to suffer from their parents. But, in the sense that the Pooh stories are about human character, Milne is not interested in portraying parental behaviour. All his satire is reserved for the 'children' – Pooh, Piglet, Eeyore, Rabbit, Owl, Kanga and baby Roo, and Tigger.[135] Each of them personifies one characteristic, one type of selfishness. Pooh puts his appetite for honey before everything, and his chief interest in life is the possibility of obtaining 'a little something at eleven o'clock in the morning' (his clock at home is stuck at five minutes to eleven, like the pub clock in *Under Milk Wood*, which always shows opening time). Piglet is only concerned to save his own skin, and is prey to every possible fear: he does his best to get out of every Woozle-hunt or Heffalump-trapping on some paltry excuse:

> 'I *think*,' said piglet . . . 'I *think* that I have just remembered something. I have just remembered something that I forgot to do yesterday and sha'n't be able to do to-morrow. So I suppose I really ought to go back and do it now.'
> 'We'll do it this afternoon, and I'll come with you,' said Pooh.
> 'It isn't the sort of thing you can do in the afternoon,' said Piglet quickly.

Eeyore is self-pity taken to such an extent that it can provoke only ridicule: '"And how are you?" said Winnie-the-Pooh. Eeyore shook his head from side to side. "Not very how," he said. "I don't seem to have felt at all how for a long time."' Tigger is exuberance and *bonhomie*136 so unbridled that they become a kind of aggression towards other people; Rabbit is bossiness exercised for its own sake: 'It was going to be one of Rabbit's busy days. As soon as he woke up he felt important, as if everything depended on him.' Owl is self-respect for one's own (non-existent) cleverness:

> Owl took Christopher Robin's notice from Rabbit and looked at it nervously. He could spell his own name WOL, and he could spell Tuesday so that you knew it wasn't Wednesday, and he could read quite comfortably when you weren't looking over his shoulder and saying 'Well?' all the time, and he could –
> 'Well?' said Rabbit.
> 'Yes,' said Owl, looking Wise and Thoughtful. 'I see what you mean. Undoubtedly.'

It is striking that Milne characterises Owl as if he were a child making first efforts at reading. But then all the characters in the Pooh books are children in their ways of reacting to the world; only the motherly Kanga has predominantly adult characteristics, and she seems to have been included in the stories so that, in her company, the other apparently grown-up characters can be seen as the children they really are:

> Before he knew where he was, Piglet was in the bath, and Kanga was scrubbing him firmly with a large lathery flannel.
> '*Ow!*' cried Piglet. 'Let me out! I'm Piglet!'
> 'Don't open the mouth, dear, or the soap goes in,' said Kanga. 'There! What did I tell you?'

The only real adult in Pooh's world is Christopher Robin: a nicely ironic inversion which puts a neat frame round the stories. But his interventions in the narrative are not usually those of a parent sorting out unruly children: instead, Milne makes him step in as a *deus ex machina*, and appoints him not merely as adult in charge, but as God. On more than one occasion he observes Pooh's muddles *from high up* – sitting in a branch of a tree – and when he comes down, to make all well again, he does so chiefly through expressions of *love*:

> Then Piglet saw what a Foolish Piglet he had been, and he was so ashamed of himself that he ran straight off home and went to bed with a headache. But Christopher Robin and Pooh went home to breakfast together.
> 'Oh, Bear!' said Christopher Robin. 'How I do love you!'
> 'So do I,' said Pooh.

Note the ambiguity in Pooh's 'So do I.' Even at this moment of tenderness he seems to be expressing self-love, the old egotism.

Christopher Robin is, in other words, the God of Love. The toys know of no other power in their lives, and their feelings for him amount to worship:

> Piglet wasn't listening, he was so agog at the thought of seeing Christopher Robin's blue braces again. He had only seen them once before, when he was much younger, and, being a little over-excited by them, had had to go to bed half an hour earlier than usual; and he had always wondered since if they were *really* as blue and as bracing as he had thought them.

But Milne is mocking this worship, just as much as he is mocking all the toys' other characteristics. Christopher Robin has been presented to us at the beginning of *Winnie-the-Pooh* not as a god, but as a child (the author's son) listening to a story about himself and his toys. And at certain points in the story we are reminded of his real nature. The 'Expotition to the North Pole', which has something about it of a pilgrimage or crusade, is led by him; it is the only adventure which he himself initiates, and the reader knows that the supposed triumph (Pooh finding a pole which Christopher Robin decides is the North Pole) is really completely ridiculous. In 'Rabbit's Busy Day' in *The House at Pooh Corner*, Christopher Robin is entirely absent from the scene – learning to read. And in the final chapter in the second book, 'An Enchanted Place', he tries to explain to Pooh that he must soon leave him and go to school.

It is difficult to remain quite unmoved by this last chapter, in which a child tries to say his farewell to childhood, cannot find the words for it, and then laughingly gives up the attempt. Coming as it does at the end of Milne's writings for children – and so at what was effectively the end of a particular tradition and movement of English children's literature – one is inclined to regard it as a kind of *envoi*, a goodbye to an entire Golden Age. But it is a false effect, a piece of whimsy on Barrie lines rather than an organic part of Milne's creation. The plain fact is that Milne wishes to be rid of Pooh and the whole *opus*, and like Conan Doyle with Sherlock Holmes at the Reichenbach Falls he must do something dramatic. In fact it was too late: Milne had become irrevocably identified with Pooh, and lived the rest of his life (he died in 1956) resenting that the public identified him almost solely with his children's books, but failing to write anything else remotely as popular. Note the irony in the title of his autobiography, *It's Too Late Now*.

But in 1928 he did not know that it was too late to try to rid himself of Pooh and Christopher Robin, so he wrote this farewell scene, in which again we are reminded of Christopher Robin's role as God to the toys; for the setting – 'an enchanted place on the very top of the Forest' – and the narrative tone has a vaguely religious connotation. Milne seems to be preparing us for some event not unlike Christ's ascension. On the other hand, he seems also to envisage a Peter-Pan-like state of perpetual continuation, in which Christopher Robin is trapped for ever within childhood:

> So they went off together. But wherever they go, and whatever happens to them on the way, in that enchanted place on the top of the Forest a little boy and his Bear will always be playing.

Quite apart from the faintly sinister implications of this – Christopher Robin as a boy who cannot grow up – there is also the inappropriateness of the statement that they 'will always be playing', for *play* is one thing that Pooh and Christopher Robin never do together in the stories. Everything that has happened to them both has been in deadly earnest.

So Milne has, at the end, lost confidence in his own creation. It is a pity, because otherwise *Winnie-the-Pooh* and *The House at Pooh Corner* are, on their own terms, more successful as works written for children than anything else produced during children's literature's Golden Age. *Alice, The Wind in the Willows, Peter Pan*, even the Beatrix Potter stories, all require some sort of adjustment before they can be taken in by young children: it is a matter partly of vocabulary but also of concept. One cannot escape the feeling with any of them that a full appreciation is only possible by adults. Milne is less ambitious than Carroll, Grahame, Barrie or even Potter: he sets out only to depict a very small fraction of human behaviour. But he manages to do so completely within a child's understanding; the Pooh books can be taken in fully by all but the smallest children, and the child reader is able to carry into adult life a perception of human character acquired from his readings of Milne. How many of us have, at one time or another, compared our friends or colleagues to Milne creations? Don't we all know an Eeyore, or a Tigger, or a Piglet? Don't we, indeed, recognise them in ourselves?

*

And yet they are not quite all of them mere types. Pooh transcends that, just a little. Certainly he is greedy. Certainly he is often a Bear of Very Little Brain. But he is also a poet, and in allowing him the dignity of being able to compose his 'Hums', Milne is allying him with the Water Rat – is portraying him as someone whose vision of the world goes at least a little way beyond selfish short-sightedness:

> Pooh sat down on a large stone, and tried to think this out. It sounded to him like a riddle, and he was never much good at riddles, being a Bear of Very Little Brain. So he sang *Cottleston Pie* instead:
>
> > Cottleston, Cottleston, Cottleston Pie.
> > A fly can't bird, but a bird can fly.
> > Ask me a riddle and I reply:
> > 'Cottleston, Cottleston, Cottleston Pie.'
>
> . . . 'That's right,' said Eeyore. 'Sing. Umty-tiddly, umty-too. Here we go gathering Nuts and May. Enjoy yourself.'
> 'I am,' said Pooh.
> 'Some can,' said Eeyore.

None of Pooh's fellow-creatures has the faintest appreciation of his artistic gift. Their reaction is that of Mole to Rat's poetry, early in *The Wind in the Willows*: '"I don't know that I think so *very* much of that little song."' And at times, one must admit, Pooh's verses are almost as reprehensible as the boasting-songs of Toad:

> > 3 Cheers for Pooh!
> > (*For Who?*)
> > For Pooh –
> > (*Why what did he do?*)
> > I thought you knew;
> > He saved his friend from a wetting:
> > 3 Cheers for Bear!
> > (*For where?*)
> > For Bear . . .

But to put even this kind of thought into rhyme goes, one feels, beyond the total self-absorption which characterises the other inhabitants of the Hundred Acre Wood. Pooh has a little of the true visionary about him.

And of course he has humility. It is he, never others, who talks of himself as 'a Bear of No Brain at All' and 'a Bear of Very Little Brain'. Both Piglet and Eeyore are in a sense humble too, and appear to have no opinion of themselves. But with Piglet this is merely a manifestation of his timidity. He really regards himself as a person of some dignity and importance, taking the broken notice board next to his 'very grand house' with its mysterious inscription TRESPASSERS W as evidence that he had a distinguished grandfather named Trespassers William, and lecturing Pooh on the subject:

> so round this spinney went Pooh and Piglet . . . Piglet passing the time by telling Pooh what his Grandfather Trespassers W had done to Remove Stiffness after Tracking, and how his Grandfather Trespassers W had suffered in his later years from Shortness of Breath, and other matters of interest . . .

By contrast we are told at the start of *Winnie-the-Pooh* that Pooh 'lived in a forest all by himself under the name of Sanders', and E. H. Shepard's illustration shows him sitting outside a front door bearing the name-plate 'Mr Sanders'. This is never enlarged upon, but seems to suggest that Pooh has little self-centred concern with his own identity. By contrast, Owl is proud that he can spell his own name (and of course he spells it wrongly), and is in the habit of festooning his front door with important-seeming notices:

PLES RING IF AN RNSWER IS REQUIRD
PLEZ CNOKE IF AN RNSR IS NOT REQID

It begins to appear that *homes* are matters of particular importance to the characters. Eeyore's self-pity has made him an outcast, albeit by his own choice, so that he not only lives in the open air but occupies a patch of thistles faintly suggestive of the Waste Land. His plight does not escape the notice of Pooh, who as usual is the only one of the animals to perceive the needs of others:

> '*You* have a house, Piglet, and I have a house, and they are very good houses. And Christopher Robin has a house, and Owl and Kanga and Rabbit have houses, and even Rabbit's friends and relations have houses or somethings, but poor Eeyore has nothing. So what I've been thinking is: Let's build him a house.'

Though perceptive, he is still a Bear of Very Little Brain, which is why
the plan to build the House at Pooh Corner goes a little awry. (The
choice of those words for the title of the second Pooh volume is
significant.) Similarly Pooh's greed, his only real fault of character, leads
to a double disaster involving houses. He gets stuck in the front door of
Rabbit's and so is unable to go home to his own. And the two episodes
in which external forces (floods and gales) threaten the lives of those in
the Hundred Acre Wood are seen entirely in terms of houses. Piglet and
Pooh are marooned in theirs, and (after the great wind) Owl's is
entirely destroyed. This last event leads Pooh to perform, in the
penultimate chapter of *The House at Pooh Corner*, his greatest act of
selflessness. Eeyore has found a 'new home' for Owl, but everyone else
knows that it is really Piglet's house, and an embarrassing situation
arises. Is the truth to be told, Owl to be deprived of a roof over his head,
and Eeyore's stupidity to be shown up? Even Christopher Robin is at a
loss; he wonders 'whether to laugh or what'. And now comes the act of
generosity, and it is not just Pooh who performs it, for by now Piglet
(the Mole to Pooh's Water Rat) has acquired at least something of
Pooh's lack of self-concern and perception of the needs of others. Piglet
has grown up, and the selfish child, the ruthless egotist, has been
replaced by a rather different figure:

> And then Piglet did a Noble Thing, and he did it in a sort of dream,
> while he was thinking of all the wonderful words Pooh had hummed
> about him.
> 'Yes, it's just the house for Owl,' he said grandly. 'And I hope he'll
> be very happy in it.' And then he gulped twice, because he had been
> very happy in it himself.
> 'What do *you* think, Christopher Robin?' asked Eeyore a little
> anxiously, feeling that something wasn't quite right.
> Christopher Robin had a question to ask first, and he was
> wondering how to ask it.
> 'Well,' he said at last, 'it's a very nice house, and if your own house
> is blown down, you *must* go somewhere else, mustn't you, Piglet?
> What would *you* do, if *your* house was blown down?'
> Before Piglet could think, Pooh answered for him.
> 'He'd come and live with me,' said Pooh, 'wouldn't you, Piglet?'
> Piglet squeezed his paw.
> 'Thank you, Pooh,' he said, 'I should love to.'

*

This is the real conclusion of the Pooh stories. The final chapter, 'In
Which Christopher Robin and Pooh Come to an Enchanted Place, and
we Leave Them There', is as we have seen a coda in a very different

mode from the rest of the narrative. But is it quite fair to dismiss it as an unnecessary piece of whimsy, a regrettably sentimental lapse? Certainly the statement that 'in that enchanted place on the top of the Forest a little boy and his Bear will always be playing' is out of place when applied to the Pooh stories themselves. But perhaps Milne is half-consciously saying goodbye not so much to his own literary creation as to the whole image of the Enchanted Place, the Arcadia, the Never Never Land, the Secret Garden. He could not have foreseen that after him would come a very different era of children's books. But in concluding his writings for children, and so in effect ending his own career as an artist, he was undoubtedly saying goodbye to the childhood that he himself had been reliving alongside his own son Christopher. The farewell at the end of *The House at Pooh Corner* is a farewell to its author's own private Golden Age. And yet at the same time, in saying that Christopher Robin and Pooh can still be found 'in that enchanted place', Milne is reminding himself that the Secret Garden is always there for those who once knew it, and who can still find the door. As Christopher Milne has said in his own book, 'For us, to whom our childhood has meant so much, the journey back is short, the coming and going easy.'

The Garden Revisited

Golden Ages can only be identified in retrospect, when they can be seen to have finished. And one can hardly be expected to give precise dates for their termination. Certainly the 'movement' of great Victorian and Edwardian writing for children petered out rather than came to an abrupt end. The First World War might have been expected to put a stop to it, but Milne wrote in the 1920s. His contemporaries Hugh Lofting and Arthur Ransome, in their 'Doctor Doolittle' and 'Swallows and Amazons' books, are Golden Age figures, too, in many readers' opinions. Yet their work is characterised by a certain plodding predictability once the general lines have been set down, and it would be hard to make out a case for it equalling Milne and his great predecessors. It seems to be in the wake of a literary movement rather than a part of it. The same may be said of P. L. Travers's *Mary Poppins* (1934), which has had huge popularity but is really a mediocre story strung round one good idea (a nanny with magic powers).

A fairly firm case *can*, in fact, be made for the First World War as the cut-off point between the classic children's books and the present day, with Milne regarded as a survivor of the Edwardians rather than belonging truly to the post-war world. It must have been harder to dream up River Banks and Never Never Lands after the experience of the Somme. Moreover, Arcadian writing for children was quite clearly part of a general tendency towards idyllic, ruralist fantasy among many English authors of the pre-war period. In his book *The Edwardian Novelists* (1982) John Batchelor lists among those who 'subscribe [d] to the myth of England as a golden rural world, a place where right feeling [was] still to be found' the names of Saki, Edward Thomas, W. H. Hudson, and Kipling. He states that 'pastoral and suburban make a fixed . . . antithesis in the Edwardian mind'. Grahame and his contemporaries were part of a wider intellectual movement.

But what, then, has happened to children's books since 1918 which makes the pre-First World War classics seem to belong to such a remote era? What is it that separates us from them? What are we giving our children to read now – what are we trying to tell them about the world that the Victorians and Edwardians weren't?

*

A subtle change of subject matter – a bridge between the Edwardians and the present time – can be found in *The Hobbit* (1937), arguably the next outstanding children's book to appear after *The House at Pooh Corner*. The story is set in an idealised landscape, and describes a journey to a long-desired place. But J. R. R. Tolkien has a very different aim from, say, Barrie or Milne. His book shows the mark of his own experiences in the trenches in 1916,[137] and could scarcely have been written before the First World War. The landscape through which the story moves is certainly made up of idealised features – cosy little villages, Alpine-style mountains, vast impenetrable forests – but it offers no security; instead there is a constant threat of physical violence. Bilbo Baggins (the hobbit) and his dwarf companions are continuously in fear of their lives, from trolls, goblins, giant spiders, a dragon, and other perils. Even those persons likely to offer them shelter – men and elves – generally prove suspicious or openly hostile. The climax of the book is not the much hoped for killing of the dragon, which happens almost offstage from the main drama, but a contest for the treasure between those who ought to have been allies. Conversely, Bilbo, the supposed hero of the book, is engaged by the dwarves as a burglar rather than a hero. His task is to steal treasure from the dragon, having made his way stealthily in by a back door. He is no warrior of medieval romance, facing his foe with drawn sword. Indeed he even performs an act of treachery against his own comrades (stealing the dwarves' priceless Arkenstone), albeit with a motive that he regards as laudable. We are confronted with a world in which old-style heroism has been rejected in favour of backstairs espionage and 'diplomatic' treachery. As Bilbo himself remarks towards the end of the story, This is a bitter adventure.' Besides, the dwarves' motive in setting out to regain their ancestral treasure from the dragon is implicitly questioned throughout the book. By the end it can be seen as a case of greed as naked as Squire Trelawney's determination to make himself rich with pirate gold in *Treasure Island*. Like Stevenson, Tolkien is questioning the accepted ethics of children's books, in the light of his own experience of the fruitlessness of conventional heroism in the trenches of a real war.

In *The Lord of the Rings*, published in 1954–5 but written between 1937 and 1949, Tolkien went on to do, entirely consciously, what many of the Victorian and Edwardian children's writers had fumbled towards: he created an alternative religion. Himself a fervent Roman Catholic, he admitted God the Creator into his fictional religious hierarchy, at the very top, but kept the deity entirely out of sight. He eliminated the figure of Christ and the notion of redemption, and posited the existence of an elaborate angelic hierarchy which partakes of the character of heathen mythologies. Yet despite these conscious efforts at religion-building, *The Lord of the Rings* is far less 'numinous' in a religious sense than is *Peter Pan* or even *The Water-Babies*.

Tolkien's 'Valar', his angelic figures, are remote from the action, and contribute little more than a sort of chilling grandeur to the tone of the story. Such religious feeling as the book does transmit comes from the rather Christ-like character of Frodo Baggins, and the distinctly otherworldly wizard Gandalf. Tolkien certainly has a religious purpose, more consciously than Barrie or Kingsley ever did. But it exists on a different plane from the things in the story that really move the reader (just as Grahame's 'Piper at the Gates of Dawn' is a piece of self-conscious religiosity which is detachable from the rest of *The Wind in the Willows*). The quasi-biblical diction of the later parts of *The Lord of the Rings* suggests that Tolkien was trying to lift the events of his tale on to an Old Testament level. In fact at the finest moments, most notably Frodo grappling with Gollum on the very brink of the fiery chasm in Mount Doom, the authorial voice slips back into ordinary un-heightened prose:

> Sam got up. He was dazed, and blood streaming from his head dripped in his eyes. He groped forward, and then he saw a strange and terrible thing. Gollum on the edge of the abyss was fighting like a mad thing with an unseen foe. To and fro he swayed, now so near the brink that he almost tumbled in, now dragging back, falling to the ground, rising, and falling again. And all the while he hissed but spoke no words.

Compare this, which is the brisk narrative style of Stevenson or John Buchan, with the self-conscious archaism of a typical passage (only a couple of pages later) where Tolkien thinks of himself as writing a religious epic:

> The Captains bowed their heads; and when they looked up again, behold! their enemies were flying and the power of Mordor was scattering like dust in the wind. As when death smites the swollen brooding thing that inhabits their crawling hill and holds them all in sway,, ants will wander witless and purposeless and then feebly die, so the creatures of Sauron, ore or troll or beast spell-enslaved, ran hither and thither mindless . . .

Tolkien was not writing the religious book that he intended to create. *The Lord of the Rings* does not provide a pantheon of alternative gods, a 'mythology for England', which was its author's avowed purpose. Like *The Hobbit*, it is largely a sustained exploration of evil. It is set in a world where evil is not merely incarnate but seems destined to triumph and destroy everything. The only acceptable course of action for the right-minded individual is to perform small acts of kindness which may have unforeseen consequences of good – such as Frodo's sparing of

Gollum, which eventually leads to the destruction of the terrible Ring. And even when, against the odds, the power of evil is destroyed, the heroes find that their own private Arcadia, the Shire, has been ravaged by another kind of wickedness, industrialisation. It is striking that at the end of *The Lord of the Rings* Tolkien attacks the very same thing against which the Arcadian movement in children's literature had reacted nearly a century earlier, the mindless industrialisation of society.

His book is a tract for its times, the work of a man who had seen two World Wars, and who anticipated a civilisation dominated by the nuclear threat. Though undoubtedly influenced by the great Arcadian children's writers – a debt to *The Wind in the Willows* is apparent in the early chapters – *The Lord of the Rings* is not a part of their movement.

Tolkien's close friend C. S. Lewis, whose seven 'Narnia' books for children appeared between 1950 and 1956, was writing more consciously than Tolkien within the Arcadian tradition. His models were George MacDonald and E. Nesbit. But *The Lion, the Witch, and the Wardrobe* and its sequels, fine as they are (particularly the later books), are governed throughout by a didactic purpose: a determination to convey to children Lewis's own affection for the narrative power of the Christian story, which he has recast in terms of a children's fantasy. He also aims to teach them his particular Muscular Christian ethics, which range from a love of beer and tobacco to a dislike of 'progressive' education and vegetarianism. At its best this didactic voice recalls Kingsley's righteous indignation:

> There was a boy called Eustace Clarence Scrubb, and he almost deserved it . . . He didn't call his Father and Mother 'Father' and 'Mother', but Harold and Alberta. They were very up-to-date and advanced people. They were vegetarians, non-smokers and teetotallers and wore a special kind of underclothes. In their house there was very little furniture and very few clothes on the beds and the windows were always open.

At its worst, Lewis's didacticism is more insidious than this. For example, his character-assassination of Edmund, who goes over to the Witch's side in *The Lion, the Witch, and the Wardrobe*, seems all too near a kind of spiritual Fascism. Edmund is a weak character because he is a weak character: there is no attempt to motivate his unpleasantness, and one has the impression in the early part of the book that he is predestined, quite simply, to damnation.

Moreover, Lewis's personal feeling is almost all for the doctrine, not the narrative. The stories are often marvellously inventive – no other children's writer can rival the sheer quantity of fantasy-ideas in the seven Narnia books, even though many of them are borrowed from recognisable sources. But the invention is always in the end a conscious embodiment of the ideas, not a potent symbol capable of being explored beyond its author's immediate intentions.

*

The stories of Tolkien and Lewis appear, therefore, to be the result of efforts to recapture the Arcadian tone and message, but in the event these efforts carried their authors in rather different directions. Both writers became hugely popular in America; but they were the last English authors for children to do so. In the mid-1950s there began in England what has often been described as a second Golden Age of children's literature,[138] but the best books produced during it, though they commanded a large following in England, did not make the same impact on America as the Victorians and Edwardians had done. Indeed, at exactly the same time America itself developed, at last, its own vigorous strain of writing for children – which in turn has had no particular appeal to English readers *en masse*. Why should America and England, the former for so long dependent on the latter for the emotional nourishment of its children, suddenly go their separate ways after the Second World War?

Up to this point America, with only a few notable exceptions,[139] had produced three general types of children's fiction: the family story, the historical novel, and the animal story. The first, modelled loosely on *Little Women*, commended the virtues of family life; the second instilled into American children a love of their country's past; and the third was often concerned with man's uneasy relationship with the unconquered landscape of America. No particular 'message' was discernible throughout this body of writing, except a vague and generally conservative patriotism, together with an implicit acceptance of morality as sanctioned by adults. But abruptly in 1951 all that changed. J. D. Salinger's *The Catcher in the Rye*, published that year, was not a children's book, but was seminal in altering American writers' attitudes to children and their relationship to the adult world and adult morality. Holden Caulfield, the novel's hero, has an aggressive, detached, ultra-critical view of adult society which appealed instantly to American teenage readers of the 1950s. Some of those readers themselves became, in following years, children's authors, and wrote fiction for the young dealing (often in a style closely resembling Salinger's) with adversity, the acceptance of responsibility, and the child or adolescent's awareness of the foibles and fallibility of adults. These subjects could scarcely have been admitted into the canon of American children's writing before 1945, except in the hands of such subtly subversive authors as Louisa Alcott and Frank Baum. In recent decades, with novels on these subjects by such accomplished 'realist'

American children's writers as E. L. Konigsburg, Paul Fox, Vera and Bill Cleaver, and Robert Cormier, the children's book in America would appear, in every sense, to have 'grown up'.

Yet though these writers (and many others) all deal with the anguish of children or teenagers coming to terms with the 'real' world, one may legitimately wonder how 'realistic' their books genuinely are. At first, American post-Salinger writing for children appears to be in direct antithesis to the English Golden Age authors, who believed in childhood as a self-contained state which is ultimately preferable to maturity. There would appear to be an enormous gulf between – on the one hand – Tom the water-baby, or Diamond in *At the Back of the North Wind*, or Peter Pan, and – on the other – the Holden Caulfield type of hero who comments in a detached, deeply cynical manner about the absurdities of adult *mores* and the psychological failings and inadequacies of the adults who surround him. Yet is there not more than a touch of the Enchanted Place about post-Salinger American juvenile fiction? Certainly it gets to grips with the adult world, and portrays grown-ups as (almost inevitably) flawed and fallible; but one sometimes feels that writers in this genre are not really preaching the virtues of growing up, but are treating adolescence as a self-contained and privileged condition, much as the Victorian and Edwardian writers in England had treated childhood. Holden Caulfield and his descendants are, in an odd kind of way, distant relatives of the Beautiful Child.

One senses this all the more when it becomes clear that, just as the Salinger influence was being felt on American juvenile fiction, American writers were also starting to create (for the first time) a large body of fantasy writing for children. Admittedly much of it has consisted of inferior imitations of Tolkien, but certain writers (notably Ursula le Guin) have shown originality and wit in their handling of Tolkien-like themes, while there have also been a few fantasies which could only have come out of America – such as Russell Hoban's *The Mouse and his Child* (1967), a tragi-comic quest story about two clockwork toys which has roots in Mark Twain and James Thurber. There has as yet been no outstanding American fantasy classic, but it does seem as if American writers have been going through a process much like that experienced by the English Victorians and Edwardians – turning away from realism to, on the one hand, self-contained escapist fantasies, and, on the other, to books which idealise the pre-adult's view of the world (in this case à la Holden Caulfield). The symptoms of the Golden Age have reappeared across the Atlantic – which leads one to suspect that America may have been going through a crisis of self-identity similar to that experienced by Britain in the late nineteenth century. Indeed, in the period beginning with the assassination of John F. Kennedy and the Vietnam War, this has quite clearly been the case. The preoccupations of recent American children's fiction demonstrate a society very ill at ease with itself.

*

Modern America has virtually no use for the modern British children's book. Compared to the enormous popularity in America of the English Golden Age classics, very little nowadays travels successfully across the Atlantic. The reason is not hard to find.

While American writers have tried to turn away from the adult world, either taking refuge in fantasy or castigating adults through teenage eyes, their contemporary British authors have been offering precisely the opposite message. At first sight the modern English children's book would seem to be continuing the themes and preoccupations of the Arcadian writers. The motifs of the Victorians and Edwardians – secret gardens, private worlds – are often discernible in their books. Yet the modern British children's author is actually encouraging children to grow up.

There is a clear statement of this in *The Borrowers* (1952) by Mary Norton, the first classic for children to emerge in England after the Second World War. The book concerns a family of tiny people, the Borrowers, who live beneath the floor of a big house and survive by 'borrowing' food and household objects from the 'Human Beans', the big people upstairs. The story is largely a social parable. The Borrowers are among the last survivors of a once large race, which still prides itself on its traditions and *tabus*, and blithely ignores the fact that it is dying out – Borrowers convince themselves that, despite the evidence, it is the Human Beans who are vanishing from the world.[140] But on another level *The Borrowers* is about family life, and in particular about parental attitudes to children.

Arrietty, the only child of Pod and Homily, lives in virtual imprisonment in her beneath-the-floors home. Her parents refuse to tell her anything about the outside world. 'My poor child,' says her mother, 'you don't know – and, thank goodness, you never will know . . . what it's like upstairs.' The way to the upper world is barred by a series of gates which are ostensibly to keep cats and other predators out, but Arrietty's father admits that they are also 'to keep you in'.

> 'To keep me in?' repeated Arrietty, dismayed.
> 'Upstairs is a dangerous place,' said Pod. 'And you, Arrietty, you're all we've got, see?'

Arrietty is at least fortunate in that she has been told that there *is* another world upstairs. Her cousin Eggletina never knew as much – 'They told her the sky was nailed up, like, with cracks in it.' Eggletina escaped and was never seen again; Arrietty comments angrily:

'I bet she just ran away because she hated being cooped up . . . day after day . . . week after week . . . year after year . . . Like I do!' she added on a sob.

'Cooped up!' repeated Homily, astounded.

Arrietty put her face into her hands. 'Gates . . .' she gasped, 'gates, gates, gates.'

To her astonishment, her mother takes her side, and declares: 'The child is right.' This disconcerts Arrietty deeply:

It shocked her to be right. Parents were right, not children. Children could say anything, Arrietty knew, and enjoy saying it – knowing always they were safe and wrong.

She precipitates a crisis when she goes upstairs with her father and is seen by a boy, one of the Human Beans. Her parents' reaction to this astonishes her:

'They are frightened,' Arrietty realized; 'they are not angry at all – they are very, very frightened.'

The Borrowers is largely an account of a child rejecting parental protection and asserting her independence. Childhood is equated not with a Golden Age of special perceptions and visions, but with a state of imprisonment. Mary Norton's book suggests that, however terrible the consequences may be (and Arrietty's actions eventually lead to the family's flight from its home), the child must break the parental bonds if it is to grow up. Moreover, the Borrowers' domain beneath the floorboards, which is in many respects Arcadian – Pod has ingeniously and lovingly fitted it out with every kind of comfort, adapted from small household objects 'borrowed' from upstairs – is characterised as above all stuffy, poky, and limiting. It is the precise opposite of Badger's kitchen: it provides not womblike security but a choking constriction.

*

A very large number of good books for children were written in England between the 1950s and the 1970s, so it is all the more striking that the greater part of children's fiction produced in this period has the same theme: the discovery or rediscovery of the past.

A typical plot from this period is likely to concern one or two children who stumble across some feature of history or mythology which concerns their own family or the place where they are living or staying, and which often involves magic or supernatural events. The children become drawn into it, usually at their own peril, and in consequence achieve some kind of spiritual, moral, or intellectual growth. This kind of plot may be found again and again in the earlier books of William Mayne, Penelope Lively, and Alan Garner, to name three of the most popular authors of the period. Even the more straightforward historical novels for children written during these years have a similar theme. For example, those of Rosemary Sutcliff, the outstanding practitioner in this genre, usually concern a maimed or handicapped individual discovering his own strengths and limitations. The same notion may be found in the quasi-historical stories of Leon Garfield.

At its worst the 'discovering myth/history and growing-up' motif can be banal; Alan Garner's *The Weirdstone of Brisingamen* (1960) and Penelope Lively's *Astercote* (1970) are examples of it at its crudest and most ridiculous. At its best, in later work by these two authors and others, it can be effective and moving. But what is striking is the unvarying emphasis throughout English children's fiction at the time on *growing up*, on coming to terms with the real world. An Arcadia may be visited by the child protagonists, but it does not offer a goal in itself. It is part of the process of the child discovering her or his identity and facing up to the challenges of life. And this process usually involves a close friendship or understanding with an adult or adults. The child is no longer occupying a separate world.

Nowhere is this theme better handled than in *Tom's Midnight Garden* (1958), a children's novel by Philippa Pearce, one of the few post-1945 books that can measure up to the best Victorian and Edwardian writing in its emotive power and the strength of its images. *Tom's Midnight Garden* is the story of a boy, Tom Long, who is obliged to spend a summer holiday with a childless uncle and aunt while his brother has measles at home. Tom finds the atmosphere in the uncle and aunt's flat oppressive, and at night is lured downstairs when an old grandfather clock strikes thirteen, to discover, outside the back door of the house which contains the flat, a large and beautiful garden which is not there in the day time. During successive midnight visits to the garden he meets and becomes deeply attached to Hatty, a small girl of about his own age. The garden and Hatty lure him back night after night, soon coming to seem far preferable to his dreary daytime existence, but he is disconcerted to find that time does not stand still in the garden, and Hatty is growing older all too fast. In only a few weeks of Tom's time she has become a grown woman, and Tom suffers the heartbreak of her turning away from him when she meets the young man she will marry. Tom had intended to stay in the Garden for ever and not return to the 'real' world, but now he cannot get into the garden at all, and he has lost Hatty. However, upstairs is old Mrs Bartholomew, the landlady in whose house the flats are, and to his astonishment Tom discovers that *she* is Hatty, grown old, and it is her dreams of her past life that Tom has been visiting each night. The book ends powerfully, with Tom hugging the old lady to him, to the astonishment of his uncle:

> 'Of course, Mrs Bartholomew's such a shrunken little old woman, she's hardly bigger than Tom, anyway: but, you know, he put his arms right round her and he hugged her good-bye as if she were a little girl.'

On its simplest level *Tom's Midnight Garden* contains the message that was found in Mrs Ewing's *Mrs Overtheway's Remembrances* – that there is a child inside every adult, every old person. But the book says much more than this. It re-examines and inverts two of the old Arcadian images, the Secret Garden and the Boy Who Wouldn't Grow Up.

Tom and Hatty's garden is childhood itself. Tom visits it every night simply because he is lonely and wants someone to play with him. Towards the end of the story he has rejected everything else in favour of it; he has decided not to grow up: 'He meant to exchange ordinary Time, that would otherwise move on towards Saturday [the day that he must return home to his parents], for an endless Time – an Eternity – in the garden.' But the book has already given a covert warning against clinging on to childhood. Tom's aunt and uncle are childless, and the aunt compensates for this by showering Tom with rich food, making coy remarks to him about fairies, and giving him her own childhood books to read. Moreover, Tom observes that his room has bars across the bottom of the window, and bursts out: 'This is a nursery! I'm not a baby!' He is trapped in a child-centred world. His escape to the garden is merely the exchange of one sort of permanent childhood for another.

He is in fact Peter Pan to Hatty's Wendy, and *Tom's Midnight Garden* is in one respect a rewriting of *Peter Pan* from Peter's point of view. In Hatty's eyes Tom is a half-spectral, unreal boy who visits her only when he chooses. (Tom goes into the garden every night, but his visits there coincide with quite differently spaced episodes in Hatty's childhood.) Just as in *Peter Pan*, the boy-visitor cannot be seen by adults who do not believe in him: he is only visible to Hatty and to Abel the gardener, a deeply religious man who regards Tom as an emanation of the Devil – a striking detail in view of the strongly religious element in the original *Peter Pan*. Thanks to his spectral relationship to Hatty's world, Tom can perform apparently supernatural feats in it: being ghostlike and weightless, he floats to earth from the branch of a tree (Peter Pan flying), and by an effort of will can force his body through an unopened door – 'Please, Tom – please come through slowly – I want to see how it's done!' cries Hatty in words reminiscent of the Darling children confronted by Peter's flying. As if to reinforce the point,

Tom's brother and *alter ego* who in his dreams shares some of Tom's experiences is called Peter. But Tom's own full name, Tom Long, seems to suggest *longtemps*, and the story's conclusion describes Tom's acceptance of what Peter Pan can never accept: that Time must be allowed to pass, and growth and even old age must be accepted as necessary and even desirable facets of human existence. As Hatty/Mrs Bartholomew tells him at the end: 'Nothing stands still, except in our memory.'

Something of the same message stands at the conclusion of *The House in Norham Gardens* (1974), one of Penelope Lively's most successful children's books, and one in which the theme of the relationship between present and past is handled with a subtlety not found in her earliest writings. The book describes young Clare Mayfield's relationship with the two elderly great aunts whose North Oxford house she inhabits, and it ends with her realisation of the importance of the aunts' lives to her own existence. She defines herself and her future in relation to the old ladies, and understands that she must grow up, change, become quite unknowable as she is now. She tries to project herself imaginatively into the future, and fails; she cannot envisage her future self, 'a stranger, familiar and unreachable'. Yet she has made the attempt, and, poised between past and future, she concludes: 'I can't make it stop at now . . . and you shouldn't want to, not really.'

*

The realisation that you can't 'make it stop at now' dominates English children's books of the modern period, and makes it possible for writers to recreate the past without indulging in nostalgia. The past exists as an enrichment of the present. If Arcadias are visited, the journey is made for the benefit of present and future. Alan Garner's outstanding *Stone Book Quartet*, four novellas published between 1976 and 1978, demonstrates this more clearly and with greater literary craftsmanship than does anything else written for children at the period.[141]

The Stone Book and its three sequels describe true details of Garner's family history. His forbears were Cheshire stonemasons and black-smiths, and he centres the narratives on certain 'sacramental moments' in the lives of several generations, showing how each action by an individual is rooted in the past and has a bearing on the future. In *The Stone Book* the child Mary ascends a church spire which her stonemason father is completing, and is also taken by him to see an ancient subterranean cave painting which one of their own ancestors, unknowable centuries before, has marked with the family's private mark. These events are echoed throughout the four books, so that, for example, in

The Aimer Gate young Robert, descendant of Mary and her father, ascends the inside of the same spire without knowing who built it, and discovers the same private mark and the family name carved high inside it, though the carver 'knew it wouldn't be seen'. Actions and words reverberate down the generations.

The Stone Book Quartet is scarcely a work of literature for children. The language is simple (apart from dialect words) but profound, and it requires several readings even by adults before anything like full comprehension is reached. The four stories virtually reject plot of the conventional sort, and even the characters are not clearly defined by the standards of children's fiction. In fact within Garner's whole *oeuvre* this makes sense, is even predictable: *The Stone Book Quartet* stands at the end of a long progression from conventional adventure-fantasy (*The Weirdstone of Brisingamen* and its sequel) via more sober, plausible, serious fantasy novels (*Elidor* and *The Owl Service*) to an enigmatic book dealing with present-day adolescents interpreting themselves through history (*Red Shift*). It is partly a process of refinement and improvement – Garner becomes a far better literary craftsman during it – but also a desire to write about what matters, to create fiction of integrity and maturity.

*

Alan Garner seems to stand at the culmination of the post-war movement in modern English children's writing. It is hard to imagine anyone bettering what he has done in *The Stone Book Quartet*, giving a finer expression to the theme of the child finding its place in the world by understanding history. Certainly nothing has appeared in recent years to suggest that English children's fiction is in the same vigorous condition that it was from the mid-1950s to the mid-1970s; that particular Golden Age seems to have run its course too. Arcadia has been visited, and now re-visited, and the two phases of notable British writing for children, with their two very different sets of conclusions about the nature of childhood, seem complete. No new theme seems to be emerging.

I am speaking here of children's books intended for readers between the ages of about seven and twelve, the group most likely to enjoy the Victorian and Edwardian classics. There is no shortage of fresh books for the very young. Modern beliefs in the importance of pre-school education have led to the wide-scale production of picture books for very small children. Instead of a modern Alice, Toad, or Peter Pan we have such ubiquitous figures as Dick Bruna's Miffy and John Burningham's Mr Gumpy. If the Beautiful Child has disappeared from popular consciousness, and has been replaced in America by the Shrewd Adolescent (out of the Salinger stable), the modern English equivalent would appear to be the Sturdy Toddler. Meanwhile, there has been a resurgence of an old, familiar element in the children's literary world. Just as Mrs Sarah Trimmer, the evangelicals, and the pioneers of the Sunday School movement concerned themselves, at the beginning of the nineteenth century, with purging children's fiction of all that seemed antagonistic to religion or to a stable social order, so modern authorities in children's books (librarians, teachers, critics and publishers) seize on the banners of Sexism and Racism, apparently in the belief that simply by ridding children's stories of these undesirable elements, and commissioning books that preach the opposite viewpoint, all will be well. So far this witch-hunt has been about as profitable for children's reading matter as was the invention of the Sunday School pamphlet.

It would appear that some sort of social change in attitudes to children has once again taken place. The Victorian age began to produce great children's books partly because family size had diminished and children were receiving greater attention. Probably the gradual disappearance of notable new fiction for children between seven and twelve reflects a loss of interest in that age group, or at least a failure to allow it any special identity. That some such change has taken place is argued by Neil Postman in *The Disappearance of Childhood* (1983), which seeks to demonstrate that the 'idea of childhood' has been largely eroded by television, a medium which makes no real distinction between childhood and adults. Television, argues Postman, deluges its audience, child and adult alike, with a flood of information. Children perceive and largely understand this information, with the result that the walls that formerly surrounded childhood – protection from the issues which dominate the adult world – are broken down.

Postman's book has not met with universal acceptance. It does not investigate demographic trends, or the current nature of family life, or even present day economic factors. His thesis also seems to be applicable only to affluent middle-class society; among poorer families it has never been customary to shield children from the 'real world'. But it is in affluent homes that children's books have been mostly read, and the perceptible alteration in the nature of writing and publishing for children in recent years does indeed suggest that something has happened to bring to an end the old-style dialogue between adult author and child audience. We do not, it appears, live any longer in a society in which adults turn to child readers to work out their private dreams on the scale of a River Bank or a Never Never Land. The Enchanted Places, the Secret Gardens, were created in an age when society, the child, and the author stood in a certain relationship to each other which has now broken down. We may revisit those Enchanted Places ourselves, but we cannot create new ones.

*

There is an odd postscript to the Golden Age, an event which, though really quite unrelated to the lives of the great children's authors, seems to stand as a kind of tombstone for them. In 1968 Cotchford Farm, the home of A. A. Milne and the setting of the Winnie-the-Pooh stories, was bought by Brian Jones of the Rolling Stones. 'Knowing the Winnie-the-Pooh stories almost by heart,' writes Philip Norman in *The Stones* (1984), 'it gave him special delight to show [friends] the sundial – under which Milne's original manuscripts are reputedly buried – and the bridge over the little stream where Pooh and Christopher Robin invented the Poohsticks game. He felt proud to be the guardian of such a shrine.'

On the night of 2 July 1969, Brian Jones was found underwater at the deep end of the swimming pool, 'lying face down on the bottom, his hair floating round him like a spread fan'. His death was no very great surprise – over the years his health had been undermined by drugs – but the newspapers made as much as they could of the ironic contrast between Milne's idyll and Brian Jones's ravaged life. The *Daily Mail* ended its obituary by quoting from Winnie-the-Pooh's search for his hidden treasure trove: '"That's funny – I know I had a jar of honey there . . ." But when he reached for it, it never seemed to be there.' Had the reporter known it, there was another far more apt image to be found in children's literature, the image of the drowned child who is not dead. Tom slips into the stream and, seeming to drown, becomes instead a water-baby. Michael Llewelyn Davies drowns in Sandford Pool but lives on in Barrie's imagination as the Boy Who Wouldn't Grow Up. 'To die will be an awfully big adventure.' But there is no death in the Golden Age, only a constant rebirth as a child, in a secret garden where no harm can come.

'So he pulled off all his clothes in such haste that he tore some of them, which was easy enough with such ragged old things. And he put his poor hot sore feet into the water; and then his legs; and the farther he went in, the more the church-bells rang in his head . . . And he had not been in it two minutes before he fell fast asleep, into the quietest, sunniest, cosiest sleep that ever he had in his life; and he dreamt about the great meadows by which he had walked that morning, and the tall elm-trees, and the sleeping cows; and after that he dreamt of nothing at all . . .'

NOTES AND REFERENCES

1 E.g. Roger Lancelyn Green, 'The Golden Age of Children's Books', *Essays and Studies* n.s. XV, 1962, pp.59–73. Mr Green dates the start of the Golden Age in the mid-nineteenth century, with such books as Ruskin's *The King of the Golden River* (1851), and declares that 'the period ends sharply with E. Nesbit'.

2 For a discussion of the various types of 'Moral Tale', with examples, see under that heading in *The Oxford Companion to Children's Literature*, compiled by Humphrey Carpenter and Mari Prichard, 1984.

3 *One Fairy Story Too Many* (1983).

4 His *Children's Books in England*, originally published in 1932, was extensively revised by Brian Alderson for the third edition (1982).

5 Silas Hocking, '*Chips*', '*Joe*', and '*Mike*' (1890); Hocking was writing after the heyday of the evangelical novel, but his stories contain sentiments that appeared from the 1840s onwards.

6 Leigh Richmond, *The Dairyman's Daughter*, originally published in 1810, but reprinted again and again throughout the nineteenth century, and circulated to Sunday Schools in America and the British colonies as well as in England.

7 See further J. S. Bratton, *The Impact of Victorian Children's Fiction* (1981), and M. N. Cutt, *Ministering Angels, a story of nineteenth-century evangelical writing for children* (1979).

8 Gillian Avery, with Angela Bull, *Nineteenth Century Children* (1965). The evangelical writers undoubtedly developed this notion of child-as-spiritual-guide partly from James Janeway's celebrated Puritan tract, *A Token for Children* (1672), which is a collection of accounts of the pious deaths of children; it was read in evangelical circles well into the nineteenth century. However, the type of evangelical book in which a poor slum child helps to convert his or her elders did not appear in any quantity until Dickens's fiction was well known. The best known examples of this type of book are *Jessica's First Prayer* (1867) by 'Hesba Stretton' (Sarah Smith), in which a poor waif brings about the repentance of a chapel attendant, and Mrs O. F. Walton's *Christie's Old Organ* (1875), in which a street-arab arranges for the religious education of a dying organ grinder.

9 One might suppose that the atmosphere of religious uncertainty in which the great children's books were written was a direct consequence of the Darwin controversy (*The Origin of Species* was published in 1859, three years before the upsurge of imaginative children's writing in England). Undoubtedly there is a connection. Yet Charles Kingsley was the only outstanding children's author who seems to have taken any direct interest in Darwin, and he fully supported the theory of evolution and adapted it into his own imaginative scheme in *The Water-Babies*. It appears that the religious doubts suffered by him and his fellow authors were more a consequence of the doctrinal liberalism purveyed by F. D. Maurice and his supporters than of Darwin's shaking of the foundations.

10 See, on this, Mark Girouard, *The Return to Camelot: chivalry and the English gentleman* (1981).

11 My definition of 'fantasy' does not precisely agree with that of C. M. Manlove, in *The Impulse of Fantasy Literature* (1983), where he defines it as 'A fiction evoking wonder and containing a substantial and irreducible element of supernatural or impossible worlds, beings or objects with which the mortal characters in the story

or the readers become on at least partly familiar terms'. While this serves adequately as a definition of the fantasy element in, say, Kingsley, Carroll, MacDonald, Nesbit, and Barrie, it does not properly describe the stories of Beatrix Potter, Kenneth Grahame, or A. A. Milne. Perhaps these should properly be classed as 'fable', in that their use of animals as human types is ultimately descended from Aesop; but they seem to me to demand consideration as part of the late Victorian and Edwardian genre of fantasy writing for children, sharing as they do so many of its motives.

12 I am thinking particularly of the 'Earthsea' trilogy by Ursula le Guin (1967–72). Most other American fantasies of the 1960s and 1970s are too plainly an attempt to scramble on the Tolkien bandwagon.

13 Quoted by Patricia Branca in *Silent Sisterhood: middle class women in the Victorian home* (1975).

14 Philippe Ariès virtually says this in *Centuries of Childhood* (English translation, 1962, p. 404) when he observes that in the modern family 'all the energy . . . is expended on helping the children to rise in the world, individually and without any collective ambition: the children rather than the family'.

15 The 'catalogues' which feature again and again in the book – nouns and adjectives in descriptions, or lists of objects – are a mannerism borrowed from Rabelais, whom Kingsley much admired. Sir John Harthover refers approvingly to Rabelais in chapter III of the story.

16 First described and quoted in Susan Chitty's 1974 biography of Kingsley.

17 A reference to *The Song of Solomon*, I.13: 'A bundle of myrrh is my well-beloved unto me; he shall lie all night betwixt my breasts.'

18 Maureen Duffy, in *The Erotic World of Faery* (1972), gives a rather crude sexual interpretation of the whole book, with Tom representing both 'the questing penis' and a foetus in its amniotic fluid. She is surely wrong to conclude that the story is chiefly about masturbation.

19 Quoted in Susan Chitty, *The Beast and the Monk*, 1975, p. 160.

20 Quoted in *Charles Kingsley, His Letters and Memories of his Life, edited by his wife*, 1901 edition, vol. I, pp.164–5.

21 Chitty, *op. cit.*, p.155.

22 *ibid.*, pp. 159–60.

23 Chitty, *op. cit.*, pp. 185–6.

24 *Charles Kingsley, His Letters (op. cit.)*, vol. III, p.141.

25 *ibid.*

26 Kingsley knew the Yorkshire terrain of the book from a holiday near Skipton, a few years before it was written. The original of Lewthwaite Crag, down which Tom clambers, was Mallam Cove, and tradition has it that small black lichen marks on its face suggested a sweep-boy's sooty footprints. On the other hand the book was largely written at Alresford near Winchester, on the banks of the Itchen, and those surroundings contribute to the description of Tom's early days as a water-baby.

27 *The Reader*, 16 May 1863.

28 Locke is among those singled out for attack in chapter IV; Kingsley objects to his rigid rationalism and disapproval of fairy stories, though he allows him to have been a 'good man and honest'.

29 *The Letters of Lewis Carroll*, ed. Morton N. Cohen, 1979, vol. I, p.4.

30 *Letters (op. cit.)*, vol. I, p.207.

31 Quoted in Derek Hudson, *Lewis Carroll*, revised ed., 1976, p.66.

32 *Letters (op. cit.)*, vol. I, pp. 12–15.

33 *Letters (op. cit.)*, vol. I, p. 121n.

34 It was quoted by S. D. Collingwood in his official biography of Dodgson (1898), but does not appear in the surviving volumes of the diary, which leads Derek

Hudson to conclude that it was found in the now missing third volume (which Collingwood had when he wrote his book), and dates from 1855.

35 Hudson, *op. cit.*, p.52. The diaries, edited by Roger Lancelyn Green, were published in 1954.

36 *The Works of Lewis Carroll*, ed. Roger Lancelyn Green, 1965, p.765.

37 *Letters (op. cit.)*, vol. I, p.34n.

38 *Letters (op. cit.)*, vol. I, p.75.

39 *Letters (op. cit.)*, vol. I, p.137n.

40 In *For My Grandchildren* (1966), p.66.

41 'Sir Gammer Vans' in Joseph Jacobs, *More English Fairy Tales* (1894).

42 For sources of 'The Great Panjandrum', see the entry for it in *The Oxford Companion to Children's Literature*.

43 *Letters (op. cit.)*, vol. I, p.53.

44 It was the first of a series of 'Wallypug' books. Other imitations of this sort include *Wanted – a King* (1890) by 'Maggie Browne', and stories by the American author Charles E. Carryl, who was moved to write them because of the similarity of his surname to 'Carroll'.

45 I owe this observation to Dr N. M. J. Woodhouse.

46 The two books of limericks known to have been published before his *Book of Nonsense* (1846) are *The History of Sixteen Wonderful Old Women* (1820) and *Anecdotes and Adventures of Fifteen Gentlemen (c.* 1821), both anonymous.

47 In *Some Versions of Pastoral* (1935).

48 This seems to be a more common childhood recollection of the books than positive affection for them.

49 This was first observed by Elisabeth Sewell in *The Field of Nonsense* (1952), to whom I am therefore much indebted.

50 Tantalisingly, there are no comments on Kingsley's book in Dodgson's diaries or letters, though he had certainly read it, and he knew the author's brother Henry Kingsley, who seems to have played some part in persuading him to publish *Alice's Adventures in Wonderland*. Nor, though he knew George MacDonald, does he have anything to say about the Curdie books or *At the Back of the North Wind*. Jealousy is not a likely motive; one suspects that Dodgson was not really very interested in children's books.

51 'The Stage and the Spirit of Reverence', originally published in *The Theatre*, June 1888; reprinted in *The Works of Lewis Carroll (op. cit.)*, p.1105.

52 Irreverence is one of the most frequent topics in his correspondence, as he gets older; see the index to Professor Cohen's edition of the *Letters*.

53 Hudson (op. cit.), p.105.

54 *The Impulse of Fantasy Literature*, 1983, p. ix.

55 Edward Salmon, *Juvenile Literature As It Is* (1888).

56 See Elizabeth A. Cripps, 'Alice and the Reviewers', *Children's Literature* (Annual of the Modern Language Association Division on Children's Literature and the Children's Literature Association), vol. XI, 1983, pp.32–48.

57 MacDonald uses the term 'bogeys' in his novel *Phantastes*.

58 Robert Lee Woolff, in *The Golden Key, a study of the fiction of George MacDonald* (1961).

59 Greville MacDonald, *George MacDonald and his wife*, 1924, p.66.

60 There were eleven MacDonald children in all: Lilia was the third to die during her father's lifetime, going to her grave in 1891 as a result of tuberculosis. The death of Lona in *Lilith* is undoubtedly a reference to this.

61 In this respect, *Lilith* bears a strong resemblance to the 'metaphysical thrillers' written in the 1920s and 1930s by Charles Williams, friend of C. S. Lewis.

62 *Adela Cathcart* (1864), the 'frame' novel within which several of his first fairy tales were set.

63 These remarks are taken from an essay on 'The Fantastic Imagination', first printed in the 1893 American edition of *The Light Princess and other fairy tales*. The essay bears a striking resemblance to Tolkien's lecture 'On Fairy-Stories' (1939).

64 Among these are *Ranald Bannerman's Boyhood* (1871), *Gutta Percha Willie* (1873), about a boy who discovers a medicinal spring, and *Sir Gibbie* (1879), whose hero is a street-arab without the power of speech.

65 'The Castle' is one of MacDonald's few predominantly allegorical pieces of writing, being a parable about the incarnation of Christ and the world's treatment of him.

66 In which respect he resembles Walter de la Mare.

67 *Dealings with the Fairies* was illustrated by Arthur Hughes, whose pictures for *At the Back of the North Wind* and *The Princess and the Goblin* made him as inseparable from MacDonald as Tenniel from *Alice*. Hughes was especially good at portraying, in his best Pre-Raphaelite manner, the long flowing tresses of the maternal North Wind and grandmother-princess.

68 A lack of overall plan is suggested by the story's title. One is tempted to ask 'The Princess and *what* Goblin?', for the book features a whole hoard of goblins rather than one in particular. *The Princess and Curdie* would be a much better title; but that was given to the sequel – which it scarcely fits!

69 An exception is Oscar Wilde, whose short fairy stories blend a moral or spiritual purpose with a rich imagination as effortlessly as do MacDonald's.

70 It has sometimes been issued under the title *The Lost Princess*.

71 Quoted in Martha Saxton, *Louisa May*, 1977, p.165.

72 I owe this observation to Madeleine Stern, editor of *Behind a Mask: the Unknown Thrillers of Louisa May Alcott* (1975).

73 The distinction of being the first American writer for girls to achieve any sort of lasting reputation seems to belong not to Louisa Alcott, but to 'Sophie May' (Rebecca Sophia Clarke), whose 'Little Prudy' series began in 1863, and remained popular for many years. *Gypsy Breynton* (1866) by Elizabeth Stuart Phelps was another early success in this genre, preceding *Little Women* by two years.

74 In the first volume, Jo tells her mother that she planned that Laurie should have married Meg – this to prevent the engagement to John Brooke.

75 Quoted by Saxton, *op. cit.*, p.365.
76 Louisa Alcott had a set of *Flower Fables* for children published in 1854, and shortly before she wrote *Little Women* a publisher had lost the manuscript of another book she had written of the same kind.

77 The principal examples of this school are Kate Douglas Wiggin's *Rebecca of Sunnybrook Farm* (1903), Eleanor Hodgman Porter's *Pollyanna* (1913), and, in Canada, L. M. Montgomery's *Anne of Green Gables* (1908).

78 It was serialised in *Aunt Judy's Magazine* in 1866, and appeared as a book three years later.

79 The chief practitioners in the genre were Yotty Osborn and Ismay Thorn, whose books about pretty dimpled toddlers, with titles like *Pickles: a Funny Little Couple* and *Only Five*, began to appear soon after the publication of '*Carrots*'. Mrs Molesworth's book was partly anticipated by Stella Austin's *Stumps* (1873), about a dimpled four-year-old who speaks baby talk.

80 I owe this suggestion to Gillian Avery.

81 There was also his boyhood enthusiasm for toy theatre melodramas, which he celebrated in the essay 'Penny Plain and Twopence Coloured' – quite literally cardboard characters in this case.

82 Quoted in Peter Green, *Kenneth Grahame* (1959), p.87.

83 Green, *op. cit.*, p.17.

84 Peter Green suggests that the ornateness and the use of archaisms crept into

Grahame's writing largely as a result of the influence of W. E. Henley, Robert Louis Stevenson's close friend, who printed many of his early pieces in his *National Observer*, and was in the habit of doctoring his contributors' style to suit his own taste, which favoured the ornate and old-fashioned.

85 Quoted in François Bédarida, *A Social History of England*, 1851–1975, 1979, p.25.

86 Originally published as 'My Schooldays' in *The Girl's Own Paper* from October 1896 to September 1897; issued in book form in 1966 as *Long Ago When I Was Young*.

87 With the inspired exception of the Ugly-Wuglies in *The Enchanted Castle* (1907), a set of scarecrow-like figures, made by children, who come alive.

88 An apparent exception is Dickie Harding, the hero of *Harding's Luck* (1909), a lame child brought up in a London slum. But thanks to time-travel, by the end of the book he is leading a very comfortable life as a seventeenth-century nobleman.

89 Even Mother in *The Railway Children*, with scarcely a penny to her name, is helped by Mrs Viney from the village.

90 Doris Langley Moore, *E. Nesbit* (2nd ed., 1967), p.127.

91 Moore, *op. cit.*, p.143.

92 *ibid.*, p.149.

93 Noël is quite simply delighted to have his poems printed, but Oswald rightly observes that 'the Editor seemed to make a game of them'.

94 In a lecture to the Children's Book History Society, London, 1982. Julia Briggs has a book on Nesbit in preparation.

95 Not altogether taken account of by Margaret Lane in her book *The Magic Years of Beatrix Potter* (1978), in which she states that the journal 'tells us a great deal about her everyday life, but about her inner experience, her feelings, very little'. In fact, the journal contains a number of passages where Beatrix talks or hints about her feelings towards her parents, her ambitions, and other 'inner' matters.

96 Quotations in this chapter are from *The Journal of Beatrix Potter from 1881 to 1897*, transcribed from her code writing by Leslie Linder (1966).

97 She first visited Sawrey in 1896, with her family; in the summer of 1905 she bought Hill Top Farm there, and four years later she acquired Castle Farm, which became her home after her marriage in 1913.

98 To whose works she appears to have been devoted, judging from a reference to *Persuasion* in a letter. One might guess this without the evidence, so Austen-like is her delineation of character and her asperity of narrative manner.

99 As is Tolkien's *The Hobbit*.

100 Compare once more *The Hobbit*, with its life-and-death riddle game.

101 In her journal Beatrix Potter mentions an acquaintance's maidservant who was dismissed for actually cutting up a cake which had been offered to guests for years; no one was expected to eat it.

102 According to evidence carefully pieced together by his biographer Peter Green.

103 Quoted in Peter Green, *Kenneth Grahame, a biography*, 1959, p.210.

104 The letters are in the Bodleian Library. Elspeth Grahame published them in *First Whispers of 'The Wind in the Willows'* (1944).

105 'On *The Wind in the Willows*', *The Hebrew University Studies in Literature*, IX, 1 (Spring 1981), p. 84. I am grateful to John Batchelor for drawing my attention to this article.

106 One should note that in William Morris's poem, *The Earthly Paradise* (1868–70), the Arcadian land itself is never reached and the quest fails.

107 Certain scenes or descriptions in *The Wind in the Willows*, and also *The Golden Age* and *Dream Days*, seem to suggest the secluded Cherwell on the fringes of North Oxford more than the broader, more populous Thames.

108 Even so, the two are really separate books, and *The Wind in the Willows* could exist quite satisfactorily (for adult readers) without Toad.

109 Quoted by kind permission from Theresa Whistler's forthcoming biography of de la Mare.

110 As to education, Badger was undoubtedly at Winchester and New College. Rat presumably went to a minor public school which had a headmaster who admired Arnold and Maurice, and Mole was perhaps a pupil at a provincial grammar school. One could imagine Toad enjoying a brief period at Eton or Harrow before being expelled.

111 There is for a start the problem of size: at one moment Toad is large enough to drive a train or a car, and to impersonate a washerwoman; the next, he is merely 'a horrid, nasty, crawly Toad' whom the bargewoman can easily throw overboard. Then there is the question of diet: Rat and Mole consume not merely ham and sardines, but 'a German sausage encased in silver paper', and Rat offers the Sea Rat a lunch which includes garlic sausage, French bread, and chianti. Not many pages distant from this, the gaoler's daughter's kindness to Toad is said to be because 'she was fond of animals as *pets*'. Rat, on his first meeting with Mole, says: 'I like your clothes awfully, old chap . . . I'm going to get a black velvet smoking-suit myself some day, as soon as I can afford it.' Peter Green asserts that children are not in the least worried by these incongruities, but this may be doubted, and in any case the book demands, in virtually all other respects, to be treated on adult terms. This problem of the animal–human relationship, coupled with the uncertainty in the narrative style, makes the trial and imprisonment sequence almost a complete failure when compared to the rest of *The Wind in the Willows*.

112 It is striking how this Muscular Christian ethic dominated the life of C. S. Lewis, and to some extent of his friend J. R. R. Tolkien, though neither was an admirer or conscious inheritor of the traditions of Maurice and the Christian Socialists. See the present writer's study of Lewis and his circle, *The Inklings* (1978).

113 Toad's obsessions are described not merely (as Peter Green has observed) in terms of classic psychological disorder, but often in a manner which has sexual connotations. The account of his playing at motor cars in his bedroom seems masturbatory, with a description of orgasm – Toad 'making uncouth and ghastly noises, till the climax was reached, when, turning a complete somersault, he would lie prostrate amid the ruins of the chairs, apparently completely satisfied for the moment'.

114 Largely but by no means totally. The language is consistently adult, full of verbal ornateness and wit. Few children are likely to understand more than a small proportion of Grahame's nuances. However, the story is so accessible that children generally acquire an affection for the book when quite young, though they probably do not read it for themselves with complete enjoyment until adolescence.

115 Quoted in Andrew Birkin, *J. M. Barrie and the Lost Boys* (1979), p.1.

116 Dialect for 'up'.

117 From *Margaret Ogilvy* (1896), which takes its title from Barrie's mother's maiden name. The book purports to be an account of her, but is almost entirely concerned with Barrie himself and his relationship with her.

118 This use of the word 'sentimental' seems to have been Barrie's own invention; the *Oxford English Dictionary* does not record it in any such sense. In Barrie's day 'sentimental' meant much the same as it does now.

119 Her childlessness has often been taken as an indication of Barrie's impotence, but no children were produced by her second marriage, either, which was to a husband who seems to have been active enough sexually, Gilbert Cannan. In fact a book that she wrote, *Dogs and Men* (1924), suggests that she was almost as odd and withdrawn a character as Barrie himself.

120 The verdict, as with Kenneth Grahame's son Alastair at Oxford the previous year, was accidental death, but in both cases some pressure was put on the inquest to discount the notion of suicide. Michael's elder brother Peter, who became a London publisher, killed himself in 1960.

121 'Never Never Never Land' in early MSS of the play; 'Never Never Land' in the final production script, and so usually in performance; 'Never-land' in *Peter and Wendy*; 'Never Land' in the published text of the play.

122 Ballantyne's book provided the outline of the story of *The Boy Castaways of Black Lake Island* (1901), a privately printed book of photographs, taken and captioned by Barrie, showing the Llewelyn Davies boys playing at shipwrecked mariners in the grounds of Black Lake Cottage, a house his wife and he had bought in the Sussex countryside. This *jeu d'esprit* was a direct forerunner of the Never Never Land adventures in *Peter Pan*. Barrie himself portrayed 'Captain Swarthy', who plays a similar part to Captain Hook.

123 Roger Lancelyn Green, in *Fifty Years of 'Peter Pan'* (1954), gives an account of Barrie's many attempts to write a final scene.

124 'The Quest for Fairyland', *The Quarterly Journal of the Library of Congress*, vol. XXXVIII, no. 4 (Fall, 1981), p.226.

125 An incident that seems almost inexplicable in the play, but which makes more sense in *The Little White Bird*, where the house protects Maimie (the equivalent to Wendy) from dying of cold in the snowbound Kensington Gardens. Did Barrie put it into the play because it has echoes of the raising of Lazarus in the tomb or of Jairus's daughter inside her father's house?

126 He also has echoes of such Shakespearian tragic figures as Macbeth and Iago, especially as played by Irving (who would surely have been the ideal Hook) and the other Victorian actor-managers.

127 That cult is described by Gillian Avery in the article cited above. It ranged from the poetry of Rose Fyleman ('There are fairies at the bottom of our garden!') to the 'Cottingley Photographs' which supposedly showed real fairies, and were taken seriously by many people.

128 Initially developed in collaboration with his brother Ken. Is there a reference to this in the fact that, in the Pooh stories, Pooh is a prolific 'poet'?

129 He was officially named Christopher Robin, but the second name was never used in the family.

130 The remarks are quoted by Christopher Milne in *The Enchanted Places*, Penguin edition (1976), p.40.

131 Christopher Milne himself dissents from his father's attitude, and writes (in the third chapter of *The Enchanted Places*) – 'Asked to choose between these two views of childhood, I am bound to say that I'm for Wordsworth . . . Maybe the infant William has fooled the middle-aged poet in the same way that the kneeling Christopher Robin fooled so many of his readers. Maybe my cynical father is right. But this is not how I feel about it.'

132 Or nearly so. It was actually preceded by two works now forgotten: *Once Upon a Time* (1917), a modern fairy story in the manner of *The Rose and the Ring*, and *Make Believe* (1918), a pallid children's play in imitation of Barrie.

133 The book resulted from a request by Rose Fyleman, a *Punch* contributor and the author of 'There are fairies at the bottom of our garden!', who asked Milne for children's poems for a juvenile magazine she was editing. Milne initially refused, then discovered that they were exactly what he wanted to write. 'Vespers' preceded the rest of the poems by several months.

134 A sequence of names that might have been found in Edith Sitwell's *Façade*, which was first performed the year before the publication of *When We Were Very Young*. Milne at his best seems to be writing Sitwellian word-music rather than conventional light verse.

Notes and References

135 Pooh, Piglet and Eeyore were real toys owned by Christopher Milne when his father began to write the stories, though their appearance was made more humorous by E. H. Shepard, Milne's brilliant illustrator. Kanga and baby Roo, and Tigger, were subsequently bought for Christopher by his parents with an eye to the part they might play in the stories. Rabbit and Owl were inventions by Milne. Winnie-the-Pooh acquired the first pan of his name from Winnie, a female bear cub at the London Zoo who was much loved by Christopher and other London children in the 1920s; 'Pooh' was originally Christopher's name for a swan encountered on a country holiday. At the beginning of the Pooh stories, Pooh is simply called 'Edward Bear'.

136 '"Bon-hommy," went on Eeyore gloomily. "French word meaning bonhommy," he explained.' (*Winnie-the-Pooh*, chapter 6.)

137 See the present writer's *J. R. R. Tolkien: a biography* (1977).

138 E. g. Virginia Haviland, 'A Second Golden Age? In Time of Flood?' in Haviland (ed.), *Children and Literature* (1973).

139 Chiefly Joel Chandler Harris's *Uncle Remus* folk-tales and Frank Baum's *The Wonderful Wizard of Oz*.

140 The Borrower family in the story, the Clocks, are distinctly lower middle class in character, but their parasitical dependence on the big people upstairs suggests a *rentier* class, a *bourgeoisie* which blinkers itself against a perception of its precarious position and its dependence on the workers.

141 The *Quartet* comprises *The Stone Book* (1976), *Granny Reardun* (1977), *The Aimer Gate* (1978), and *Tom Fobble's Day* (1977), here listed in the order in which they are intended to be read.

INDEX